Marxism, Mysticism and Modern Theory

Edited by

M AND M

Suke Wolton
St Antony's College, Oxford

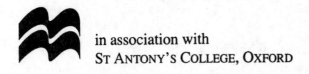

in association with
ST ANTONY'S COLLEGE, OXFORD

First published in Great Britain 1996 by
MACMILLAN PRESS LTD
Houndmills, Basingstoke, Hampshire RG21 6XS
and London
Companies and representatives
throughout the world

This title is published in the *St Antony's Series*
General Editor: Alex Pravda

A catalogue record for this book is available
from the British Library.

ISBN 0–333–65900–7 hardcover
ISBN 0–333–65901–5 paperback

First published in the United States of America 1996 by
ST. MARTIN'S PRESS, INC.,
Scholarly and Reference Division,
175 Fifth Avenue,
New York, N.Y. 10010

ISBN 0–312–15940–4

Library of Congress Cataloging-in-Publication Data
Marxism, mysticism and modern theory / edited by Suke Wolton.
p.   cm.
Includes bibliographical references and index.
ISBN 0–312–15940–4 (cloth)
1. Socialism and society.   2. Socialism and religion.   I. Wolton,
Suke.
HX542.M343   1996
335—dc20
                                        95–53921
                                          CIP

10   9   8   7   6   5   4   3   2   1
05   04   03   02   01   00   99   98   97   96

Printed in Great Britain by
Ipswich Book Co. Ltd, Ipswich, Suffolk

For Judith, my inspiration

Contents

Acknowledgements

This book originated from a series of seminars in the spring of 1995. I would not have been able to organise these seminars without the help and support of Dr Phyllis Ferguson and Professor Terence Ranger. I would also like to thank all those who attended the seminars and stimulated discussion and clarification. It is the contributors to the book, however, who have put in a great deal of work and who never complained at my schedule, whom I thank for helping me complete this project. It has been a thorough team effort. I am especially indebted to James Heartfield for his help and instruction in editing the book. Finally, I thank all the friends who read over these pages, spotting errors and thinking of questions. Since this book was an idea of mine I take full responsibility for its coherence and any errors.

Notes on the contributors

Andrew Calcutt is a journalist who has written on youth culture and the computer porn panic for *Futures* journal, *The Modern Review* and elsewhere. A former record producer, he is particularly interested in the relationship between new media and changing forms of social control.

GA Cohen is Chichele Professor of Social and Political Theory in the University of Oxford and a fellow of All Souls College. In 1979 he was awarded the Isaac Deutscher Memorial Prize for *Karl Marx's Theory of History: A Defence*. Since then he has published *History, Labour and Freedom: Themes from Marx* and *Self-Ownership, Freedom and Equality*.

James Heartfield is the book reviews editor at *Living Marxism* magazine and recently edited and introduced a new edition of VI Lenin's *State and Revolution*.

Ellie Lee has been an active campaigner around women's rights since 1987. In Leeds she initiated the 'Bitter Pill' campaign to maintain free contraception. She is a regular writer for *Living Marxism* magazine on the issue of women and society.

Peter Ray is editor of the Originals edition of works by Marx, Engels and Lenin.

Lynn Revell is researching the nature of community and identity within the Church of England for her postgraduate studies at the University of Kent. Before beginning her current studies she worked for the Commission for Racial Equality and taught religious education in Buckinghamshire and Cheshire secondary schools.

Keith Teare founded, with others, the Cyberia café in September 1994 and is a director of Easynet Ltd, the Internet service provider. During the 1980s he led Workers Against Racism, a national campaign against immigration controls and wrote, under the pseudonym Keith Tompson, *Under Siege: Racial Violence in Britain Today*.

Suke Wolton is currently a doctoral student with Terence Ranger at St Antony's College, Oxford, researching the Anglo-American debate on race and empire during the Second World War. She recently helped to start the Close Campsfield Campaign which coordinates opposition to the imprisonment of refugees in the Oxfordshire immigrant detention centre.

Introduction

Suke Wolton

My intention in putting together this book was to make a first step towards the reappropriation of Marx's theory of alienation—not through an exegesis of his text, but through an examination of contemporary ideology. By uncovering the shifting relationship between changes in society and the development of ideas about society, the arguments presented here together give an outline of the form of modern alienation and argue for the contemporary relevance of the theory.

This theme was largely dictated by my passion for this theory. For me, it seems easy to say this is a sick society. It is more inspiring to locate the crazy logic of capitalism in the precise form of current social interactions. The other impulse for this book came from discussions with various friends (who were then persuaded to participate in this project) on the way that new studies of society emphasised the importance of 'social' effects while employing a very different concept of society from our own. This, we thought, would be interesting to pursue in a series of seminars which I organised in Oxford. The discussions at these seminars helped to clarify ideas further and each of those papers has been reworked to become the chapters of this book. Underscoring each chapter's different subject matter is the particular form in which alienation is expressed in different contemporary social theories.

Marx's development of the concept of alienation was instrumental in enabling him to revolutionise the understanding of capitalist society. Not only did the theory of alienation capture the specific nature of capitalism, it also explained the misunderstanding and mystification of capitalist social relations by other theories about society. For Marx, alienation was the estrangement of man from himself, from his life activity and creativity, and, at the same time, the reappearance of that collective work in an atomised, distorted and mystified form. So that although man is individually rational, the impact of human intervention as a whole is made irrational under capitalism.[1] This irrationality is clearly expressed in the strength of mysticism in society, not because people are gullible, stupid or even irrational, but because mysticism makes sense in a world where human relationships are mysterious, hidden and apparently other-worldly.

The transformation of human activity by the specific form of capitalist social relations means that society is mysterious, not because we are incapable of understanding complex human interactions, but because relations in society are themselves mystified, made 'absurd' (*verrückt*), by commodity production.[2] Marx sums up the mystical connections in society when he explains commodity fetishism, the religion, if you like, of capitalism, writing in *Capital* that:

> the labour of the individual asserts itself as a part of the labour of society, only by means of the relations which the act of exchange establishes directly between the products, and indirectly, through them, between the producers. To the latter, therefore, the relations connecting the labour of one individual with that of the rest appear not as direct relations between individuals at work, but as what they really are, material relations between persons and social relations between things.[3]

In brief then, relations between people appear as free and equal when really, under capitalism, some are 'more equal than others'. Wealth, material objects, measures the social position of any individual. But it is not just that relations between individuals do not *appear* as social relations, it is that they *really are* transformed into material relations in capitalism. This is a theory of the way that capitalist society is not only mysterious, it is, by its very nature, self-mystifying.

The fact of this relationship between real society and its mystification means that the latter, although one-sided and often idealised, can give us insights into understanding this self-contradictory system. For example, running through this book is the theme of evaluating 'social constructionism'; a theory of how social norms are established by emerging ideologies. The point of these criticisms of social constructionism is not to dismiss the theory out of hand, but rather through a critique of it, to fully appropriate its insights into the fluidity and relativity of human institutions and arrangements, and the importance it gives to the role of human agency. Social constructionism captures these elements of the social world, but presents them in their idealised, other-worldly form, ascribing changes simply at the level of attitudes and culture. By grounding these ideas in objective social circumstances we hope to outline a picture of the totality of today's social relations. The weakness of social constructionism is that, ironically, it lacks a theory of society and so ends up mystifying the 'social', the very element it seeks to emphasise.

Marx made the point against Feuerbach's demystification of religion that it is not enough simply to show how religious ideas are the celestial and idealised form of man's aspirations for himself, that, for example, Protestant ideas were an attempt to clean the Catholic church of hierarchy and opulence. But rather one needs to show also why the religious form of the social conflict is the only form through which those social conflicts (of the sixteenth century) could be expressed.[4] Marx, in the fourth thesis on Feuerbach, sets out the argument for the real work to be not merely revealing the secular foundation for mysticism, but demonstrating that this mysticism is the necessary appearance of irrational social relations.

> Feuerbach starts out from the fact of religious self-alienation, the duplication of the world into a religious, imaginary world and a real one. His work consists in the dissolution of the religious world into its secular basis. He overlooks the fact that after completing this work, the chief thing still remains to be done. For the fact that the secular foundation detaches itself from itself and establishes itself in the clouds as an independent realm is really only to be explained by the self-cleavage and contradictory character of this secular basis.[5]

The passage that Enlightenment rationality, as represented here by Ludwig Feuerbach, takes—crashing through the mystical illusions to get to a hidden reality—is, according to Marx and Engels, the easier part of the process. The really difficult thing is then to explain why it is that reality should and must give rise to *these* mystical appearances.

Marx inverted Hegel's mystical presentation of history as an ideal development. In the process of standing Hegel on his feet (and off his head), Marx, as Jerry Cohen explains in his chapter, found the rational kernel in Hegel's philosophy—that there is development in human affairs. However, according to Marx, Hegel mystified this real development as the movement of the Absolute Spirit through history. Cohen makes clear that Marx's critique of Hegel substituted the this-worldly development of modern industry for the other-worldly development of the Spirit, as the guiding principle of history. Here Marx is in keeping with the Enlightenment critique of idealism.

The social constructionist theory that James Heartfield investigates has also rejected the Hegelian concept of a universalistic essence. Under the banner of 'anti-essentialism', social construction theorists have dismissed essences as mystical and illusory, preferring instead the concrete, tangible phenomena of modern society. The problem, however, for the social constructionists is that the more that they reject mystical essences, the more they find that the real detail of society runs through their hands like grains of sand. Without an explanation of how the real society lends substance to such essences, they must omit the other half of the task before us. Their resulting examination of social institutions fragments and crumbles as if it were just made of sand.

Social constructionism simply rejects the mystified essence of a Hegelian idealism as so much illusion. But this viewpoint rejects a notion of a real essence because, as Heartfield explains in his chapter, it fails to understand the contradictory nature of capitalist society that gives rise to real mystifications.

Capitalist social relations are the material foundation of a world which really makes the appearance of interrelationships mystical. The distinction between reality and appearance is a result of real conditions. This is pointed out by Robert Wolff in *Moneybags Must Be So Lucky* with the example of a straight stick which looks bent when dipped in water. Insisting that the stick is still straight misses half of the picture. It is the property of the light in water, as opposed to air, that makes the stick appear bent. The rejection of the distinction between appearance and essence is as mystical as the assertion that the water does not bend the stick when all our senses tell us that it does. The key to understanding is to explain how it appears to be this way.

At the heart of the mystification endemic to social constructionism is its failure sufficiently to distinguish the standpoint of the individual from the standpoint of society as a whole. The misconception of society by social constructionists, who have adopted the sociological conception of society as an aggregate of individuals, ends up condensing the 'social' into many individuals. Their idealised society makes for an idealised individual, who they then argue can be freed from the constraints of society. In reality the processes governing society appear on one level to be affected by individual action, while at the same time, the overall effect is governed by processes independent of rational decisions. As Engels explained:

> The ends of the actions are intended, but the results which actually follow from these actions are not intended; or when they do seem to correspond to the end intended, they ultimately have consequences quite other than those intended. Historical events thus appear on the whole to be likewise governed by chance. But where on the surface accident holds sway, there actually it is always governed by inner, hidden laws and it is only a matter of discovering these laws.[6]

To try to describe society in rational terms, when that society is not rationally organised, necessarily leads to confusion. Andrew Calcutt's chapter shows that criminology is dominated by just this confusion. The relationship of crime and punishment is at heart irrational. The rationality of judgement is, in the courts, a rationality that comes after the event and necessarily so. It is a specific feature of a market society that social organisation is mediated through the free choices of isolated individuals. Implicit in that atomised, anti-social manner of social organisation is the possibility of crime—the freedom of the individual gone sour. In these circumstances the court's judgement is revenge writ large.

The great weakness of criminology is that it attempts to understand these anti-rational relations in the pseudo-rational categories of sociology. The work that reason ought to do is to capture the spontaneous movement of society in thought. In that way it builds a bridge between the blindly operating laws of the market and their rational reflection. Simply to impose a rational framework on an irrational society only elevates that irrationality to an ever greater height. The impasse of moral relativism that Calcutt investigates in the theory of deviance is the unavoidable outcome of such a bogus rationalism.

In my chapter, I focus on how cultural studies academics have captured the fluidity and development of social life but idealise its processes. Recent identity studies emphasise the role of individuals and the exchange of ideas between people to explain their sense of the movement of society. The debate between the idea that race is 'invented' by the ruling establishment and the idea that race is 'imagined' as a cultural no-go area, a site of resistance, expresses the way in which ideas are involved in social development. Engels placed a premium on the understanding of life as a process, but his view emphasised the underlying movement that occurs beneath the surface of apparent accident and chaos.

> The great basic thought that the world is not to be comprehended as a complex of ready-made *things*, but as a complex of *processes*, in which the things apparently stable no less than their mind images in our heads, the concepts, go through an uninterrupted change of coming into being and passing away, in which, in spite of all seeming accidentality and of all temporary retrogression, a progressive development asserts itself in the end.[7]

But there is a confusion in cultural studies which mixes surface phenomena with changing social conditions, and so loses the distinction between the conscious intentionality of individuals and the apparently purposeful, but actually irrational, movement of society towards division and fragmentation. The idealised conception in the social constructionist view of race misinterprets the rationalisation of experience after the event, with a consciously planned strategy.

The misunderstanding of the way that capitalism manufactures a one-sided understanding of society has been a fatal flaw for the women's movement. The social division between the genders was accepted by the founding feminists as the dominant social relation. From that perspective the individual experience of women was assumed to be sufficiently cohering and uniting for the women's movement to be based on it. For example, many women looked to the self-discovery of consciousness-raising groups to create unity and a common purpose. But, while the social relations of capitalism systematically put women in an inferior position, the everyday experience of each woman is different and diverse. Not all women feel themselves a victim of violent men. Not all women care about fashion pressures and male attentions, and not all women give up their careers for the children. Each of us leads our own life with all its particularities, whatever are our similarities from the standpoint of the totality of society. As Ellie Lee describes, however, the fragmentation of the women's movement has shown that the differences between women have come to be regarded as more rather than less important.

The women's movement confused the appearance of women's oppression in the form of male domination with the reality of their oppression. They saw form and mistook it for content. Their focus on the everyday was a way of grasping reality. But there is more to social reality than what is apparent in the everyday experiences of women (and men for that matter). In the end the variation and diversity at that level encouraged fragmentation. And feminism's attempt to make the one-sided partial experience of the individual into its cohering creed proved to be fatally flawed. As a consequence today, feminist theory has gone furthest in its fragmentation and in its rejection of singular explanation. It used to be at the forefront in creating a social movement, now it is at the cutting edge of developing ideas about difference.

The sense of a more atomised and individuated existence today is most clearly expressed in the rise of New Age religion which has even influenced the established Anglican church. As Lynn Revell explains, New Age demonstrates the way in which belief has become fragmented. The loss of legitimacy and relevance of the older religions has been mirrored by the rise of the New Age, centred on a new form of authority for belief. Instead of looking to some celestial sphere, some common God, for their spirituality and the *raison d'etre* of their religion, the New Agers seek a new truth to be found within themselves as different individuals. For them, the true understanding should be discovered by self-awareness, not self-evaluation (as with the original idealist Plato), because all that is true is already there.

The new mysticism thus reveres what already exists, because that appears to have some solidity and tangibility, and rejects that which is aspired to or dreamed of. As the New Age makes the secular, the body, sacred so it illustrates the idealisation of the mundane and everyday that makes sense in a world where old icons have no meaning and 'All that is solid melts into air, all that is holy is profaned'.[8]

According to Peter Ray, social constructionism can be seen to have idealised the gay identity. Social constructionists have shown how the concept of the homosexual emerged through debates and moral panics in the nineteenth century. The discussion concerning homosexual activity, in parliament, in the press and in the courts, has often been very vocal and polarised. This has lent credence to the idea that this discourse alone is responsible for creating sexual identities. Even this characterisation has, however, proved problematic since the outcome of the clash of competing discourses appears arbitrary.

It is only by looking at society in its totality that we can elucidate the shifting position and components of such an identity. Not only do social constructionists lack a methodology to cut through surface appearances, but they insist that there is nothing beneath surface appearances. For them, it is the ideological practices themselves that are the perpetrators of the criminalisation of gay men. But, Ray argues, it is only by bringing out the relationship between the material determinants of homosexuality and those of the family that it is possible to understand both the moral certainties of the past and the current sense of contingency surrounding sexual relations in general and the changing meaning of gay identity in particular.

Keith Teare's chapter on the Internet examines the mystification that has taken place around the network of communication technology and in particular how the dreams of global interconnectedness have been translated into fibre-optic cables and satellite link-ups. In a society that takes an increasingly fragmented and atomised form, the idea of rebuilding networks of people, brought together through electronic messages, appears to be a concrete and practical suggestion. The real economic barriers to technical development form, however, a minimal part of the popular debate about the Internet. Teare argues, as a result, that the global dream of the Net enthusiasts is idealistic and other-worldly. The very celebration of the form of communication as the solution to social divisions is a mystification that simply incorporates the modern fascination with the interaction of words, images and talking.

Finally, in the last chapter, I have tried to show how alienation in contemporary society is best summed up in the prevalence of anti-humanistic prejudice. Recent social theories emphasise the role of human agency in the formation and shaping of modern society. But this understanding, without a broader critique of society that challenges the social relations of capitalism, becomes distorted and remains partial and one-sided. Today, many people focus on what seems most specific and immediate, and yet this turns out to be what is most intractable. What is most immediately to hand is, ironically, what is most deceiving. As with those who cannot see the wood for the trees, or think that the world is flat because they cannot see around its curvature, appearances deceive. In each case real understanding demands a distance from the immediate sense perception, and that distance is reason. Against all our intuition we get closer to the truth of the thing by moving further away from our sense impressions of it.

The elevation of the immediate appearances over considered reality is intrinsically related to the elevation of the standpoint of the individual over the standpoint of society. The current fascination with personal relationships,

the body, spiritual and physical health are testimony to the degree of atomi-
sation in society, and also the search for something that seems to be close at
hand and controllable.

In contrast, Marxism aims to transcend immediate and individual
experience. It uses the theory of alienation to understand the way that
capitalist society systematically mystifies itself in other social theories. By
putting our common humanity to the fore, Marxism tries to overcome one-
sidedness. The argument for humanism, in this book as a whole, takes the
form of a critique of contemporary social theories.

We need to understand how modern theories about society express some
real, although one-sided facet, of social relations today. As an atomised
individual, less connected to the old social organisations such as trade unions,
political parties and old-style religions, the movement of the surrounding
society appears particularly destabilising and confusing. Marxist theory,
rather than overturning in the stream of social change, tries to reproduce that
movement in thought. 'From this standpoint' Engels explains:

> the demand for final solutions and eternal truths ceases once for all; one is
> always conscious of the necessary limitation of all acquired knowledge, of the
> fact that it is conditioned by the circumstances in which it was acquired....One
> knows that these antitheses have only a relative validity; that that which is
> recognised now as true has also its latent false side which will later manifest
> itself, just as that which is now regarded as false has also its true side by virtue
> of which it could previously be regarded as true.[9]

The development of knowledge is not about piling up static and eternal
truths, it is about understanding the developing society around us so that we,
collectively, are in a position to effect change rather than simply be affected by
it. In this way we can begin to grasp a changed situation, not in a relativistic
way, where all ideas are valid and none are true, but in a real way as a whole
process including the self-mystifying character of an alienated society. The
modern social theories both describe, as they reflect, and mystify, in their
idealisation, the real movement of social relations in this society.

It is important to recognise that knowledge is not a static body of
information. Knowing is the activity of people trying to understand the world
around them. We make use of information in such a way as to demonstrate
that aspects of our world are no longer beyond our reach. Engels, in *Ludwig
Feuerbach and the End of Classical German Philosophy*, explained this process
in reference to Kant's concept of the 'thing-in-itself' which referred to the
limitations of human understanding which, according to Kant, could only be
overcome by the transcendental knowledge of the world by God. But, said

Engels, Kant's limits were the boundaries of the eighteenth century, and as such were not permanent, but were being superseded by the development of humanity:

> If we are able to prove the correctness of our conception of a natural process by making it ourselves, bringing it into being out of its conditions and making it serve our own purposes into the bargain, then there is an end to the Kantian ungraspable "thing-in-itself". The chemical substances produced in the bodies of plants and animals remained just such "things-in-themselves" until organic chemistry began to produce them one after another, whereupon the "thing-in-itself" became a thing for us, as, for instance, alizarin, the colouring matter of the madder, which we no longer trouble to grow in the madder roots in the field, but produce much more cheaply and simply from coal tar.[10]

This is not some crude pragmatism. The development of organic chemistry involved great conceptual leaps, in which what really became the 'thing-for-us' was the rebuilding of an image [*abbilder*] of real things that we could use.[11] For example when Kekulé dreamed of snakes circling to eat their tails he grasped the movement of the electrons in the molecular structure of benzene. In so doing he enabled organic chemistry to take a step forward in understanding the relationship between the structure of the molecule and the physical and chemical properties of the substance.

This example also demonstrates how truth is not some mere character of the image, it is governed by an active relationship with the objective world. No 'correspondence' can be measured by a photofit mechanism. Truth is evident only in the real world of practical activity. Moreover, it is those practical consequences that encourage new ideas, new conceptual tools and thereby new insights. At the same time, however, the realisation of ideas into activities and things is a process that involves the social organisation of people as a whole. Even the inventor, working alone in a basement, uses tools and materials and concepts that have been produced by others before him. 'If I have seen further', Isaac Newton acknowledged, 'it is by standing on the shoulders of giants.'[12] Advancing knowledge involves wider society in the broadest sense.

Since the goal of knowledge is ultimately to improve the lot of humanity, so a positive outlook for humanity provides the inspiration for creativity and inventiveness. Today, however, economic impasse dominates society. The sense of limits has, therefore, a foundation which both bounds our imagination and our experiments. Without the practical spur of a dynamic economy, the sense of a common humanity appears to be so distant as to require a leap of faith to suppose its existence.

For me, the fact that the McDonalds logo is now better known than the

Christian cross is a contemporary example of how the self-mystifying character of capitalist society creates its own religious icons.[13] The McDonalds M-sign, if a new icon of today, is, however, a symbol of mere marketing success rather than a trademark of industrial growth and dynamism. It is hardly that McDonalds is popular, it is rather that there is little else to inspire.

With the exhaustion of the political traditions of left and right, many of the old ideas and assumptions regarding social organisations are called into question. In many ways these changes have been itemised and examined by the now popular school of social constructionism. But the way that the new social theorists have interpreted these changes both mystifies real society because social relations are hidden from us, and yet at the same time, indicates by what is idealised, the real secular self-cleavage in modern society. The important point, however, is that the new insights, because they are localised and focused on the role of human consciousness, are in fact a greater mystification than ever before. The ability of social constructionism to describe the contingency of contemporary society has made its perspective increasingly popular. The new social theories are successful because they capture modern life and speak to us as individuals with a relevance that the old ideas cannot match. But their narrow focus on consciousness mystifies the role of ideas in effecting social change. Uncovering the real relationship between consciousness and society must be our new starting point.

NOTES

1   As Robert Wolff eloquently puts it: 'As the rational becomes real, the real becomes ever more irrational.' Robert Paul Wolff, *Moneybags Must Be So Lucky: On the Literary Structure of Capital,* University of Massachusetts Press, 1988, p76

2   Karl Marx, *Capital,* Vol1, Lawrence & Wishart, 1983, p80

3   Karl Marx, *Capital,* Vol1, Lawrence & Wishart, 1983, p78

4   Frederick Engels and Karl Marx, *Ludwig Feuerbach and the End of Classical German Philosophy and Theses on Feuerbach,* Progress Publishers, 1978, p57

5   Karl Marx, 'Theses on Feuerbach No4' in Frederick Engels and Karl Marx, *Ludwig Feuerbach and the End of Classical German Philosophy and Theses on Feuerbach,* Progress Publishers, 1978, p66

6   Frederick Engels and Karl Marx, *Ludwig Feuerbach and the End of Classical German Philosophy and Theses on Feuerbach,* Progress Publishers, 1978, pp48-49

7   Frederick Engels and Karl Marx, *Ludwig Feuerbach and the End of Classical German Philosophy and Theses on Feuerbach,* Progress Publishers, 1978, pp44-45

8   Karl Marx and Frederick Engels, *Manifesto of the Communist Party,* Foreign Languages Press, 1973, p37

9   Frederick Engels and Karl Marx, *Ludwig Feuerbach and the End of Classical German Philosophy and Theses on Feuerbach,* Progress Publishers, 1978, p45

10   Frederick Engels and Karl Marx, *Ludwig Feuerbach and the End of Classical German Philosophy and Theses on Feuerbach,* Progress Publishers, 1978, pp24-25

11   See Frederick Engels and Karl Marx, *Ludwig Feuerbach and the End of Classical German Philosophy and Theses on Feuerbach,* Progress Publishers, 1978, p44

12   Isaac Newton, letter to Robert Hooke, 5 February 1675

13   Market Research Survey result for the Olympic Games Committee reported in *Guardian,* 2 August 1995

1
The three sources and component parts of Marxism

GA Cohen

In 1913, Lenin wrote a brilliant short sketch called 'The three sources and component parts of Marxism'.[1] I shall here indicate, following Lenin, what those components were. But I shall strive to do a bit better than Lenin (in this particular respect!) by displaying more clearly than he did how the three parts of Marxism that he identified were so combined by Marx as to make each part far more illuminating and consequential than it was in the isolated condition in which Marx found it.

The three sources of Marxism come from three European countries, in each of which a single one of them was most highly developed. And each source was a field of thought which presented itself as distinct from the other two, so that it was an act of supreme genius on Marx's part to bring all three together. In the order in which Marx appropriated the three elements, they were: first, the dialectical mode of analysis, which he drew from the philosophy he studied as an adolescent and as a young man in his native Germany; second, French socialist ideas flourishing among intellectuals critical of capitalism in the France of his day, the France which was the country of his first exile; and, finally, the classical political economy, or economics, of Marx's final exile, in Great Britain.

I start where Marx started, with the philosophical component, the dialectical idea. The words 'dialectic', 'dialectical', 'dialectically' and so on have been used with undisciplined abandon across the Marxist tradition, but I shall mean one reasonably precise thing by the 'dialectical idea' here. The idea that I have in mind appears in embryonic form in many episodes in the history of philosophy, but its most powerful exponent was the German philosopher GWF Hegel, who died in 1830, less than 10 years before Marx became a student of law and philosophy in a Germany intellectually still under Hegel's shadow.

This dialectical idea is that every living thing, every functioning thing, every live thing, including not only the literally living things studied by biology, but also live systems of ideas of trends in art or developing societies or families; every such thing develops by unfolding its inner nature in outward forms, and, when it has fully elaborated its own nature, it dies, disappears, is

1

transformed into a successor form precisely because it has succeeded in elaborating itself fully. So the fundamental dialectical idea is the idea of self-destruction through self-fulfilment.

Examples: The flower runs to seed. The family brings the children to maturity and thereby dissolves itself. The form of painting flourishes when it is not yet entirely explored and becomes stale and dead when it is. Every developing thing is a victim of its own success.

Now the most dramatic field within which Hegel applied the dialectical idea was world history, where, in his view, the units of development are spiritual entities, in a broad sense of 'spiritual', which is to say that they are the cultures, in a broad sense, which characterise successively higher societies. The story of history is the story of the world-spirit, which is God in His manifestation on Earth in human consciousness. What happens in history to the world-spirit is that it undergoes growth in self-awareness, and the vehicle of that growth at any given time is a culture, a culture which stimulates the growth of God's self-awareness, and therefore of human self-awareness, and which perishes when it has stimulated more growth than it can contain. (God knows himself only in human beings, so that His self-knowledge is their self-knowledge, and their knowledge of Him is their knowledge of themselves.) So, for example, the civilisation of feudal Europe perfects itself in its visual arts, in its manners, in its religion, in its literature and is then as a result ripe for transformation into modern post-Catholic Europe.

A one-sentence summary of the Hegelian philosophy of history:

> History is the history *of the world-spirit and, derivatively, of human consciousness,* which undergoes growth in *self-knowledge,* the stimulus and vehicle of which is a *culture,* which perishes when it has stimulated more growth than it can contain.

In that summary, the dialectical idea of self-destruction through self-fulfilment plays a key role: the culture destroys itself by perfecting itself. Later, I shall indicate how Marx preserved the dialectical idea and, therefore, the structure of Hegel's account of history, while transforming its content (the italicised part of the foregoing summarising sentence) from a spiritual one into a materialist one.

Marx encountered the second source and component of Marxism in his French exile. This was the socialist project, as propounded by such authors as Etienne Cabet, Henri de Saint-Simon, and Charles Fourier, a vision of a better society, one lacking the manifest injustice and misery of capitalism, one, too, that was rational in its workings because planned, rather than anarchic because market-driven and, therefore, irrational, as was capitalism.

This French socialism was, however, Utopian, which means, among other things, that it was undialectical, in the sense of 'dialectical' that I have expounded. French socialism was undialectical because it was not accompanied by a critique of capitalism which showed how capitalism would transform itself and generate socialism as its own proper supersession. It is Utopian and undialectical to represent the socialist project as one of clearing away capitalism to produce an empty plane on which socialism is constructed. That is a Utopian way of construing the relationship between political ideals and political practice.

The dialectical analysis of transition requires a narrative of how capitalism will transform itself so that socialism is the inevitable or near inevitable replacement of it. Of course, the French socialists offered a deep critique of capitalism, but it was a moralising rather than a dialectical critique, showing the evils and irrationalities of capitalism without pointing out how capitalism would supersede itself. And the associated Utopian practice would be on the technocratic engineering model of alteration from without, whereas dialectically inspired political practice is a matter of working with the forces within capitalism itself which are destined to transform it. Hence the socialist revolution for Marx is not, as it is for the French socialists, merely for the proletariat, to relieve their misery, but by the proletariat, the proletariat being the force within capitalist reality that subverts it, the creation of capitalism than overturns its creator.

But that application of the dialectical idea to capitalism so as to generate socialism, that synthesis of German philosophy and French socialism, remains schematic without provision of a third component, an analysis of the economic dynamic of capitalism, and that was the major intellectual appropriation of Marx's second exile, in Britain, where he studied the classical political economists with a thoroughness probably never equalled by anyone. Classical political economy was undialectical. In its more vulgar form it depicted capitalism as a continually self-reproducing system, destined for lasting success. In its more tragic and truly classical form it indeed depicts a development for capitalism, but one culminating not in a higher form of economy, but in the stationary state, at which development stops. Marx refashioned the classical analysis so as to show how capitalist competition abolishes itself by creating enterprises of implicitly social character in which the capitalist becomes obsolete, so that little but his removal is needed to establish socialism. Engels elaborated that thought in his *Socialism: Utopian and Scientific*.[2]

In this way capitalism was placed within the dialectical frame that Hegel used to describe cultures, as an entity with a principle of self-development within it that was also a principle of self-destruction and self-transcendence into a higher form. But Marx generalised that account of social self-transformation to the universal plane of history as a whole, and thereby generated the theory of historical materialism, which, as I said, preserves the structure of the Hegelian philosophy of history but alters its content. The content is now materialist, since history is not, as in Hegel, the history of the world-spirit manifesting itself in human consciousness, but of human industry. Correspondingly, the central growth is not, now, in self-awareness, but in productive power, in sovereignty over nature rather than over the self; and the unit of development is not, now, a culture, but an economic structure. So the sentence given below both conveys the theory of historical materialism and displays how it alters the content of Hegel's theory while preserving its structure:

> History is the history of *human industry,* which undergoes growth in *productive power,* the stimulus and vehicle of which is an *economic structure,* which perishes when it has stimulated more growth than it can contain.

The human problem is here seen as lying in humanity's relationship to the world, not to itself. The problem is to turn the world into a home for humanity, by transcending the scarcity in the relationship between humanity and nature which generates class conflict at the level of social organisation. Scarcity generates class conflict because scarcity means repugnant labour and a consequent class division between those whose lives must be given over to that labour and those whose good fortune it is to see to it that the former perform it. With the massive productive power generated by capitalism, repugnant labour is no longer required, which means that class division loses its progressive function.

Lenin was right that Marx's teachings 'arose as a direct and immediate continuation of the teachings of the greatest representatives of philosophy, political economy and socialism', and that Marxism 'is the legitimate successor of the best that was created by humanity in the nineteenth century in the shape of German philosophy, English political economy and French socialism'.[3]

You can measure the immensity of Marx's theoretical achievement by considering how restricted, how one-sided, each of the three components that he brought together is, in its original isolated form.

The Hegelian philosophy was, of course, profound and fertile. But it was really a fantasy that could only have been produced in a country bewitched by its romance with philosophy, so bewitched, indeed, by its romance with philosophy that German idealism could ignore the material base of human existence and picture history as a succession of states of consciousness. That deviation into abstracted other-worldliness is corrected by the this-worldly focus of French socialism and British political economy, which Marx united with the revolutionary dialectical idea.

French socialism, in its turn, provided the necessary vision of a better reality, but with the French it was nothing but a vision because of the French lack of the dialectical idea on the one hand, and of British political economy on the other, which could be used to produce a realistic application of the dialectical idea to capitalism. Socialism then emerges not as a mere vision, but as a realistic projection of the future of capitalism itself.

Finally, British political economy lacked the vision of a better future and condemned humanity to capitalism precisely because it lacked the German dialectical principle which counselled search for self-transcendence in self-destructive self-development, and also because it lacked the socialist ideal which France had provided.

NOTES

1   VI Lenin, *Selected Works,* Vol1, Progress, 1977, pp44-48
2   Frederick Engels, *Socialism: Utopian and Scientific,* Junius, 1995 (orig. 1880)
3   VI Lenin, *Selected Works,* Vol1, Progress, 1977, p44

2

Marxism and social construction

James Heartfield

Today the proposition that identities are socially constructed is common place. A hundred years ago, characteristics like sex, race, nationality, generation and social class would have been seen as natural characteristics. Now, just as unassailably, these self-same characteristics are no longer seen as natural, but rather attributed to a social process of the construction of identity. In some cases these characteristics are renamed to signify their social origins: race becomes ethnicity, sex becomes gender. It is not just that these social categories are supposed to overlay natural properties, the proposition is that there is no discrete natural foundation to identities, rather socially constructed identities are the real content of the characteristics once attributed to nature.

Even where there is no terminological change, the meaning of a category like 'generation' is just different from the meaning of the same word a century previously. The sociologists and journalists who have coined the term 'Generation Y' have probably forgotten that the word generation once referred to a process of natural growth.[1] At the turn of the century, the authorities were alarmed at the apparent incapacity of the British working man to fight. These fears of 'degeneration' were, literally, fears of the physical depletion of the national stock. Today, however, a generation is readily assumed to mean a social or cultural formation. No naturally inherited characteristics distinguish the beat generation from slackers. Similarly the characteristic of 'good breeding', that today could only be employed with ironic quotation marks once literally meant good breeding. So too did true-born Englishman mean something more physical than a juridical concept.

Today, however, it is largely accepted that these identities are socially constructed rather than natural—that is that they are generated in society. There are different ways of presenting the argument. Some stress the way girls are, from an early age, socialised into pre-given patterns of behaviour that are deemed appropriate for their gender. More recently some authors and commentators, especially on the gay scene, have stressed that identities are wilfully self-constructed.[2] Others have emphasised the plurality of identities that any one individual may perform.[3] All of these different nuances are issues within the theory of the social construction of identity.

This paper, however, is not concerned with the different nuances of social construction, but with the theory as such.[4] It aims to test the idea of social construction against Marxism. Over and above the familiar idea of a social construction of identity, as outlined above, it examines the more pointed claim of the theorists that, in the words of the sociologist Alfred Schutz, 'reality is a social construct'.

The proposition that reality is a social construct would less readily win assent than the narrower proposition that identities are socially constructed. Nonetheless the basis of the idea that identities are socially constructed rests on the broader proposition that *all* meaning is created socially and that there is no discrete world of experience that is not filtered through social interpretation. Despite the counter-intuitive nature of the broader theory it is widespread among all kinds of thinkers, from sociologists like Jurgen Habermas, Anthony Giddens, Peter Berger and Pierre Bordieu, anthropologists like Clifford Geertz, Peter Winch and the late Claude Levi-Strauss, philosophers like Richard Rorty, the late, older Ludwig Wittgenstein as well as whole hosts of post-structuralist and deconstructionist thinkers in France and elsewhere. It would not be an exaggeration to say that, in the Humanities at least, the 'reality-is-a-social-construct' theory is the orthodoxy.

The origins of the theory that reality is a social construct lie in the German historical school of law in the latter part of the last century, people like Wilhelm Dilthey, Leopold von Ranke and Heinrich Rickert. They were among the first people—apart from the Marxists—to look at history rather than nature as the basis of society. But it is in the philosophy initiated by Edmund Husserl, which he called phenomenology, that the idea was most clearly elaborated. Husserl influenced sociologists like Max Scheler, Alfred Schutz and Raymond Aron, and philosophers like Martin Heidegger and, through him, Jean-Paul Sartre.

The idea of phenomenology was in part an attempt to overcome the conflict between empiricism and idealism that had divided philosophy for more than a century. Scepticism about the existence of a natural world outside of man's thinking remained unresolved. Husserl's avowedly temporary resolution was to set the problem aside. We cannot know whether our ideas are real representations of an objective world, he said, so let us simply bracket that question for the time being and examine what we can know. The phenomena of experience are without doubt real. If we experience phenomena we cannot doubt that we are experiencing phenomena—only whether these refer to something objective beyond themselves.[5]

Bracketing the traditional understanding of 'objectivity' as referring to a material world outside of consciousness, Husserl elaborated a distinction between subjectivity and objectivity in the 1936 essay 'The origin of geometry'.[6] This exercise in 'bracketing' contains the basic elements of the theory of a socially constructed world.[7]

To Husserl the term 'subjective' refers to that which is held by one consciousness alone. 'Objectivity' means those views and perceptions that are verified by their common possession among a community. In 'The origin of geometry' Husserl reinterprets the question of objectivity. He sets aside the empiricist idea of an objective world. Instead Husserl introduces the phenomenological idea of an objective consensus between subjects.[8]

In his last full work *The Crisis of European Sciences and Transcendental Phenomenology* Husserl elaborated the sphere of objectivity as a consensus between subjects, or intersubjectivity, that he called the 'life-world'.[9] And, formulating the theory of the social construction of reality, Husserl says 'in this regard we speak of the "intersubjective constitution" of the world'.[10] (It was the concept of the life-world that was later taken up by the German sociologist Jurgen Habermas.)

Despite the initial implausibility of the argument that the world is constituted intersubjectively, it has proved fruitful for research as well as being persuasive to the educated. Indeed the theory of the social construction of reality is ultimately compelling. The argument does not demand that there is no objective world, only that for us there is no experience that is innocent of social interpretation. Instead the theory says that only socially generated meanings allow us to make sense of our experience. Naming things, and fixing them in narratives, is very important in the social construction theory. These cultural activities create codes of meaning through which we interpret our world. The very idea of a 'nature' separate and apart from man is questionable. More commonly than our ancestors we use the term 'environment' where they might have used the word nature. After all, there are hardly any areas of the world left that we could truly call wilderness. And contemporary environmentalism reminds us that the whole world is subject to man's influence in myriad, often unforeseen, ways. So rather than talking of a nature separate and apart from man we talk instead of that which surrounds us: our 'environs', which might include the built environment, moral environment and so on.

Context is everything. Karl Marx makes a similar point in the first volume of *Capital: An Analysis of Capitalist Production*: 'Under certain circumstances a chair with four legs and a velvet covering may be used as a throne.'[11] But this chair does not become a throne by virtue of its usefulness as an object, but because of the social relationships in which it is placed.

Similarly 'one man is a king only because other men stand in the relation of subjects to him. They, on the contrary, imagine that they are subject because he is king.'[12]

Common sense rebels against the wider theory of a socially constructed world, however much it is the basis of more accepted notions of identity. But what is the alternative? To reject the theory that reality is a social construct we would have to return to a naive empiricism, where ideas are made anew by individuals on the basis of their bare perceptions. That might do for unreflective thinking but it does not bear scrutiny. What experience is not shaped by our foreknowledge and conceptual apparatus? Even such things that we readily assume to be physical characteristics like perspective can be dated as human inventions. Foreshortening, the decreasing size of faraway objects, the vanishing point—all of these are ways that we arrange our visual world, ways that were created by artists of the Italian Renaissance.[13] Before then, in the art of the Egyptians for example, it was normal for the size of a figure on paper to represent the subject's importance, rather than his place on a notional grid of diverging lines of perspective. Arguably primitive peoples literally saw importance as size, accounting for the near universal accounts of an age when giants ruled the land.

There are other reasons why we should favour the theory that reality is a social construct over the alternative view that social life is determined by laws of nature. Where natural necessity is seen as the governing principle of social life, perverse conclusions ensue. The authority of the idea that ethnicity or gender are better categories than race or sex is not just a question of theoretical development. Theories that attribute human characteristics to nature are suspect because of the reactionary purposes to which such theories were put. Race laws in Germany, colour bars in the British colonies and the southern states of America were premised upon racial, often pseudo-scientific, theories of natural difference. Today those policies are generally held to be reprehensible, and the theories that supported them rightly held to be untenable. In 1994, Charles Murray and the late Richard Herrnstein sought to breathe new life into the generally discredited theory of inherited intelligence, and in particular into the prejudice that black people are naturally inferior to whites.[14] Pointedly, Murray and Herrnstein's arguments were broadly rejected by reviewers across the political spectrum.

Not just race, but all sorts of nature-based theories of society are held to be suspect today. It is not so long ago that women's exclusion from society was justified largely on natural grounds, or that homosexuality was considered to be a medical disorder. Today those views might still be held in private but they are increasingly untenable in public discussion. The naturalistic view of human institutions is in abeyance because it is difficult to maintain in the face of the evidence. This is not just an argument from results. Racial science was bad science. Forcing questionable moral categories into the straitjacket of natural science was a poor way to understand the world. As an alternative, social construction theory has introduced a subtlety that was not previously available. Its researches are its justification.

Furthermore the theory that reality is a social construct seems unassailable from the perspective of empiricism. Ideas precede and inform experience. However, there is another point of attack from which the theory should be tested, and that is its assumed concept of society and the social. In the passages that follow I reconstruct the theory of the social in sociology that I take to be the premise of social construction theory. It is the sociologists' concept of society that, I suggest, is the basis of social construction theory and it is that that I want to reconstruct now.

Society and intersubjectivity

> Social action, which includes both failure to act and passive acquiescence, may be oriented to the past, present or expected future behaviour of others. Thus it may be motivated by revenge for a past attack, defence against present, or measures against future aggression. The 'others' may be individual persons, and may be known to the actor as such, or may constitute an indefinite plurality and may be entirely unknown as individuals.[15]

Max Weber's definition of social action implies a definition of society. Social action is action oriented towards others. It embraces action oriented towards those 'others' known to the actor and those unknown. The picture of society here is reached through an implied sequence from the interpersonal relations that are clear to us, like familial relations, for example, to a broader set of relations, relations with 'an indefinite plurality'. Is this a legitimate leap? A relation to an individual person known to the actor is something that is quite easy to imagine. A relation to 'an indefinite plurality [who] may be entirely unknown as individuals', however, is less easy to picture. The weight of Weber's definition rests on the leap from interpersonal relations to a relation to something called 'society'.

The sociologist George Simmel, like his contemporary Weber, a pioneer of the science, dealt with the expansion of interpersonal relations into social relations through his discussion of the 'dyad' and the 'triad', in the 1908 work, *Sociologie, Untersuchungen über die Formen der Vergesellshaftung*.[16] The dyad, a relation of one to one, stands in the position of the interpersonal. The step towards the triad is supposed to represent the transition from the interpersonal to the social:

the difference between the dyad and larger groups consists in the fact that the dyad has a different relation to each of its two elements than have the larger groups to their members. Although for the outsider, the group consisting of two may function as an autonomous super-individual unit, it usually does not do so for its participants. Rather each of the two feels himself confronted only by the other, not by a collectivity above him. The social structure here rests immediately on the one and on the other of the two, and the secession of either would destroy the whole. The dyad, therefore does not attain that super-personal life which the individual feels to be independent of himself. As soon, however as there is a sociation of three, a group continues to exist even in case one of the members drops out.[17]

Thus Simmel usefully describes the difference between an interpersonal relationship between individuals and one that involves a larger 'sociation'. Simmel emphasises the way that relations between persons are interdependent, suggesting that voluntarism and consent are pre-requisites of the dyadic relation. By contrast, larger groups create the possibility of a loss of control as a 'super-personal life' intercedes, which the individual feels to be independent of himself. Georg Lukacs recalls that the idea of alienation was in the air in Germany in the early twentieth century.[18] Here we can see it in Simmel's discussion of dyad and triad.

However, Simmel's development of the concept of sociation, and of the development of a super-personal life is not satisfactory. In this telling it is simply the introduction of a third partner that forces the step from interpersonal relations to social relations. A merely quantitative numerical change does not seem sufficient to occasion the qualitative shift from interpersonal relations to a social relation. In this version society is an extension of the sequence: Individual...Dyad...Triad, recalling the apocryphal tribe whose number system consisted of 'one...two...many'. As with Weber, social relations are an extension of interpersonal relations, or an extrapolation from the same, as if the mere aggregation of persons would bring into being a society. The vernacular expression 'the world and his wife', could stand as an example of the necessarily incomplete character of the series that leads from the interpersonal to the bad infinity of the social. The logical conclusion of the transition from social action, as action oriented towards others, through 'dyadic' and 'triadic' relations is society, but society understood as an intersubjectivity.

In the work of Edmund Husserl, the theory that reality is a social construct is first advanced. The concept of society that Husserl employs can be seen to be that of the sociologists, of the social as an intersubjectivity.

Husserl's description of the social consensus makes it clear that he is talking of an intersubjectivity: 'Before even taking notice of it at all, we are conscious of the open horizon of our fellow men with its limited nucleus of our neighbours, those known to us.' He continues:

> We are thereby conscious of the men on our external horizon in each case as 'others'; in each case 'I' am conscious of them as 'my' others, as those with whom I can enter into actual and potential, immediate and mediate relations of empathy; this involves a reciprocal 'getting along' with others; and on the basis of these relations I can deal with them, enter into particular modes of community with them, and then know, in a habitual way, of my being so related.[19]

Here is the developed sociologists' version of society that is implicit in the concept of social action as action oriented towards others. Incorporated within it, without being reformulated, is the relation of 'I' to 'my' others. Society is a reciprocity, a 'getting along' with others. This reciprocity is an intersubjectivity.

Jean Francois Lyotard's 1954 exposition of phenomenology explains well Husserl's argument, citing Husserl's *Cartesian Meditations:*

> When he writes that 'transcendental subjectivity is intersubjectivity', or that the spiritual world has an absolute ontological priority over the natural world, we are led to believe that the *Einfülung*, or coexistence with the Other which is an understanding of the Other, brings about a relation of reciprocity where the concrete transcendental subject grasps itself as Other in that it is 'an other' for the Other, and introduces an absolutely original element into this subject: the social.[20]

However, good as Lyotard's reading is, that last move, from 'the Other' to 'the social' is illegitimate. In fact 'the social' described here is no more transcendent of the reciprocal relation of the subject and its other than 'transcendental subjectivity is intersubjectivity'. No transcendence is taking place. The myriad relations of subject and other, remain what they were from the outset, reflex categories: the one is other to the other, the other is other to the one. Intersubjectivity is only an advance on subjectivity in the most formal sense of an addition of other subjectivities.

The sociological concept of society does not transcend subjectivity. Despite its scientific invocation of a logos, it is closer to the religious teachings of the existentialist Martin Buber. In his 1921 work *Ich und Du (I and Thou)* Buber elaborates a theology from the counterposition of the twofold attitude of the I-it of the natural world, on the one hand, and of the I-thou on the other. As with the sociologists, it is the relation of I-thou that is taken as elemental to man's worth. Buber insists that 'the relation to the Thou is direct. No system of ideas, no foreknowledge, and no fancy intervene between I and Thou'.[21] Nonetheless there is a spiritual transcendence contained within the relation of I and Thou:

> In every sphere in its own way, through each process of becoming that is present to us we look outward to the eternal Thou; in each we are aware of a breath from the eternal Thou; in each Thou we address the eternal Thou.[22]

Martin Buber's anti-rational theology is not logically that different from the sociological concept of society. Both extrapolate outwards from inter-subjectivity; I and Thou in Buber's case, social action in Weber's. Weber hopes to reach society, Buber aims at eternity. Buber's eternity is as near and as far as Weber's society.

Sociology takes intersubjectivity to be society. What is lost in the sociological definition of the social? We can find out by contrasting the sociological concept of the social with Karl Marx's concept of society.

The anti-social society

The first thing to notice about Marx's concept of society is that he has no general concept of society.[23] In so far as he reflects upon society in general he remains very much in the Enlightenment way of talking of man, rather than society. Indeed history to date is to Marx only the 'pre-history of human society'. Not only does Marx quite insistently decline to characterise society as such, preferring to talk of specific societies, but he insists that society has no real existence under the capitalist mode of production, the subject-matter of his life's work; *Capital: A Critical Analysis of Capitalist Production* published in 1887.

> A commodity is therefore a mysterious thing, simply because in it the social character of men's labour appears to them as an objective character stamped upon the product of that labour; because the relation of the producers to the sum total of their own labour is presented to them as a social relation existing not between them, but between the products of their labour.[24]

The theory of commodity fetishism outlined above is not simply a theory of the values of commodities, but a theory of the totality of social relations under the capitalist mode of production. Marx's developed point is that all social relations under capitalism are relations of exchange. Where markets predominate, every aspect of human society is ordered through exchange. Not just products for consumption, but the whole of society's productive apparatus, land, funds for investment and even the productive abilities of individuals are subsumed under the market as commodities to be traded.

Consequently social relations—which for Marx are substantially relations of production—are not directly social. Rather they take place through the medium of private property and the relations between private individuals of the exchange of private property:

> In other words, the labour of the individual asserts itself as a part of the labour of society, only by means of the relations which the act of exchange establishes directly between the products, and indirectly, through them, between the producers. To the latter, therefore, the relations connecting the labour of one individual with that of the rest appear not as direct relations between individuals at work, but as what they really are, material relations between persons and social relations between things.[25]

Karl Marx's theory of commodity fetishism was not without precedent. Adam Smith, the founder of English political economy made the point in his *Wealth of Nations*: 'It is not from the benevolence of the butcher, the brewer or the baker that we expect our dinner, but from their regard to their own self-interest.'[26] The political economists grasped that the social division of labour was established through the 'invisible hand' of the market. It was through regard to their self-interest that men's social nature was realised.

The German philosophy that the young Marx studied was already translating the insight of the political economy into broader philosophical terms. In his *Idea for a Universal History with a Cosmopolitan Intent* Immanuel Kant's 'Fourth Thesis' opens:

> The means that nature uses to bring about the development of all man's capacities is the antagonism among them in society, as far as in society the end of this antagonism is the cause of law-governed order in society. In this context I understand antagonism to mean men's unsocial sociability, ie, their tendency to enter into society, combined, however, with a thorough-going resistance that constantly threatens to sunder this society.[27]

The most developed form of the theory in German idealism, however, was Hegel's. In *Phenomenology of Spirit* and *The Philosophy of Right* Hegel develops the idea of the 'cunning of reason'. As Hegel tells it, a super-individual reason attains its purposes through the apparently free acts of individual men, who are unaware that through their free will a greater force operates. It is the Hegelian conception of the 'cunning of reason' that Marx translates back into the this-worldly language of the capital accumulation process. For Marx the laws of capitalist production operate 'behind the backs of the producers', as with Hegel, but they are not thereby granted a spurious intentionality. On the contrary, they operate blindly, spontaneously. As a spontaneous process, capital accumulation is the opposite of rationality for Marx.

Of course the sociologists were aware of the process of 'commodification'. But for them it is not the defining feature of social relations under capitalism. Rather it is a discrete influence, another factor in society. Hence for Weber, the money relation is just one example of the way that social action may be oriented towards an unknown plurality.[28] Similarly, Simmel writes of 'the money economy' as 'another source' of the blasé attitude that prevails in the modern metropolis.[29] What explains the specific character of capitalist society is reduced to one descriptive feature of the eclectic mix of the modern metropolis.

Certain things flow from Marx's version of the social. First, in the words of David Hume and Margaret Thatcher, 'there is no such thing as society'— at least not immediately.[30] The whole point of the anti-social character of capitalist society is that man's sociability is not reached directly, but mediated through the relations of private appropriation. This is quite a distinct version of the relationship between the intersubjective and the social, from that advanced in sociology. In sociology, as we saw above, the social is an extension of the intersubjective. It is the end point 'many' of the sequence 'one...two...many'. By contrast, intersubjective relations are, for Marx, the immediate appearance of the social relation of capital accumulation. Put the other way round, intersubjective relations, relations of exchange, are the form through which social relations are mediated. Consequently, in the Marxist system, relations generally appear only in a mediated form. For example, the rate at which the ruling class exploits the working class has no immediate existence, but is instead reflected in the rate of return on the capital of independent investors. Nonetheless, Marx maintains, the former is determinant, the latter is derivative.

The second thing that flows from the Marxist concept of capitalism's anti-social society, is that the surface appearance of intersubjectivity is distinct from its underlying, and hidden social essence. Indeed Marx says 'all science would be superfluous if the outward appearance and the essence of things directly coincided'.[31] By contrast, the phenomenological roots of social construction theory rule the question of an underlying essence outside of the matter under investigation. Hence Husserl 'brackets' the question of whether the phenomena of social experience have an external referent. Social construction theorists consider it 'arrogant' to assume that there is a true picture beneath the perceptions of the community under examination. Marx, on the other hand, remains in the spirit of the Enlightenment with his insistence that beyond ordinary understanding lies developed reason.

Thirdly, reducing the social to the intersubjective, must, as a consequence, mystify the real operation of social relations. To take the superficial relations between subjects for society itself could only lead to a reduction of the latter to the former: but intersubjectivity is not society. Consequently the mediating links between the underlying social determinants and their immediate form as relations between persons are collapsed into each other. Just as the social is reduced to the intersubjective, so too is the mediated whole, capitalist society, reduced to its immediate parts, market relations. With their origins in the process of capitalist accumulation obscured, market relations appear to be arbitrary, contingent and free.

In sociology any number of determinants can be granted the status of social determinants. Peer group pressure, ethnic identification, class, gender, generational identification, educational background, neighbourhood—all of these disparate phenomena are placed on a par as social forces.[32] In fact none of the above is a social determinant, rather they are only intersubjective phenomena.

Karl Marx had no knowledge of the phenomenological 'bracketing' that Edmund Husserl was to undertake after his death. Still Marx does, by accident, anticipate the argument in his discussion of money, where he rejects the view that money is a social convention:

> But if it be declared that the social characters assumed by objects, or the material forms assumed by the social qualities of labour under the regime of a definite mode of production, are mere symbols, it is in the same breath also declared that these characteristics are arbitrary fictions sanctioned by the so-called universal consent of mankind. This suited the mode of explanation in favour during the eighteenth century. Unable to account for the origin of the puzzling forms assumed by social relations between man and man, people sought to denude them of their strange appearance by ascribing to them a conventional origin.[33]

One advantage of the Marxist conception of a society whose social content is masked by its anti-social form is anticipated here. The concept of society as a social construct, or convention, takes unconscious processes for conscious processes. Who is doing the constructing? In Marx's example eighteenth-century writers treated a spontaneous and non-rational process as if it were rational.

So too do the theorists of social construction talk as if social phenomena were rational constructs. But where is the forum in which society is constructed?

At the level of interpersonal relations, deliberation prevails. Severally we are all free. But 'society' is not a conscious entity. Rendering unconscious social processes as if they were rational conflates the intersubjective with the social, and appearance with essence. There is an implied denial of a distinction between essence and appearance that is anti-essentialist.

Anti-essentialism

The reduction of the social to the intersubjective implies a reduction of the mediate to the immediate, and of essence to appearance. Indeed the fully developed social construction theory forbids an investigation from appearance to essence under the slogans of 'anti-essentialism' or 'anti-foundationalism'.

Anti-essentialism, the idea that there are no underlying essences, is strong today. It is argued that what were once seen as objective foundations to knowledge are in reality only subjective ways of organising the material under investigation. Pejoratively, such essentialist or foundationalist theories are called 'grand narratives' or 'metaphysics'. And the proper attitude to such grand narratives is one of incredulity.[34]

For radical-minded people it often seems attractive to dispense with essence because such essences are usually naturalistic essences, like the supposed genetic superiority of whites over blacks. There is a kind of similarity between Marx's critique of classical political economy and the social construction theory's critique of naturalistic social theory. Marx rejects the classical economists' prejudice that the laws they uncovered, such as the theory that value is embodied labour, were laws of nature. Instead, Marx insists that these laws are laws of capitalist society.

There is, however, also a clear difference between Marx's critique of classical political economy and the social construction theorists' assertion that there are *no* essences, natural or otherwise. Firstly, Marx also criticised the 'vulgar' theory of value: that values are simply subjective expressions of the desires of the purchasers. By contrast, he insists that the superficial and relative expression of value in exchange must reflect objective values. For Marxists, the theory that there are no essences throws the baby out with the bathwater. Because there are no natural essences, it does not follow that there are no essences whatsoever. On the contrary, science is necessary because essence and appearance do not coincide.

Radical critics of Marx follow through the logic of the anti-essentialistic theory and apply it to Marx. In his *Mirror of Production* Jean Baudrillard asserts that Marx has not successfully extricated himself from the outlook of the classical economists. Though Marx has extricated himself from the directly naturalistic concept of the economy, Baudrillard says, he remains implicated in the underlying assumptions of classical economy. For Marx, like Adam Smith and David Ricardo, shares the prejudice that productivity is the goal of the economy. 'Productivism', according to Baudrillard is the common, essentialistic presupposition of the Marxists and the classical economists.[35] And, of course, if one accepts the argument that all essences are reactionary, then Marx too is a reactionary. But there is no reason to accept any such thing.

Implicit in the anti-essentialistic character of sociological categories is a tendency towards indeterminacy and eclecticism. As explanations of the way that people interact, a theory of intersubjectivity can only ever serve as a description. In the initial concept of social action outlined by Max Weber the striking thing is the indeterminacy of the definition. Social action is defined too broadly to delimit an area of investigation. The question of what kind of social action is postponed. This indeterminate character carries through all the categories of sociology: norm and dysfunction, traditional and modern societies, groups and sub-groups. As categories these all put the work of delimiting an area of investigation off into the future. By contrast the specification of the capitalist mode of production fixes on a characteristic that Marx sees as a defining one.

It should not be assumed, however, that because the categories of sociology are non-specific that its investigations remain equally abstract. On the contrary, the very abstract nature of sociological categories means that the real world intrudes spontaneously as these categories take up an empirical content. The problem is that the manner in which empirical reality is present in sociology is eclectic, that is, it does not accord to any logic, either of the investigation or of the subject-matter, but accidentally as verification, or illustration of the matter in hand. So one begins with 'groups' as a category, and then finds real groups to illustrate the phenomena. The collection of groups remains eclectically related under a wholly formal category, 'groups'.

This spontaneous empiricism is particularly debilitating for social construction theory. Social construction theory purports to give an explanation of the way that identities and mores are socially constructed. But, with its deficient concept of the social, it is incapable of doing so. Rather it can only describe how in their relations to one another, certain identities prevail, and certain interpretations of reality predominate. To ask of social construction theory the question why, say, gender relations are constructed the way they are is to ask an interminable question: young girls and boys are socialised into their gendered roles with Barbie dolls and Action Men. Their mothers, too, were taught these roles by their mothers before them. And so the sequence extends ever further backwards to a prehistoric patriarchy. It is clear why there can be no explanation of the cause of sexual stereotypes: causality is ruled out of court. Only the particular prejudices of men are offered as explanation of the particular subjugation of women. But that is to describe everything and explain nothing.

The indeterminacy of sociological categories arises from the discipline's character as a register only of the intersubjective. Intersubjective relations may seem to have a local logic of their own, such as investigated in psychology. However, to become meaningful as social phenomena intersubjective relations must be understood as themselves mediations of social determinants. The Marxist concept of commodity fetishism explains how interpersonal relations of exchange mediate the laws of development of capitalist society. This picture has been assumed to be rather forbidding by the social scientists after Marx. It is taken as a picture that excludes human agency. That, however, is to substantially misunderstand Marx.

Marx's investigation of the inner laws of capitalist society is not intended to set them in stone. On the contrary, Marx's concept of social law is dynamic. By investigating the movement of capitalist society, Marx intends to isolate those trends that imply a supersession of that society, and those limitations that stand in the way of social development. Marx's theory is not idle. It is intended to illuminate the barriers to human development so that they may be overcome, in fact, through the conscious intervention of men. For Marx, necessity is the mother of invention. Self-determination both arises out of and overcomes determination.

But for sociology, and especially for the theory of the social construction of reality, it is very different. Here the appearance is one of great freedom. Agency is at hand, not obscured by talk of social laws. But because agency remains at the level of mere intersubjectivity, it is peculiarly local and partial. At the level of interpersonal behaviour we are the authors of our situation, as negotiated with other actors. But any wider arena of society is closed to us. Indeed for sociologists it is questionable whether any such arena exists.

Consider Max Weber's distinction between what is and is not a legitimate area of sociological investigation; 'There are', he warns us 'statistics of processes devoid of meaning such as death rates, phenomena of fatigue, the production rate of machines, the amount of rainfall'. Now, barring the last, it should be apparent that the other three 'processes devoid of meaning' were questions of great importance to the socialists and Marxists of Weber's day. Those men were concerned with such social questions as overwork, the unrewarded productivity of their mechanised labour, and the mortality rates that reflected their social disadvantage. Nor indeed are these questions closed today.

On the other hand, there are, according to Weber, statistics that are susceptible to sociology and therefore 'meaningful'. Examples of these are 'crime rates, occupational distributions, price statistics, and statistics of crop acreage'.[36] It is pointed that, apart perhaps from crime, the social dimensions cited hold at the level of the market. Here Weber's conception of society is analogous to the micro-economic focus of neo-classical economics. Only the immediate relations of exchange that hold in the markets for labour, commodities and land can be considered as an arena of 'meaning'.

So for sociology, agency obtains at the level of the intersubjective, which we associate with the level of the market, but beyond the immediate relations of one to one, we may not enquire. Society sketched any further than immediate relations between persons is a closed book. Here agency relates to necessity not by overcoming it, but as its limit point. Freedom here is not like Marx's recognition of and leap from necessity. It is less a picture of a diver and his diving board, and more a square peg in a round hole. The space between peg and hole is the arena of freedom in which we rattle away.

A contemporary example of a sociologist who holds to the idea that reality is socially constructed shows just how limited is this sense of agency. In *Beyond Left and Right: The Future of Radical Politics*, Anthony Giddens writes about a reflexive modernity that echoes Edmund Husserl's concept of the life-world. What Giddens means by 'reflexive modernity' is that the kind of society we have is changing because it is having to deal with its own consequences for the first time. The argument is that the advanced industrial societies of the nineteenth and early twentieth century were all going in one direction: higher productivity, greater scientific understanding and better standards of living. By contrast, in his view, modernisation becomes reflexive when the productive and social processes begin to react back upon modernisation itself.

Here Giddens borrows from Ulrich Beck's concept of a 'risk society'. The 'risks' proliferate the more society develops. In large part Beck draws upon his knowledge of industrial pollution to illustrate his point. Industrial processes create unforeseen circumstances, like poisonous waste, that undermine our capacity to anticipate the future.[37] Giddens goes further. 'Our daily actions are', he writes 'thoroughly infected by manufactured uncertainties' which continue to describe 'open and problematic futures which we have, as it were, to work on as we go along in the present'. 'We influence processes of change', he adds 'but full control of them chronically eludes our grasp'.[38]

Giddens' sociology meets his political project here. *Beyond Left and Right* is not just an analysis of society, but also a political, or rather an anti-political, tract. His argument is that since those 'processes' 'chronically elude our grasp', politics must abandon its goal of planning the future. Giddens' earlier works were intended to be an alternative to 'historical materialism'. *Beyond Left and Right* resumes that task and Giddens attacks Marx because he presumes the greatest degree of human control over society: 'The Promethean outlook which so influenced Marx should be more or less abandoned in the face of the insuperable complexity of society and nature.'[39]

This is a deeply conservative and apologetic argument. The 'risk society' cannot be overcome, only anticipated and prepared for. It is also a mystification. Risk, or 'manufactured uncertainty' is a characterisation that removes all culpability. But the risks faced by building workers or tube drivers are not in any way 'chronically elusive' in their origins, but due principally to cost-cutting and over-long working hours pursued by their employers. And work-related injuries remain the highest risk in the world.

Giddens writes as if society had only recently run out of control. But capitalist society, ordered around the allocation of labour through the market, has always been a spontaneous social order. Far from being inescapable, though, 'manufactured uncertainty' is a compelling reason to replace the market with a rationally planned society. But instead Beck and Giddens continue to conflate the real problems of unemployment and exploitation with the fears of unknown dangers ahead.

There is, however, another side to Giddens' argument that is less pessimistic. Although Giddens denies change at the level of society, he does endorse change at the level of the individual. Indeed, Giddens protests that he is no traditional conservative. Rather, he says, individuals not only can, but must take control of their own lives to deal with manufactured uncertainty. This is a return to the ideas of his earlier work, *The Transformation of Intimacy,* in which Giddens wrote about how people can reinvent themselves to accommodate new and unfamiliar circumstances.[40]

For Giddens, then, the indeterminacy at the social level is the precondition for freedom at the level of the individual. He thinks that the risk society should be embraced as an arena where the individual can find his true metier. But accommodating oneself to risk seems to be a poor idea of freedom. After all, insisting that society is indeterminate is not the same thing as transcending real determinations. As Heraclitus said 'The more one puts oneself at the mercy of chance, the more chance will involve one in the laws of necessity and inevitability.'[41]

In *Beyond Left and Right,* the project of accommodation begins to sound like apologetics, as Giddens invites us to foster the 'autotelic self'. Striking a Thatcherite note he explains 'The autotelic self does not seek to neutralise risk or to suppose that "someone else will take care of the problem"'. The language is New Age—'risk is confronted as the active challenge which generates self-actualisation'.[42] Underneath the jargon, Giddens is saying that you can make it, though he is careful to talk about psychic happiness, instead of material success. His proposition that 'happiness and its opposite bear no particular relation to either wealth or the possession of power' sounds suspiciously like the old cliché, money can't bring happiness.[43]

Of course, there is nothing inherently wrong with taking responsibility for changing your circumstances. But Giddens' argument, like that of other apologists for capitalism, restricts the arena of change to that of the individual and his or her immediate connections with wider society. He presumes that change at the level of society is beyond our grasp.

The point made earlier was that the sociologists' arguments echoed those of neo-classical economics, in demarcating the intelligible arena of inter-personal relations from the opaque, and allegedly fictitious realm, of social determination. But while sociology's method is similar to micro-economics, it is not the same. Modern economics is preoccupied with interpersonal relations as market relations. The demarcation of sociology as a special science separate from economics tends to justify the way that economics is considered apart from its social content, as though prices were only expressions of desire or technical information. Economics with the social aspect taken out is reduced to a statistical inquiry.

Sociology, too, is one-sided. It restricts its investigations to interpersonal relations, but looks at these less as economic relations, than as cultural, institutional or ideological relations. The raw material of sociology is found in the public institutions that are established to cope with market failure or that exist at the perimeters of the spontaneous operation of the market. Much excellent research has been undertaken by social constructionists investigating the way that the family is informed by institutional supports, or that racial identities are cohered by processes of regulation, either official or semi-official.

Rich as these investigations are, they tend only to see the end-point of the process of fixing, or 'constructing' identities. The social constructionists strength is in the treatment of the way that social trends are consolidated in institutions and ideologies. But unfortunately, it is the submerged pre-history of these institutional or cultural forms that social construction theory neglects. That pre-history is unfortunately ruled out of court as an 'essentialist' or 'foundationalist' explanation.

The theory of social construction is not wrong, only limited. It reflects the growing recognition of the contingency of capitalist social relations. To that extent it is a belated but welcome concession to Marx's theory of historical change. But, in so far as it seeks to understand society, it is constrained by the sociological reduction of society to intersubjectivity. Surprisingly, it is society itself that remains a closed book to the theory that reality is a social construction.

NOTES

1 Though Helen Wilkinson uses the less naturalistic term 'cohort' in her *Demos* pamphlet *Genderquake.*

2 'As consuming citizens we seek to purchase our fetishised individual unique sexual identities and lifestyles within the increasingly self-imposed confinement of sexual communities.' David Evans in Angelia Wilson (Ed), *A Simple Matter of Justice?*, Cassell, 1995, p116. He also writes of '"cultural scenarios" in the form of intra- and inter-personal scripts' p115.

3 At a demonstration against cuts in education in London in March 1995 I heard a platform speaker repeat a familiar sociologist's inventory of social roles. She introduced herself as 'a school governor, a mother and a teacher'.

4 See Suke Wolton, 'Racial identities: the degradation of human constructions', given as a paper in this seminar series and reproduced in this volume.

5 Georg Lukacs recalls: 'Once during the First World War Scheler visited me in Heidelberg, and we had an informing conversation on this subject. Scheler maintained that phenomenology was a universal method which could have anything for its intentional object. For example, he explained, phenomenological researches could be made about the devil; only the question of the devil's reality would first have to be "bracketed". "Certainly", I answered, "and when you are finished with the phenomenological picture of the devil, you open the brackets and the devil is standing before you". Scheler, laughed, shrugged his shoulders and made no reply.' Georg Lukacs, 'Existentialism', in *Marxism and Human Liberation*, Delta, 1973, p246. Today the proposed research might be published under the title of *The Invented Devil: A Study in the Social Construction of Evil.*

6 Edmund Husserl, *The Crisis of European Science and Transcendental Phenomenology*, (Trans D Carr) Northwestern University Press, 1970, pp353-78.

7 A contemporary version of Husserl's bracketing of the natural world can be found in Jeffrey Weeks, *Sex, Politics and Society*, Longman, 1989 (2nd ed). In Chapter 6, 'The construction of homosexuality', Weeks brackets the question of a natural foundation to sexual difference when he writes that, 'even if primary differences were biologically formed, this would not fundamentally alter the argument', p97.

8 Husserl's researches were not without precedent. Followers of Immanuel Kant in southern Germany had granted a greater role to history in the development of ideas. For example, Heinrich Rickert wrote: 'From philosophical standpoints "nature" itself—in other words, the conception of reality with respect to the general, or the nomological nexus—becomes a product of the historical *work of culture.*' Heinrich Rickert, *The Limits of Concept Formation in Natural Science*, Cambridge University Press, 1986 (orig 1902), p226

9 Edmund Husserl, *The Crisis of European Sciences and Transcendental Phenomenology*, Northwestern University Press, 1970, pp121-23

10 Edmund Husserl, *The Crisis of European Sciences and Transcendental Phenomenology*, Northwestern University Press, 1970, p168

11 Karl Marx, *Capital*, Vol1, Penguin, 1976, pp997-98. All other citations are to the Lawrence & Wishart edition

12 Karl Marx, *Capital*, Vol1, Lawrence & Wishart, Moscow, 1983, p63

13   Fillippo Brunelleschi is widely credited with the invention of perspective, circa
     1420. See N Kelly Smith, *Here I Stand: Perspective from Another Point of View*,
     Columbia University Press, 1994

14   Richard Herrnstein and Charles Murray, *The Bell Curve*, The Free Press, 1994

15   Max Weber, *The Theory of Social and Economic Organisation*, (Talcott Parsons
     Ed), William Hodge, 1947 (orig 1922), p102

16   Reprinted in Kurt H Wolff (Ed), *The Sociology of George Simmel*, The Free Press,
     1950

17   Kurt H Wolff (Ed), *The Sociology of George Simmel*, The Free Press, 1950, and
     cited in Kenneth Thompson and Jeremy Tunstall (Eds), *Sociological Perspectives:
     Selected Readings*, Penguin, 1971, p80

18   See Lucien Goldmann, *Lukacs and Heidegger: Towards a New Philosophy*,
     (Trans WQ Boelhower), Routledge & Kegan Paul, 1977

19   Reproduced in Thomas Luckmann (Ed), *Phenomenology and Sociology*,
     Penguin Modern Social Readings, 1978, p48

20   Jean Francois Lyotard, *Phenomenology*, State University of New York, 1991, p75

21   Martin Buber, *Ich und Du (I and Thou)*, Collier Books, 1987 (orig 1921), p11

22   Martin Buber, *Ich und Du (I and Thou)*, Collier Books, 1987 (orig 1921), p6

23   There is a sketch of a theory of society as such in the *Introduction to the Critique
     of Political Economy*, though its main purpose is to highlight the formal charac-
     ter of transhistorical social categories. See Marx and Engels, *Introduction to the
     Critique of Political Economy* in *The German Ideology*, Students edition,
     Lawrence & Wishart, 1970

24   Karl Marx, *Capital*, Vol1, Lawrence & Wishart, 1983, p77

25   Karl Marx, *Capital*, Vol1, Lawrence & Wishart, 1983, p78

26   Adam Smith, *Wealth of Nations*, Penguin Classics, 1987 (orig 1776), p119.
     Smith in turn developed his point from Bernard Mandeville whose polemical
     poem *The Fable of the Bees: or, Private Vices, Publick Benefits*, written in 1714,
     imagines the economy as a hive of bees where 'every part was full of Vice/ Yet
     the whole Mass a Paradise'. 'And Vertue, who from Politicks/Had Learn'd a
     Thousand cunning Tricks/Was, by their happy Influence/Made Friends with
     Vice: And ever since/The Worst of all the Multitude/Did Something for the
     common Good', Bernard Mandeville, *The Fable of the Bees*, Penguin, 1970
     (orig 1714), pp67-68.

27   Immanuel Kant, *Perpetual Peace and Other Essays*, Hackett, 1988 (orig 1784),
     pp31-32.

28   Max Weber writes: 'Thus "money" as a means of exchange which the actor
     accepts in payment because he orients his action to the expectation that a large
     but unknown number of individuals he is personally unacquainted with will be
     ready to accept it in exchange on some future occasion.' Cited in Kenneth
     Thompson and Jeremy Tunstall (Eds), *Sociological Perspectives: Selected
     Readings*, Penguin, 1971, p138

29   Georg Simmel, *The Metropolis and Mental Life*, cited in Kenneth Thompson
     and Jeremy Tunstall (Eds), *Sociological Perspectives: Selected Readings*, Penguin,
     1971, p87

30 Margaret Thatcher; 'I don't believe in society. There is no such thing, only individual people, and there are families.' Quoted in an interview with *Women's Own*, 31 October 1987

31 Karl Marx, *Capital*, Vol3, Lawrence & Wishart, 1984, p817

32 Take this example from the Frankfurt school 'The specification of the human being as a person implies that he always finds himself in *specific interpersonal roles* within the social relations in which he lives, before he is even aware of this. Because of this, he is what he is in relation to others: a child of a mother, student of a teacher, member of a tribe or of a profession; this relation then is not external to him, but one within which and in terms of which he defines himself as specifically this or that.' The Frankfurt Institute, *Aspects of Sociology*, Heinemann Educational Books, 1973, p28

33 Karl Marx, *Capital*, Vol1, Lawrence & Wishart, 1974, p94. Marx cites V de Forbonnais, 'Elements du commerce', tII, p143 and p155 (1766) and Montesquieu, 'Esprit des lois', tII, p2 (1767). If he were writing today he could add his own less than attentive student Alain Lipietz, 'Reflections on a tale', *Studies in Political Economy*, No26, 1988, who imagined a society with a conventionally agreed currency, in apparent ignorance of this passage.

34 Jean Francois Lyotard, *The Postmodern Condition*, Manchester University Press, 1984. Lyotard summed up the modern as 'any science that legitimates itself with reference to a metadiscourse...making an explicit appeal to some grand narrative, such as the dialectics of Spirit, hermeneutics of meaning, the emancipation of the rational or working subject or the creation of wealth.' (p*xxiii*) And, furthermore, postmodernists must show 'incredulity to metanarratives' (p*xxiv*).

35 See Jean Baudrillard, *The Mirror of Production*, Telos Press, 1975 and Scott Meikle, *Essentialism in the Thought of Karl Marx*, Open Court (and Duckworth), 1985

36 Max Weber, *The Theory of Social and Economic Organisation*, (Talcott Parsons Ed), William Hodge, 1947 (orig 1922), p91

37 Ulrich Beck, *Risk Society: Towards a New Modernity*, Sage, 1992

38 Anthony Giddens, *Beyond Left and Right: The Future of Radical Politics*, Polity Press, 1994, p79

39 Anthony Giddens, *Beyond Left and Right: The Future of Radical Politics*, Polity Press, 1994, p79

40 Anthony Giddens, *The Transformation of Intimacy: Sexuality, Love and Eroticism in Modern Societies*, Polity, 1992

41 *Heraclitus and Diogenes*, translated from the Greek by Guy Davenport, Grey Fox Press, 1976, p23

42 Anthony Giddens, *Beyond Left and Right: The Future of Radical Politics*, Polity Press, 1994, p192

43 Anthony Giddens, *Beyond Left and Right: The Future of Radical Politics*, Polity Press, 1994, p181

3
Uncertain judgement: a critique of the culture of crime

Andrew Calcutt

By day they talk loudly and intimately in public places, larding their language with swear-words and pushing through doors in front of their elders and betters. On buses they sit tight on their seats chewing gum while little old ladies sway in front of them. Headphones and Walkmans cut them off from the ordinary world and tune them into totally unintelligible radio stations which batter their eardrums with crude jungle rhythms. At night they glue themselves to TV programmes and videos in order to absorb what seems to be an alarming amoral mix of violence and sexuality, now on tap for 24 hours a day. Electrocution, impaling, squishing into liquid pulp and puffing apart in a cloud of stars are all a fingertip away for Gameboy and Nintendo cyberneticides.[1]

Commenting on the killing of James Bulger on Merseyside in February 1993, *Sunday Telegraph* columnist Christina Hardyment sought to locate the origins of youthful criminality in terms of mannerisms, consumption and lifestyle. The picture she painted amounts to a culture of crime in which real-life events parallel the brutal fantasies of popular iconography.

Hardyment is not so crude as to assert that computer games and/or rap music lead directly to the murder of children. But she equates aggressive music with aggressive behaviour, and suggests that these two mutually reinforcing elements combine to create a kind of anti-civilisation—a lifeworld which desensitises and disinhibits all those who enter into it. Her message is that bad manners and violent images are only a 'fingertip' away from violent crime, and anyone who adopts the lifestyle associated with the former is likely to become a perpetrator of the latter. She offers no evidence with which to substantiate this claim, but—in today's climate at least—its lack of substance in no way diminishes its purchase on public opinion.

Hardyment is only one of many subscribers to the notion that there is a culture of crime, and that crime can best be understood as a culture. 'From millions of car stereos and boom boxes, gangsta rappers and skinhead semi-demi-quasi-neo Nazis give the nation its most persistent defining soundtrack', warned Peter Hamill in the New York edition of *Esquire*. 'Rob the weak, they croon. Stomp the soft...pop culture both feeds and reflects the larger society'.[2] Fellow American Michael Medved projected 'the seeds of evil sown on our screens' as the most virulent element in the growth of a culture of crime.[3]

In the *Independent*, James Style connected 'illegality' with the 'gangster and gun culture' celebrated in the lyrics of 'jungle music'.[4] Bryan Appleyard cited footballer Eric Cantona as the icon of a culture of violence: 'to his fans, his crimes are accessories, the essential kit of the existentially pure, authentic soul that is ooh-ah Eric.'[5] Both these commentators were content to overlook the distinction between real violence and fantasy. Introducing the necessary distinction would have undermined their attempts to conceptualise violence as a lifestyle choice which some people are apparently predisposed to make.

In March 1995, the *Sunday Times* suggested that: 'the availability of drugs and violent videos' has given birth to 'the savage generation'.[6] A month earlier, the *Sunday Times* claimed that 'television culture' had contributed to a 50 per cent rise in mental illness among children. The culture of crime, it is alleged, makes young people both mad and bad.

The notion of a media-driven culture of crime stretches from old-style right wingers such as Theodore Dalrymple ('the lost children of the video nasty age'[7]) to erstwhile members of the Communist Party of Great Britain. Prominent ex-Stalinist Beatrix Campbell warns that delinquent 'lads' are 'surrounded by macho propaganda...soaked in globally transmitted images and ideologies of butch and brutal solutions to life's difficulties'.[8] A new consensus seems to have emerged around the tired, old notion that life imitates art.

Mensch ist was er isst, says the German proverb: man is what he eats. In his 1953 essay, 'The phantom world of TV', postwar German critic of mass culture Gunther Anders was among the first to relocate the proverb on to the terrain of cultural consumption. With the assertion, 'it is through the consumption of mass commodities that mass men are produced', Anders was suggesting that we are what we watch.[9] He was already wary of the allegedly poor taste and potentially anti-social tendencies of 'mass men'. Forty years on, these misgivings have been amplified enormously. It is now widely assumed that the consumption of images of criminality converges with criminal activities to produce a 'culture of crime'.

The Bulger case reactivated a long-standing debate about which comes first: criminal behaviour or media images of criminality. The debate continues, but both sides have already agreed that violent images and anti-social activities together comprise a culture which is criminogenic. Once this notion has been arrived at, it is then called upon to account for a wide range of anti-social activities. At best, this is a description of crime as an activity which individuals learn from social interaction. Of course it is true that each criminal does not invent crime anew. John Donne's observation that 'no man is an island' applies as much to the lawbreaker as to the poet who hears the funeral bell. But why should there be a propensity to learn crime rather than, say, hard work and self-discipline? The description of crime as a culture offers no explanations for this. It stalls at the level of surface appearances, yet it is often advanced as if it were the last word in penetrating analysis.

It is my contention that the culturalisation of crime is a tautology which merely serves to confirm the prejudices of its authors. It is a substitute for analysis in an age when self-serving descriptions proliferate but social critique is singularly lacking. However, if the 'culture of crime' is banal, it is also true to its time; that is, no other social context could have given rise to its current usage. If it is tautologous, it is also an entirely appropriate expression of a society which is perhaps best described as a vicious circle. The pervasiveness of the notion of the culture of crime is indicative of a social system which is both stagnant and opaque. It is therefore worthwhile to investigate the notion of crime as culture in so far as it is an expression of contemporary society in all its contradictions.

We're all criminals now

One of the most striking characteristics of contemporary society is the widespread eagerness to identify the particular cultures which allegedly predispose their participants to a life of crime. So many particular cultures, however, have been identified as criminogenic that, taken together, they add up to a universe of criminality. What begins as an attempt to isolate the exceptional and unacceptable finishes as an index of flaws and failings which seem to have permeated the whole of society. The spontaneous and uncontrollable expansion of the term 'yob culture' is a case in point.

In September 1994, prime minister John Major 'declared war on Britain's "yob culture"'. In a speech to the Social Market Foundation, a beleaguered premier called for 'a national "anti-yob culture"' with parents and teachers instilling discipline and respect, and more councils using their powers to stamp out excessive public drinking'. There would be 'a crackdown on those who made the streets a frightening place' because, according to Major, people avoided city centres through fear being jostled, jeered at or made to feel insecure by rowdy and offensive behaviour.[10]

In this depiction, the perpetrators of 'yob culture' in the nineties would seem to be the younger brothers of the 'lager louts' of the late eighties. The *Spectator's* photofit highlighted the same features: 'yobs...fight in the stadiums, they get drunk on trains, they riot in the streets'.[11] Likewise in the *Daily Telegraph*, Hardyment identified the 'unskilled, randomly violent...potentially murderous misfits who make the well-meaning mass of good citizens quail' in an article entitled 'Have men got worse?'.[12]

Hardyment's 'misfits' are as testosterone-driven as Campbell's 'lads'. In the latter's eyes, criminal culture is almost exclusively male, and undirected masculinity is the defining element in the culture of crime. But other commentators are already concerned that criminogenic culture has leaked beyond the boundaries of its all-male, inner-city habitat.

'Are girls turning meaner?', enquired American journalist Andrea Jones. 'Since half the people in the world are women, I used to think that half the world was safe. Now I don't think that way. It seems to me that women are getting meaner and meaner, and that the youngest ones—the girls my age— are the worst.' Jones situates the new culture of aggression among young women alongside recent developments in fashion: 'popular culture also has decided it's "in" for girls to be rough. The hottest fashion for girls is the thuggish look, prison blues.'[13]

'Suddenly yob woman is everywhere', complained Anita Chaudhuri in the *Guardian*, 'spanning the whole lout spectrum from *Birds of a Feather* to cartoon-yobs 'Tank Girl' and the 'Fat Slags', to sporting yobs such as Tonya Harding and cruel violent yobs like the two females who received life sentences for their part in the torture and murder of Suzanne Capper'.[14] Chaudhuri conflates fiction and fact into a folk she-devil which she dubs 'yob femme', and claims to have encountered this cultural demon in the form of the stilettoed woman who spiked her foot in a bar in Hampstead. When film starlet and fashion model Elizabeth Hurley was robbed in a west London street by four young women, tabloid journalists conveyed the notion of 'yob femme' to a much larger reading public under the label 'girl gangs'.

Chaudhuri felt at risk, even in the heights of Hampstead. Is there no stratum immune from the culture of crime? Apparently not. In the *Sunday Times*, John Davison and Annabel Heseltine reported that 'crack, the street drug associated with inner-city ghettos, has penetrated the English upper classes' (Heseltine should know about the upper classes: she bears the same family name as president of the Board of Trade, Michael Heseltine).[15] Jones and Chaudhuri were apprehensive about the behaviour of women. The headline writer in the *Los Angeles Times* felt the same way about children: 'Who are our children? One day they are innocent. The next they may try to blow your head off.'[16] Similar uncertainties were expressed throughout Britain when it emerged that the killers of James Bulger were barely in their teens. The killing of a child by other children is extremely rare yet not unprecedented. In most years since the Second World War there have been one or two such instances.

But the Bulger murder was widely perceived to be uniquely horrific, and at the same time symbolic of a general loss of innocence and security.

It would seem that nothing is sacred and nowhere is safe from the culture of crime—not even the family. Gertrude Himmelfarb, the Republican social commentator and distinguished American academic,[17] has noted that the family 'is now seen as pathological, concealing behind the facade of respectability the new "original sin", child abuse'.[18] Hitherto regarded as synonymous with moral rectitude, the family, in today's exaggerated accounts, is often portrayed as the home of secret vices of the most odious kind. Himmelfarb is not alone in lamenting the fall from grace of this, the most revered of social institutions.

Old-fashioned communities now seem to be as prone to the culture of crime as inner-city ghettos. In Britain, it emerged that serial killer Frederick West lived within sight of Gloucester cathedral, in a street which appeared to be a bastion of tradition and respectability. There is no sanctuary from moral blight, even in the great plains of America. Idyllic images of fair-skinned, fair-minded people in the rural mid-West were irretrievably shattered in April 1995 when members of the unofficial Michigan Militia bombed the federal offices in Oklahoma City, killing 176 people and injuring many more. Commentators were forced to conclude that there are criminal cultures lurking in the rural heartland as well as the inner cities.

In Britain, the term 'yob culture' has even been applied to the unprincipled journalists who first put it into circulation (and this from one of their own, none other than Associated Newspapers chairman and former *Daily Mail* editor Sir David English).[19] This is the reflexive spiral of today's moral recrimination.

Each of the examples cited above highlights a particular culture which is alleged to be especially criminogenic. But taken together they indicate the implausibility of ascribing criminality to any particular culture. On the contrary, it would seem that the whole world has been incorporated into a culture of crime which is well-nigh universal. In the end, the attempt to locate the problem of crime by means of cultural coordinates only underlines the feeling that every section of society has already been tainted by a general culture of anti-social behaviour and criminality.

The 'culture of crime' would appear to be ubiquitous. But this only intensifies the pressure to identify its origins and track down the culprits. Once again, the spiral of recrimination repeats itself. Almost every expression of moral condemnation has a tendency to rebound on those who voiced it; and what started out as an attempt to specify criminogenic culture ends as an indictment of society and an expression of general self-doubt.

For example, John Major had hardly uttered his rallying cry against 'offensive behaviour' when Roy Chapman, chairman of the Headmasters' Conference, 'blamed the country's traditional leaders for encouraging "yob culture"'.[20] Chapman claimed that the failure of Britain's leaders to uphold standards had created a generation of selfish youngsters unable to tell the difference between right and wrong.

Chapman is head of the prominent public school, Malvern College, and chair of the normally right-wing community of headmasters. He is not the type of person who might be expected to attack a Conservative government for the poverty of its morals. The fact that this outburst came from such an unexpected quarter epitomises the contemporary spiral of corrosive self-doubt. Chapman's speech derided almost every traditional institution:

> The family no longer provides either the cohesive force or the base line in standards of behaviour. The church seems prepared to accept anything except intolerance, while the government seems to operate on the basis of political expediency, rather than on coherent policies, much less principle....Is there not something profoundly wrong with our values when there is a public debate about whether or not leaders of our country, be they senior politicians, civil servants, servicemen or sportsmen, should resign if they have been caught in an untruth or an indiscretion?[21]

Chapman blamed the senior politicians and church leaders. Christie Davies, sociology professor at Reading University, directed his ire at fellow academics: 'progressives' who 'created a culture not merely of moral confusion, but of moral excuses'.[22] 'We've been betrayed by the intellectuals', echoed professor Norman Dennis of Newcastle University.[23] In her contribution to the *Sunday Times* British Underclass Forum, Himmelfarb pointed the finger of blame in the same direction: 'the underclass...is not only the victim of its own "culture of poverty" but also the victim of the upper class culture around it.'[24]

Other commentators are less hostile to intellectuals and more concerned about the activities of marketing departments and especially their corrupting influence on children. In the aftermath of the Bulger killing, Greg Neale alleged in the *Sunday Telegraph* that 'the biggest change in the child's world is the extent to which he is now targeted by the commercial media'.[25] On BBC2's *The Late Show*, *Observer* features editor, Melanie Phillips, warned that 'the culture cynically sets out to exploit children..[and] tells them they are entitled to demand instant gratification'.[26] Computer games 'only use a dialectic of bish-bash', concurred feminist author and critic Marina Warner. Phillips concluded that there would soon be 'two nations', one of 'successful' adults from 'emotionally stable backgrounds', with the 'other nation' born into 'moral vacuum'.[27]

Dr Edward Luttwak, senior fellow at the Centre for Strategic and International Studies in Washington went even further in the direction of self-doubt. Under the headline, 'Crime: it's their best option', he reaffirmed the concept of *anomie* propounded by Emile Durkheim and nominated capitalist dynamism as the source of instability and criminogenic culture: 'today's turbo-charged capitalism gives us a dynamic economy at the expense of a disordered society.'[28] Reformed right winger, John Gray, now writing for the *Guardian* and *New Left Review*, has also targeted the 'market individualism of the eighties as a major source of the soiled and frayed Britain we see before us in the nineties'.[29] All in all, the apportioning of blame has turned out to be as boundless and corrosive as the notion of the culture of crime itself.

Under the heading 'The nation searches its soul', the leader writer of the *Independent* noted that 'the causes of crime are complex and multifarious, and no two psychologists, criminologists or sociologists agree on which components are the most important'.[30] As the headline would suggest, the problem which this editorial refers to is far more significant than mere differences of opinion among academics. At issue here is the conundrum which at times threatens to incapacitate the policy-makers and political leaders of Britain, namely; the universal desire to establish a new moral order, concomitant with a pervasive inability to establish what such an order might consist of, who would be party to it, and who would be excluded.

Throughout Western societies in the 1990s, there is a genuine demand for order. This demand is derived from a widespread and perhaps exaggerated sense of social instability. Every time it is expressed, however, the demand for order only serves to highlight the problems which it sets out to address. Likewise, the prolific attempts to identify and exclude those who are culturally predisposed to crime has the unintended effect of including every section of society in what appears to be an all-embracing 'culture of crime'.

Beyond left and right

The consensus for moral rearmament cuts across traditional political divides and consigns them to the past. Thus the *Daily Telegraph* congratulated Tony Blair (then Labour shadow home secretary) when he first spoke out about the 'threat' of moral chaos and the need to teach the value of right and wrong. The *Telegraph* leader-writer declared that 'Mr Blair's words' were the way to 'sanity and ultimately recovery' and promised to 'adopt them as our own'.[31] Written in February 1993, this was an early indication of the convergence between institutions which for generations have stood on either side of the left/right divide.

Following John Major's rallying cry against 'yob culture', the *Sun* published a special feature on 'The new barbarians' which noted the common ground between 'right-wing American Charles Murray and British Professor Norman Dennis, a lifelong member of the Labour Party'.[32] Leaving behind the traditional enmity between their respective political traditions, Murray and Dennis 'agreed' that 'the civilising process that begins in infancy and is completed by marriage cannot occur in societies where the two-parent family is not the norm'. Matching statements from Murray and Dennis were soon to be mirrored by identical-twin speeches on the part of Labour leader, Tony Blair, and the Conservative social security minister, Alistair Burt, both of them expounding the view that two-parent families are more conducive to social stability.

Almost alone among mainstream commentators, Ros Coward has noted another important convergence: the scapegoating of masculinity common to the likes of Murray and erstwhile left-wingers such as Beatrix Campbell. In a penetrating article in the *Guardian*, which stands out against the everyday prejudices of that newspaper,[33] she explained how post-feminists and former right wingers have converged upon young working class men as the 'Whipping boys' for the failure of society.[34]

The demand for a moral consensus was epitomised by Blair in his statement that 'fighting crime is the ultimate public good undertaken by a community which believes in itself as a community'.[35] Blair's declaration sounded pregnant with aspiration but empty of policy. Commentators such as the American critic Sykes have noted the discrepancy between the desire for consensus and the absence of any foundation upon which consensus might be built. Sykes has pointed out that there can be no 'community of interdependent citizens' when 'we lack agreed upon standards to which we can refer our disputes'.[36]

In the absence of 'agreed-upon standards', some pundits have resorted to declaring that new standards need to be found, or that old standards can be rediscovered. Geoff Mulgan, director of left-of-centre think-tank *Demos*, would like to do both: 'we need new criteria to appraise which government policies contribute to fulfilled lives and a balanced ecology';[37] and 'humans are born with a built-in moral capacity, rather like our genetic capacity to learn language'.[38] But neither of these rhetorical flourishes can hide the policy vacuum alluded to by Gray, who asks 'But what does the idea of community mean for public policy?', and notes the 'lack of concrete proposals' in the host of recent attempts to reinvent the idea of community.[39]

The problem of how to arrive at shared values in an atomised society has been addressed by moral philosopher Alasdair MacIntyre. His *Whose Justice? Which Rationality?* was written for 'the type of post-Enlightenment person who responds to the failure of the Enlightenment to provide neutral,

impersonal, tradition-independent standards of rational judgement by con-
cluding that no set of beliefs is therefore justifiable'.[40] But even MacIntyre is
stymied by the apparently unbridgeable gap between the self-evident interests
of a particular individual and the elusive common interests of society as
a whole: 'Such a person is confronted by the claims of each of the traditions
which we have considered as well as by those other traditions. How is it rational
to respond to them? The initial answer is: that will depend on who you are
and how you understand yourself.'[41]

Despite his attempts to extricate his readers from the prison of the particular,
MacIntyre's momentary reclamation of the universal is itself subsumed by the
personal predilections of the individual subject. Having tried to recover universally applicable 'neutral' standards, MacIntyre finds himself confined to
the terrain of the individual's integrity.

Financial Times columnist Joe Rogaly found himself equally non-plussed
by the proliferation of competing values:

> Values are cheap, everyone sprouts them, including the leader of the Labour
> Party, the prime minister, the youngest of the putative leaders of the
> Conservative Party, the chief rabbi, the president of the United States, an
> acquaintance I met while on holiday on Cyprus, and I swear from the look
> in its eyes, our cat Milou. All of the above-listed creatures, save perhaps the
> last, would if held upside down, produce a unique definition of values, each
> distinct from the rest.[42]

Rogaly is describing the moral impasse in contemporary society. Everyone
seems to have become a minor moral philosopher, each with their own individual solution to the lack of common agreement. In this vortex of apparently
disconnected values, one person's rectitude is another's deviancy, and the eye
of the beholder is as much judgement as can be brought to bear on any
subject. The overall effect is a hubbub of competing moralities and the seeming
acceptance of moral relativism.

In her polemical 1995 essay, 'The de-moralisation of society', Himmelfarb
made a vigorous attack on this proliferation of competing values.[43] She called
for the reintroduction of virtue, an attribute of the Victorians which she characterises as singular and absolute, where values are multifarious and relative.
But hers is a semantic sleight of hand which merely reposes the conundrum
under a different heading, as Rogaly noted in his review of Himmelfarb's
book. 'The world needs virtues, but whose?', was as much of a conclusion as
he felt able to draw from her work.[44]

Rogaly's question is the most succinct summation of the simultaneous
yearning for morality and the increasing elusiveness of moral principles with

a general application. At least he is honest enough to admit that he has no ready answer to the conundrum.

The flip-side of the same conundrum is expressed in the attempt to locate and define the 'culture of crime', coupled with the expanding usage of the term to the extent that it becomes generally applicable to all sections of society. In the nineties, it seems, there is no basis for a universal moral order, but anyone and everyone can be included in the various manifestations of the anti-moral disorder known as the 'culture of crime'. This is a singular state of affairs. For the first time, the search for consensus is beset by a three-headed monster: the impossibility of absolutes; the inability to sustain a compromise; and the widespread recognition of this conundrum. All this is in complete contrast to the situation of two and a half centuries ago, when universal moral certainty gave Immanuel Kant cause for rejoicing: 'Two things fill the mind with ever new and increasing admiration and awe, the oftener and more steadily we reflect on them—the starry heavens above and the moral law within.'[45]

The harmony of social development

> Hence in this identity of the universal will with the particular will, right and duty coalesce, and being in the ethical order a man has rights in so far as he has duties, and duties in so far as he has rights.[46]

Echoes of this famous passage from Hegel's *Philosophy of Right* are audible in many of today's political speeches on the theme of crime and the community. For example, the correlation between rights and duties was asserted more than 20 times in the Labour Party leader's speech to the *Spectator* dinner in April 1995. But the grand historical changes of Hegel's time gave him grounds for believing in the correlation between universal and particular will. Today's bowdlerisers, however, are merely asserting this correspondence in the face of contemporary experience dominated by competing antagonisms and a prevailing sense of social fragmentation.[47]

Two centuries ago, Hegel's high opinion of humanity was widely shared. The English radical William Godwin declared: 'There will be no war, no crimes, no administration of justice, as it is called, and no government. Every man will seek, with ineffable ardour, the good of all.'[48] And Tom Paine talked of 'the brotherhood of man' and was exiled from Britain for doing so. Political economist Adam Smith maintained that the maturation of economic man would be marked by a harmony of self-interests: 'society may subsist among different men, as among different merchants, from a sense of its utility'.[49]

Thomas Malthus, whose fatalism finds much resonance today, countered the boundless optimism of the Enlightenment with his theory of natural limits to social development. But even he felt the need to dilute his original emphasis on the fixed character of human nature. As Himmelfarb has noted, in the second, revised edition of *On Population,* Malthus suggested that 'the laws of human nature were less inevitable and the principle of population less inexorable'.[50]

From today's vantage point, at a time when change is perceived as synonymous with conflict, it is tempting to conclude that this notion of society as the confluence of complementary self-interests must have arisen from a period of unique stability. Nothing could be further from the truth. It was the momentum of economic development which generated such harmonious currents; and, in the last instance, it is today's lack of economic momentum and the absence of a clear future which underpin the difficulties in conceptualising a harmonious existence.

In Britain the first half of the nineteenth century was a period of untrammelled development. The motive force of economic expansion impacted upon more and more people, until the whole population was drawn for the first time into a universal system of social relations. In the age of Adam Smith, it looked as if economic development would proceed indefinitely, generating wealth for increasing numbers of people. In this way the emergence of a new mode of production—capitalism—provided the basis for the widespread feeling that this was, or soon would be, the best of all possible worlds, and that everyone was, or soon would be, in a position to enjoy its benefits. It was the expectation of continued progress which underpinned the atmosphere of self-confidence that is characteristic of the period. Likewise, the expectation of everyone eventually sharing in the fruits of industry gave a foundation to the idea of a universally shared understanding of right and wrong. Certainly for those in power, it was generally agreed that the continuation of progress was 'right', and 'wrong' described that which prevented change for the better.

Nowadays, however, there is no such expectation. 'Progress', as columnist Julie Burchill has remarked, sounds as out of date as the steam engine; and the cohering effect of economic dynamism is noticeable by its absence.[51] In these conditions, we are left with the moral fragmentation which everyone is seeking to address but failing to resolve.

The sense in which economic development fuelled the moral certainty of the early Victorian age was demonstrated by the mid-nineteenth century novelist and critic Charles Kingsley: 'The spinning jenny and the railroad, Cunard's liners and the electric telegraph are...signs that we are on some points at least in harmony with the universe.'[52] The climax of this mood, and its most extravagant expression, was the Great Exhibition at Crystal Palace in

1851, described by Himmelfarb as 'a single nation sharing a single ethos and exulting in the monumental product of that ethos'.[53]

Penal reform kept pace with the breakneck speed of economic development. Jeremy Bentham, one of the two exemplars of the classical school of criminology (Beccaria being the other), was described by his former pupil John Stuart Mill as 'the great subversive' in the vanguard of social change.[54] Bentham contributed to the rationalisation of law in keeping with the development of a new social order. Where the old order had been arbitrary and particular, the new order was systematic and general. Parochial isolation gave way to participation in an all-embracing social system. This was the white heat of development in which were forged both modern society and the modern individual.

At the high point of its dynamic, the new society was regarded as the manifestation of rationality expressed in each and every individual, including the criminal. This has been referred to by subsequent historians as the 'rationalistic error'.[55] Bentham's theories of punishment were based on the assumption that the criminal is above all a calculating individual. Hegel also maintained that the criminal's 'action is the action of a rational being'.[56] Hegel described anti-social activity as the knowledge of what is right combined with the failure to act upon it: 'It consists then in this, that it knows the objective ethical principles but fails in self-forgetfulness and self-renunciation to immerse itself in their seriousness and to base action upon them.'[57] For Hegel, the criminal act is the denial of individuality. As the criminal goes against the general order so he acts, according to Hegel, against himself as the partial embodiment and expression of the general Will. For the offender to be reformed, he must be made aware (forcefully and forcibly) of the errors of his ways.

The notion of a 'culture of crime' could not have existed in such a context. 'Culture' did not then connote the exclusive behaviour of a particular anti-social group. At a time when it was thought, as Lord Salisbury noted, that 'civilisation is constantly tending towards unity', the term 'culture' referred to the aspiration on the part of the vast majority of the population towards the development of commonly held standards which would be open and applicable to all. Thus for Her Majesty's inspector of schools, Matthew Arnold:

> Culture seeks...to make the best that has been thought and known in the world current everywhere; to make all men live in an atmosphere of sweetness and light, where they may use ideas, as it uses them itself, freely nourished and not bound by them. This is the social idea; and the men of culture are the true apostles of equality.[58]

According to Arnold, each individual could become part of the social whole if instructed in the shared knowledge of the world by 'men of culture'. The latter were the standard-bearers of 'equality' inasmuch as all men who had been inducted into this world of ideas would become equal participants in it. This was the ethos of a professional educationalist who was confident that he had something to teach the rest of the world, and equally confident that the rest of the world can be fitted into his classroom.

During Arnold's lifetime, the existence of crime was often attributed to the as yet incomplete distribution of culture. Charles Dickens, who is sometimes referred to as the first 'crime novelist', might also have expected to be the last of this genre. For Dickens maintained that 'ignorance causes crime' which in turn would be remedied by the establishment of a state system of education.[59]

Henry Mayhew—one of the earliest investigative journalists, whose work became a reference point for social reform in the mid-nineteenth century— regarded criminality not so much as a temporary aberration on the part of an otherwise rational individual, but more as the isolated activity of a minority of blighted individuals born from inferior stock. He accounted for the crim- inogenic street-folk of London by describing them as the remnants of an out- dated species—'the nomad', distinguished 'from the civilised man by his repugnance to regular and continuous labour'.[60] Mayhew anticipated the work of Cesare Lombroso, the Italian physician and anthropologist who is often cited as the father of positivist criminology. In *L'Uomo Delinquente*, Lombroso declared that 'the atavism of the criminal...may go back beyond the savage even to the brutes themselves'.[61]

Lombroso subscribed to the new school of Darwinian naturalism. He regarded certain individuals as predisposed to criminality primarily as a result of their physical characteristics, which were then compounded by environmental influences. These 'criminaloids' would require treatment from professionals trained to ameliorate or possibly correct their condition. This is the origin of the pathological approach to crime.

Naturalistic explanations of human behaviour—criminal or otherwise— are ostensibly the opposite of Enlightenment accounts in which a Spirit or Will is accorded the primary role. But both these apparently contradictory accounts share a common optimism which is noticeable by its absence today. In either account of criminal behaviour, idealist or naturalist, those so afflicted were almost always assumed to be in a tiny minority, and there was no suggestion—as there is today—that the whole of society might be engulfed in a tidal wave of criminality. The self-confidence which was characteristic of the nineteenth century had little foresight of this sort of doomsday scenario.

Himmelfarb has commented on the small numbers of Mayhew's subjects: '*London Labour and the London Poor*, in spite of its ambitious title, focused on a small segment of the poor...40 years later, the "Mayhewian" poor has so shrunk in size as no longer to constitute a "race" or even a major social problem.'[62] Mayhew himself talked of 'a fortieth part of the entire population of the metropolis getting their living in the streets'.[63] Despite his pre-occupation, there is no suggestion in Mayhew that this particular culture and its environs could not be penetrated by civilised society and absorbed into a world of universal standards. In Mayhew's worldview the anachronistic habits of the 'street-folk' were a curious exception to the undisputed, generally accepted standards of the day. Mayhew would never have dreamed of suggesting that they were both equally valid.[64]

The early Victorians assumed that crime was an unnatural exception to the organic development of society. According to the precepts of classical criminology, the criminal was a rational member of a rational society, who had become temporarily dislodged from the universal Will, but would respond rationally to the reassertion of Will in the form of punishment. Among the school of thought dubbed 'positivist criminology', the criminal was regarded either as a degenerate form of the human species or a throwback to a more primitive stage in the evolutionary process. He was not fully in control of his faculties, but those in authority felt very much in control of the situation. Both the classical and nineteenth-century positivist schools were confident that society was vigorous enough to override the anti-social tendencies manifested in a small minority of criminals. There was nothing inevitable about crime, and the idea that society could be enveloped in a series of criminogenic cultures would have been inconceivable.

In sharp contrast to the optimism of the early Victorians, the contemporary culturalisation of crime assumes that anti-social behaviour will spontaneously reproduce itself for as long as particular cultural patterns remain extant. Within the narrow horizons of the contemporary mindset there is little or no scope for overcoming cultural particularism, which means that this unstable state of affairs is now expected to continue indefinitely. The 'crime problem' is taken as given, as are the separate, impenetrable cultures which allegedly give rise to it.

Seeds of doubt

Towards the end of the nineteenth century, the eminent sociologist Emile Durkheim was among the first to exhibit the seeds of doubt which have since grown into a dense thicket of moral confusion. Durkheim found himself unable to sustain the assumption that the same moral absolutes would eventually assert themselves in all circumstances and for all time. He recognised that morality is derived from the particular context in which it operates.

His emphasis upon the historical and cultural limits of differing moralities was itself derived from the curtailment of the progressive dynamic of capitalism. The social system which had been the basis for universalism, was already embarked upon the process of compromising itself—a process which included new tariffs and regulations to curtail the workings of its own market. But Durkheim remained confident that compromise could be made to work, and that the whole of society should be encouraged to enter into it.

Durkheim's work coincided with the deceleration of the spontaneous dynamic of the capitalist economy, and the inauguration of the newly enlarged machinery of the state as the means to keep it on course. He is characteristic, therefore, of a new age in which capitalism was compelled to transcend its own forms and transgress its own principles. However, the unforeseen problems which emerged towards the end of the nineteenth century were perceived as arising not from the shortfall, but from the overspill of the market economy. This accounts for Durkheim's antipathy towards the apparently immoral workings of its unseen hand: 'thereupon the appetites thus excited have become freed of any limiting authority....Ultimately this liberation of desires has been made worse by the very development of industry and the almost infinite extension of the market.'[65]

In 1980, Stewart Clegg and David Dunkerley summarised the task which Durkheim set himself: 'Durkheim, rather than praising the market as the ethical foundation of a natural order, was more concerned first to delineate the role of the market as a possible source of disorder, second to specify the conditions under which order would be possible, and third, to determine the reason for its absence in contemporary industrial society.'[66] Durkheim's concern was to establish a new moral order to take the place of pre-capitalist traditions. His attempt to assert morality against the grain of the market economy should be seen as the first of many attempts to harness morality in compensation for the shortcomings of the capitalist dynamic.

On matters of crime and morality, Durkheim was a transitional figure standing halfway between the absolute optimism of the mid-nineteenth century and the relative pessimism of the twentieth. Thus in *The Rules of Sociological Method*, the onset of doubt was expressed in the following terms: 'One should abandon the still too widespread habit of judging an institution, a practice, or a moral standard as if it were good or bad in and by itself, for all social types indiscriminately.'[67] But the recognition that morality is conditional upon 'social facts' and therefore relative to particular circumstances is countered by a reaffirmation of faith in the best of all possible worlds. With regard to the 'social conditions that are most generally distributed', Durkheim notes that it would be 'incomprehensible if the most widespread forms [were not] the most advantageous'.[68]

Durkheim did not renounce positivism so much as qualify it. Cambridge criminologist Colin Sumner has stressed the ambiguities in Durkheim's writing on crime and law.[69] Durkheim introduced the idea that crime might be inevitable and indeed essential to the function of society, while retaining the belief that moral order could be established by means of professional intervention into the vicissitudes arising from a market-led economy. In Durkheim, such contradictions are finely balanced. But those who came after him have focused their attention on the aspects of Durkheim's work which reflect the onset of doubt. His residual sense of self-confidence now seems almost as anachronistic as the spinning jenny.

With Durkheim, Sumner notes, 'the supposed universality of morality has melted into air'.[70] Here was the onset of what Himmelfarb describes as the 'De-moralisation of society'—the sinking of universal Victorian 'virtue' into the quicksand of relative 'values'.[71] This is a process which originated in Durkheim's Europe. But it became even more pronounced in the USA, where the momentum of capitalist development had been faster than anywhere else, and the effects of its deceleration came to be felt all the more intensely.

The American compromise

In the early years of the twentieth century, the relative dynamism of the American economy was in sharp contrast to the ragged and increasingly uneven character of capitalist development elsewhere. Hence the continued desire to emigrate to the USA on the part of the huddled masses of Europe. But even in 'God's crucible'[72] there were limits to the integrative capacity of the capitalist machine. This was the context which prompted moves to limit immigration on the part of the United States authorities, coupled with more intensive policing of those groups of immigrants which had been allowed to enter the promised land. Against this background, the Chicago School of sociology first came to international prominence during the 1920s.

Established in 1895, the sociology department at the University of Chicago was the first in America, and it soon came to play a leading role in the development of sociology both as an academic discipline and a policy tool. Under the direction of Robert Park, the Chicago School became associated with the detailed field study of subcultures, not for their own sake, but in order to devise social policies which would facilitate their integration into mainstream society.

Citing the 1989 edition of the *Oxford English Dictionary* as her authority, Himmelfarb says that the term 'values', in the plural, was first used in *The Polish Peasant in Europe and America*, 1918, by Chicagoans William I Thomas

and Florian Znaniecki.[73] This influential study anticipated the detailed observation of immigrant cultures, sometimes with an apparently high disposition
towards crime, which was to become the trademark of the Chicago School.

Ironically, the notion of particular cultures with their own values, separate
and distinct from Arnold's concept of a singular, shared culture and its unifying effect, first arose in the melting pot of America. However, as the term
'melting pot' would suggest, the early Chicagoans assumed that particularity
and criminality were residual. Criminality was regarded as a sign of
insufficient acculturation. It would be bred out of subsequent generations as
they made inroads into the American way of life (and away from ethnicity).
'The Chicago School saw high crime rates optimistically', notes Sumner, 'as
a temporary imbalance in the process of evolution of modern
societies....Once ethnic groups settled down and established themselves on
a suitable territory their crime rates were supposed to diminish naturally.'[74]

In the late sixties, long after the early assumptions of the school had been
discredited, radical sociologist David Matza summed up 'the Chicago dilemma'
as 'how [to] describe the fact of diversity in urban America, yet maintain the
idea of pathology'.[75] For Matza, recognition of difference is antithetical to the
exercise of moral judgement. Criminologists of his generation felt they had to
choose between the two. But this is a dilemma of the 1960s and 1970s which
Matza has applied retrospectively. In the 1920s, by contrast, immigrants could
still expect to better themselves economically. They aspired to be admitted
into the American Way of Life. Likewise, sociologists and criminologists
regarded themselves as social engineers with a positivist part to play in the
integration of immigrants into mainstream America. They aspired to the role
of professional, quasi-medical agents in a process of cultural treatment—
acculturation—which was assumed to be mutually beneficial. Both parties
tended to regard ethnic difference as an outdated skin to be shed in the light
of a more advanced society and a generally superior morality.

The Chicago School thus expressed a recognition of cultural difference
offset by the assumption that such differences would be eroded in the long-
term, and in the interests of the common good. This was, in practical terms,
the sort of compromise which Durkheim had been feeling his way towards.
But it was not unassailable. With the onset of the Depression and the intense
atmosphere of doubt and distrust arising from it, criminological literature
began to show a heavier emphasis on cultural difference. Questions arose as
to whether mainstream society had either the capacity or the moral authority
to override such differences. This ethos of scepticism became more pronounced alongside the growing recognition that official morality embodied
not the tradition of disinterested universalism so much as the venal self-
interest of those in authority. The contours of the new criminology are first

exemplified in the 1930s pioneering work of Chicago sociologist Louis Wirth. Wirth painted a picture of society as a patchwork of cultural differences:

> Whatever may be the physical, psychological and the temperamental differ-
> ences between various races and societies, one thing is certain, namely that
> their cultures are different. Their traditions, their modes of living and mak-
> ing a living, the values that they place upon various types of conduct are
> often so strikingly different that what is punished as crime in one group is
> celebrated as heroic conduct in another.[76]

The earlier sense of difference disappearing as the social fabric is woven together, is itself disappearing; and Wirth expresses this departure in formu-lating the emerging criminological problem of his age—the novel difficulty of arriving at a definition of crime which is applicable to everybody. Whereas Durkheim retained a consensual view of law, Wirth was struck by its prejudi-cial character:

> Not until we appreciate that the law itself...is an expression of the wishes of
> a social group, and that it is not infallibly and permanently in accord
> with the cultural needs and definitions of all the social groups whom
> it seeks to restrain, can we begin to understand why there should be crime
> at all.[77]

As well as recognising the difficulty of arriving at a generally applicable definition of crime, Wirth hints that the attempt to impose inappropriate definitions may itself be the real problem: 'Human conduct presents a prob-lem only when it involves a deviation from the dominant code or the gener-ally prevailing definition in a culture, ie, when a given society regards it as a problem.'[78] According to Wirth, the crime problem facing society is to some extent self-imposed: 'The official conception of crime [fails to] see misconduct in the relative perspective of the cultural setting in which it occurs and which makes it into the peculiar problem which it is.'[79]

In the ethos of the new Chicago school, following Wirth, the 'dominant code' lacked the capacity to integrate other cultures.[80] Nor did the dominant culture possess the moral authority to pass judgements upon others.[81] In the light of this, Wirth expunged words like 'criminal' and 'degeneracy' from the language of criminology, replacing them with the concept of deviance. Borrowed from psychology, the sociological usage of deviance (originally 'deviate behaviour') connotes interpersonal activity other than that which conforms to the 'dominant code', but without the moralistic condemnation which such behaviour might previously have attracted. Deviance, in short, is a de-moralised concept of crime and anti-social behaviour. The substitution of 'deviant' for criminal is the terminological expression of the call by EM Lemert to 'abandon once and for all the archaic and medicinal idea that human beings can be divided into normal and pathological, or, at least, if such a division must be made, to divest the term 'pathological' of its moralistic, unscientific overtones.'[82]

Soon after Wirth and the new generation of criminologists stopped seeing the criminal in terms of a degeneracy model, they began to apply terms akin to degeneracy to the society which had given birth to the deviant. Thus in *Society as the Patient: Essays on Culture and Personality,* LK Frank described society, not the criminal, as pathological:

> The disintegration of our traditional culture, with the decay of those ideas, those conceptions, and belief upon which our social and individual lives were organised, brings us face to face with the problem of treating society, since individual therapy or punishment no longer has any value beyond the mere alleviation of our symptoms.[83]

Frank went on to describe deviancy as the straightforward expression of a twisted society, and he argued that this was the only way to make sense of an otherwise meaningless existence. It was the fault of science and technology, according to Frank, that robbed people of purpose and a sense of loyalty.[84]

Published in 1938, *Crime and the Community* by Frank Tannenbaum pursued the new Chicago line but applied it in a more polemical fashion. He concluded that crime was not separate from respectable society, but a vivid expression of its inadequacies. In so doing, he began to undermine the capacity of respectable society to reshape outsiders in its own image. Throughout the 60 years since Lombroso first appeared on the scene, successive generations of criminologists had assumed that they had a right and a duty to extinguish or at least ameliorate the predisposition towards criminal behaviour, whether culturally or biologically derived. In so doing, they believed they were acting as the professional embodiment of a civilised society engaged in the process of treating its weakest members and teaching them to aspire to the standards required of civilised human beings. Tannenbaum, however, was suggesting that the problems facing America might be the result of the American Way, rather than the result of failure to live up to it:

> The amount of crime in the United States responds to all the factors and forces in American life—it is one way of describing our politics, our police, our civil and judicial administration, our immigration policy, our industrial

and social conditions, our education, our morals, our religion, our manners, our culture. It is just as much one aspect of America as baseball or divorce or anti-union industry or unemployment or Fords or movies.[85]

In introducing the idea of crime as the extension of respectable society by other means, Tannenbaum also brought into question the role of the state, and its professional agents, in colonising and incorporating those subcultures whose apparent criminality had hitherto been associated with their un-American origins. Instead of immigrants becoming criminals because they were insufficiently American, as had been widely assumed, the implication of Tannenbaum's breakthrough was that criminality was made in the image of America. It follows, therefore, that the correctional agencies which personified the American Way of Life had no positive role to play.

The notion of crime as a reflection of respectable society was subsequently reinforced by Edwin Sutherland's investigations into white-collar crime in the 1940s. Sutherland's contemporary Donald Taft provided the most succinct formulation of this new tendency: 'we get the criminals we deserve'.[86] But it was Tannenbaum who pursued this line of argument to its logical conclusion. He declared that when society intervened against deviancy it was making matters worse, and in making this declaration he sounded an alarm bell against positivist intervention and the various agencies which had applied this approach for more than half a century:

> The person becomes the thing he is described as being. Nor does it seem to matter whether the valuation is made by those who would punish or by those who would reform...the way out is through a refusal to dramatise the evil. The less said about it the better. The more said about something else, still better.[87]

Tannenbaum moved towards the idea that crime and deviancy are the result of the imposition of inappropriate correctional models. Taken to its logical conclusion, this means that deviants are not only portrayed in stereotypical terms, but that stereotyping actually creates deviance in its own image. This amounts to the breakdown of the long-established and generally assumed relationship between positivism and progress—a breakdown which was to be even more intensely expressed in the radical criminology of the 1960s and 1970s.

Two sides of the criminological coin

After Tannenbaum, criminology came to be dominated by debates between those who continued to endow the state and its agencies with the capacity to ameliorate crime and associated social problems, and those who responded to the inability of the state to alleviate social problems by directing their criticism against it. These debates were to continue along the same lines for nearly 40 years. However, even though none of the participants would ever have admitted it, the differences between the two sides were often outweighed by what they held in common.

Throughout this period, proponents of positivist intervention felt the need to be highly critical of its previous track record, while those who directed their energies against positivist social engineering were never able to come up with an alternative means of social improvement. Indeed these critics may be said to have existed only as a reaction to policy failure, while depending on the renewal of similar policies for their continued existence as social critics. The opponents of positivism came to be known as laissez-faire or left idealists. But they were essentially the radical wing of positivism, responding to its decreasing efficacy and expressing the inner logic of its own failure.

Among the prominent criminologists and social commentators of the period, none was prepared to lend uncritical support to capitalist society and its laws. But then neither was the bourgeoisie itself. As Lord Annan remarked in *Our Age,* 'the brave new world was to be a pluralist world. People should acknowledge that there was no single model of belief and behaviour such as that of the gentleman in bygone days'.[88]

In establishment circles there was a warm welcome for *The Authoritarian Personality* by Theodore Adorno, leader of the Frankfurt School. Adorno claimed that the quest for progress had produced repressed personalities which were predisposed towards fascism. In the *Sociological Imagination,* C Wright Mills complained that the suburban conformists of middle America were 'cheerful robots',[89] and William H Whyte made similar complaints against those whom he dubbed 'Organisation Man'. At the time, the reproduction of bourgeois mores in their traditional form was widely regarded as problematic and even dangerous.

The self-criticism of this period is indicative of a capitalist society which was under pressure to reinvent itself in order to guarantee its continued existence. Among criminologists, the recasting of capitalist society was expressed in the growing trend towards the appreciation of deviant subcultures. The latter were increasingly regarded as a necessary splash of colour in a world which might otherwise revert to the gun-metal grey of totalitarianism. This sympathetic approach was pursued by both positivists and radicals.

Radical American sociologist Alvin Gouldner was contemptuous of positivism, even in its new guise.[90] Yet the chief target of Gouldner's ire was fellow American, Howard Becker, whose work shares at least some of Gouldner's radicalism, and who is often credited, alongside David Matza,[91] with developing the 'appreciative' sociology of deviance. Indeed it was Becker who had distilled EM Lemert's labelling theory into the well-known formulation: 'the deviant is one to whom that label has been consistently applied; deviant behaviour is behaviour that people so label'.[92] Ostensibly on opposite sides of the fence, Gouldner and Becker were united in their criticism of old-fashioned authority and the apologetic character of traditional, positivist criminology.

This was the common ground shared both by reforming positivists who gave critical support to the agency of the state, and by the laissez-faire or left idealists who pointed out that the interfering state made matters worse. From 1945 to 1975, criminological debate remained within these parameters.

Looking back on this period in 1979 (by which time he was already installed at Middlesex Polytechnic but had not yet taken the conservative turn which was to become known as 'left realism'), Jock Young summarised the debates among postwar criminologists as follows:

> My colleagues and I have the continuing task of trying to situate, historically and intellectually, the developments in the theory of crime and punishment since the war. On one side, this has involved an examination of the official criminology of reformism, on the other the plotting of the pendulum away from positivism towards the idealism of the new deviancy theory in the mid-1960s.[93]

Young noted the elements of continuity throughout this period: 'the theoretical structures remained in fact scarcely altered. Thus the laissez-faire idealism of labelling theory became replaced by a left idealism of the new criminologists in the early 1970s.'[94] According to Young, the latter-day positivists applied themselves to the sickness of society as well as that of the criminal. They aimed 'simultaneously to intervene in the realms of normality to maintain and increase freedom, whilst protecting, treating and attempting to reintegrate the deviant into the body politic'.[95] Thus Young's 'reformists' regarded both society and the deviant as their patients.

This was to extend the range of positivist intervention, but it was also inextricably linked with a dilution of the professional self-confidence previously associated with positivism. While continuing to emphasise the role of the professional reformer, the latter-day positivists felt it necessary to continually question and qualify their own assumptions.

Meanwhile the 'laissez-faire idealists' favoured a policy of 'radical non-intervention'.[96] They reserved their criticism for 'the conventional and conforming members of society who identify and interpret behaviour as deviant'. According to the American radical sociologist J Kitsuse, it is the 'responses' of the conformers 'which sociologically transform persons into deviants'.[97] From this outlook, conformity and its agents transform the otherwise creative input of deviancy into a social problem.

The laissez-faire idealists originated in the USA. Their stance, in which 'positivism...is seen as the main ideological enemy' was recapitulated by the left idealists, many of whom were British. *The Politics of Deviance*, a collection of papers to the National Deviancy Conference edited by radical criminologists Ian Taylor and Laurie Taylor, demonstrates this approach. Its editors introduced the collection by declaring that 'the argument that holds this book together is that the concept of and the reality of crime is created through political action by those groups and institutions which possess the power to enforce their will'.[98] This is a distillation of the 'conflict approach' to crime, which seeks to explain crime as a manifestation of the conflictual nature of class society, and which sees the law solely as the *post-hoc* rationalisation of the self-interest of the capitalist class.

In the introduction to *The New Criminology*, Taylor *et al* went even further, to the point of calling for the abdication of the state to ensure the abandonment of its correctionist powers.[99] Although the 'laissez-faire and left idealists' went further along this route than the 'reformists', it is important to realise that both wings of postwar criminology were voluble in their criticism of authority, and to some extent prepared to suspend 'conventional morality' in order to 'appreciate the variety of deviant enterprises' and their 'intrinsic, ineradicable and vital part in human society'.[100]

Not only is it the case that the two wings of postwar criminology shared a great deal of common ground, it is also the case that the left-wing colour of the idealist camp was dependent upon the continued efforts of the positivist reformers. The idealists were left wing in so far as they posed a challenge to the attempts by the state to act as the engineer of a universal society. Thus they provided a critique of the bogus universalism of state policy. By the mid-seventies, however, the failure of social engineering was becoming apparent to all, and the collapse of the Great Society anti-poverty programme in the United States marked the beginning of the end of state attempts to induce universality. In criminology, as in every other field, the latter-day positivists began to reduce the scale of their project, and in doing so they shifted the political coordinates of the idealist camp.

The aim of the radicals had been to expose the failure of the integrationist state, and highlight its capacity only to make matters worse. As part of their critique of state intervention, they had tended to stress the impenetrability of deviant cultures. For example, KT Erikson suggested that deviants were created by authority, and that, once made, the deviant would stay that way for life:

> The community's decision to bring deviant sanctions against the individual...is a sharp rite of transition at once moving him out of his normal position in society and transferring him into a distinctive deviant role....An important feature of these ceremonies in our culture is that they are almost irreversible.[101]

In pursuing a critique of officialdom, Erikson had developed a concept of the deviant as someone who is beyond the reach of reasoning as well as coercion or correctional treatment. He had marooned the deviant in an apparently irreversible social role.

Likewise, Stan Cohen (renowned for his seminal study *Folk Devils and Moral Panics*) and Laurie Taylor described the self-enclosed culture of deviants whom, in the style of Matza, Becker and company, they had set out to appreciate:

> We did not accept that he was the possessor of an inadequate or flawed or undeveloped consciousness, but rather believed that the matters to which he attended, and possibly the style in which he attended them, were evidence of his existence within a different life-world.[102]

In the 1970s, the Birmingham Centre for Contemporary Cultural Studies characterised youth subcultures as 'cultures of resistance', in contradistinction to the parent culture of the working class and in opposition to bourgeois hegemony.[103] For the Birmingham school in the early seventies, the separation of youth cultures from the mainstream was something to be celebrated. But the celebration of 'cultures of resistance' turned out to be the precursor of the notion of youth culture as anti-civilisation, as propounded by Hardyment *et al.* In the new context, in which positivism on a grand scale is noticeable by its absence, 'cultures of resistance' have come to be described as cultures which are resistant to civilised values. It seems that Gouldner was entirely apposite in criticising 'the zoo-keepers of deviance' for creating a 'comfortable and humane Indian Reservation, a protected social space, within which these colourful specimens may be exhibited, unmolested and unchanged'.[104]

Cohen, Taylor and the Birmingham school were keen to criticise the positivist notion of deviance as pathology. In its place they posited the idea of deviance as a 'different life-world', as equally valid as it was utterly impenetrable to the concerns and motivation of respectable society. But, as it turned out, the radicalism of their supposition depended on the continuation of large-scale positivist intervention, albeit in a qualified and self-critical form. When this mode of social policy came to an end, the radicalism of the sixties and seventies metamorphosed into what was to become the new fatalism of the nineties.

The new fatalism

Roger Graef has described the beginning of the end of postwar positivism:

> in 1974 a team of researchers led by American criminologist Robert Martinson studied a variety of rehabilitation programmes in Britain and North America. Their report What Works? Questions and Answers about Prison Reform concluded that nothing could be proved to divert offenders from crime.[105]

The idea that 'nothing works' hit the cover of *Time* magazine and soon made inroads into popular consciousness. As soon as the high expectations of state intervention were extinguished, the notion of 'a different life-world' began to be translated into the 'culture of crime'. Without a credible agent of social reform to extricate the deviant from his culture, or to integrate his culture into the overall framework of society, it could only be assumed that he would remain walled-up within it for the rest of his natural life. The now-pervasive influence of this assumption has been acknowledged by *Newsweek* feature-writers Jonathan Alter and Pat Wingert:

> One current popular argument is that the culture of the underclass is so different and isolated that it will not respond to the same incentives as the rest of society.[106]

The influential notion of an irretrievably 'different...isolated' culture of crime is fatalism writ large. But contemporary fatalism does not fit into the long-standing debate between champions of conservatism and advocates of social change. It cannot fit into this debate, because such a debate no longer exists. In today's society, there is no longer even the semblance of a rift between radicals and conservatives. Everyone agrees that something ought to be done, but that nothing much can be accomplished.

The conservative tradition arose in reaction to the Enlightenment and the French Revolution. It utilised the concept of the fixed nature of mankind to attack the liberal emphasis on nurture. Godwin (nurture) and Malthus (nature) were among the first opponents in this battle of ideas. Where Godwin argued that the birth of a new society meant that everything was achievable, Malthus maintained that nature would have the last word. This is the essence of the left/right divide which was to remain in existence for 200 years.

The progressive aspects of the liberal tradition were derived from the recognition that the paramount influences upon humanity are also made by humanity; from which followed Condorcet's doctrine of 'the perfectibility of man'. This means that what humanity has made of itself, humanity can also un-make and make better. Towards the end of the nineteenth century, the revised version of the liberal tradition stated that even if individuals turned out to be unequal to this task, it could nevertheless be accomplished by agents of social engineering such as the state. It was this, revised version of liberalism, which was so heavily discredited in the seventies.

In the 1990s, the new fatalism maintains the liberal emphasis on nurture. Its stock in trade is culture rather than biology. However, in the wake of the failure of the integrationist state, and in the light of the findings of radical criminologists from the sixties and seventies, the social and environmental factors grouped under such headings as the 'culture of crime' are now regarded as inviolable and irreversible. These factors are alleged to give rise to a cultural codification of human behaviour which is as fixed and limiting as any genetic code, and susceptible to damage limitation at the very most. The result is a nurture-based outlook which holds that social activity is fixed and limited. It depicts humanity in the sort of rigid posture which used to be a projection exclusive to the nature-based theories of traditional conservatism.

The irony is that the reactionary implications of the new fatalism are more readily derived from the fragments of the liberal tradition rather than old-style conservatism. Thus, at the level of ideas, the development of the notion of permanently criminogenic cultures owes far more to the sociology of deviance than it does to the crude biologism of someone like Charles Murray.[107] Meanwhile the stagnation of the economy and the failure of the integrationist project of the bourgeois state provide the material basis for the convergence of both liberal and conservative traditions around fatalistic assumptions.

Virtue out of necessity?

Moral philosophers and criminologists are now attempting to devise theories of crime and punishment in the absence of anything approaching the integrationist impetus of the Great Society anti-poverty programme. 'Anglo-American moral philosophy', explained Martha Nussbaum in the *Times Literary Supplement,* 'is turning away from an ethics based on Enlightenment ideals of universality to an ethics based on tradition and particularity'.[108]

Theoretically, this would entail the devolution of moral authority to the particular community. For example, the Australian criminologist John Braithwaite seeks to avoid the pitfalls of 'both professional technocracy and laissez-faire' by means of 'community moralising'.[109] His theory of 'reintegrative shaming' would equip the community 'to allure and inveigle the citizen to attend to the moral claims of the criminal law, to coax and caress compliance'.[110] In the wake of Braithwaite's theories, *Newsweek* explained that 'conformity' is the practical aim of 'the return of shame': 'the goal is not mere retribution, but conformity—good conformity, the kind that makes it easier for people to form communities.'[111]

Braithwaite is trying to make a virtue out of the end of large-scale social engineering. In the formulation, 'we should be intolerant and understanding', he endeavours to combine the inevitability of separate cultures and the capacity for moral condemnation. But his theory comes up against the same unanswerable question posed by Rogaly: 'the world needs virtues, but whose?'

The moral authority of the early phase of capitalism originated neither from tradition nor community, but in its universalising dynamic. In today's society the intensifying quest for moral authority and the equally frantic attempts to single out 'cultures of crime' should be recognised as pathetic substitutes for the dynamism that is long since exhausted. Likewise the celebration of community is an attempt to find local refuge from the intractable problems of global capitalism. 'Moral community', 'criminal culture'—both of these notions are equally fantastic. But they are also real expressions of a society which has lost the momentum which used to endow it with some form of coherence.

Throughout its history, capitalism has wrestled with the contradiction between the individual and society. It is a contradiction which this society could never have resolved, because it is derived from the paradox inherent in the capitalist mode of production; between, on the one hand, the production and reproduction of the universal world of social endeavour, and, on the other hand, the alienation of particular individuals one from another as a consequence of the recurring transformation of social endeavour into private property.

Thus the system in which we live both creates society, and in the same moment destroys it—giving rise to the anti-social society. It is this contradiction which finds its everyday expression in crime. The history of the past two centuries is of this society's diminishing capacity to override its own contradictions—a diminishing capacity which prompts compensatory efforts whose effectiveness is in turn diminished. The history of this degeneration finds partial expression in the attenuation of theories of crime and punishment, from the rationalism of Hegel to the cultural mystification of the present day.

NOTES

1   Christina Hardyment, 'Liverpool's murder: the finger points at parents', *Sunday Telegraph*, 21 February 1993

2   Peter Hamill, 'Endgame', *Esquire* (US edition), December 1994

3   Michael Medved, 'The seeds of evil sown on our screens', *Sunday Times*, 28 November 1993

4   James Style, 'Rhythm of the jungle', *The Independent*, 5 October 1994

5   Bryan Appleyard, 'Poetry soaked in blood', *The Independent*, 26 October 1994

6   Ian Burrell, 'The "savage generation" hits Britain', *Sunday Times*, 5 February 1995

7   Theodore Dalrymple, 'The lost children of the video nasty age', *Daily Telegraph*, 20 February 1993

8   Beatrix Campbell, *Goliath: Britain's Dangerous Places*, 1993, cited in Ros Coward, 'Whipping Boys', *Guardian Weekend*, 3 September 1994

9   Gunther Anders, 'The phantom world of TV', *Dissent*, Vol3, 1965, pp14-24

10 Philip Webster, 'Major declares war on Britain's "yob culture"', *The Times*, 10 September 1994

11 'Kicking against the Picts', *Spectator*, 17 September 1994

12 Christina Hardyment, 'Have men got worse?', *Daily Telegraph*, 9 March 1995

13 Andrea N Jones, 'Are girls turning meaner?', *YO! (Youth Outlook)*, San Francisco, Spring 1993

14 Anita Chaudhuri, 'Deadlier than the male', *Guardian*, 13 October 1994

15 Annabel Heseltine and John Davison, 'Aristocrats hooked on crack for kicks', *Sunday Times*, 30 October 1994

16 Headline from the *LA Times* quoted in Jennifer Vogel, 'Juvenile offenders are the Willie Hortons of the 90s', *Utne Reader*, Minneapolis, July/August 1994

17 Currently *Emeritus* Professor of History at the Graduate School of the City University of New York

18 Gertrude Himmelfarb, 'The de-moralisation of society: from Victorian virtues to modern values', *Institute of Economic Affairs*, 1995, pp235-36.

19 'M[ail] o[n] S[unday] slams Fleet Street "yobs"', *UK Press Gazette*, 1 May 1995

20 Howard Smith, 'Head attacks failure to combat yob culture', *London Evening Standard*, 14 September 1994

21 Roy Chapman speaking at the Headmasters' Conference in Bournemouth, September 1994

22 Professor Christie Davies, Reading University, 'Poverty should not be scapegoated for lawlessness: our culture excuses social deviance', *Sunday Times*, 21 February 1993

23 Professor Norman Dennis, Newcastle University, quoted in 'The new barbarians', *The Sun*, 10 September 1994

24 Gertrude Himmelfarb, 'The British Underclass Forum', *Sunday Times*, 11 September 1994

25 Greg Neale, 'Switched on to choice', *Sunday Telegraph*, 21 February 1993

26 Melanie Phillips, speaking on BBC's *The Late Show,* 5 December 1994

27 Melanie Phillips, speaking on BBC's *The Late Show,* 5 December 1994

28 Edward N Luttwak, *Daily Telegraph,* February 1995

29 John Gray, 'Hollowing out the core', *Guardian,* 8 March 1995

30 'The nation searches its soul', *Independent,* editorial, 20 February 1993

31 'Right and wrong', *Daily Telegraph,* editorial, 22 February 1993

32 Chris Mycroft-Davies, *Sun,* 10 September 1994

33 At the 1995 conference of the Campaign for Press and Broadcasting Freedom (Congress House, March 1995), *Guardian* journalist Seumas Milne admitted that his paper displayed an 'anti-working class bias'.

34 Ros Coward, 'Whipping boys', *Guardian Weekend,* 3 September 1994

35 Tony Blair, then shadow home secretary, speaking at the National Crime Debate jointly organised by *Tribune* and the *Daily Mirror,* Church House, Westminster, 19 January 1993

36 C Sykes, *A Nation of Victims: The Decay of the American Character,* St Martin's Press, 1992, cited in Colin Sumner, *The Sociology of Deviance: An Obituary,* Open University Press, 1994

37 Geoff Mulgan, 'Money doesn't make the world go round', *Independent,* 27 February 1995

38 Geoff Mulgan, 'Our built-in moral sense is the basic we must go back to', *Guardian,* November 1994

39 John Gray, 'Hollowing out the core', *Guardian,* 8 March 1995

40 Alasdair MacIntyre, *Whose Justice?, Whose Rationality?,* Duckworth, 1992

41 Alasdair MacIntyre, *Whose Justice? Whose Rationality?,* Duckworth, 1992

42 Joe Rogaly, 'Politicians of easy value', *Financial Times,* 22 April 1995

43 Gertrude Himmelfarb, 'The de-moralisation of society: from Victorian virtues to modern values', *Institute of Economic Affairs,* 1995

44 Joe Rogaly, 'Politicians of easy value', *Financial Times,* 22 April 1995

45 Immanuel Kant, *The Critique of Pure Reason,* (Trans TK Abbott) Longman Green & Co, 3rd ed, 1883

46 GWF Hegel, *The Philosophy of Right, Encyclopaedia Britannica,* Chicago, 1982, Ethical Life, p57

47 Ulrich Beck, *The Risk Society,* Sage, 1992

48 William Godwin, *Enquiry into Political Justice and its Influence on Morals and Happiness,* (Ed FEL Priestley), Penguin, 1985 (orig 1798), Book I, p86

49 Adam Smith, *An Enquiry in the Nature and Causes of the Wealth of Nations,* Oxford University Press, 1976, Book1, pp26-27

50 Gertrude Himmelfarb, *The Idea of Poverty: England in the Early Industrial Age,* Faber & Faber, 1985, p120

51 Julie Burchill, *Ambition,* Corgi, 1989

52 Charles Kingsley, 'Yeast: a problem', *Fraser's Magazine,* London, Autumn 1848

53 Gertrude Himmelfarb, *The Idea of Poverty: England in the Early Industrial Age*, Faber & Faber, 1985, p365

54 John Stuart Mill, 'On Bentham', from *Dissertations and Discussion*, Vol1, 1859. JS Mill also wrote 'who, before Bentham (whatever controversies might exist on points of detail), dared to speak disrespectfully, in express terms, of the British Constitution, or the English law? He did so; and his arguments and his example encouraged others...Bentham broke the spell'.

55 Philip Collins, *Dickens and Crime*, Macmillan, 1965, p18

56 GWF Hegel, *The Philosophy of Right*, Encyclopaedia Britannica, Chicago, 1982, Ethical Life, p37

57 GWF Hegel, *The Philosophy of Right*, Encyclopaedia Britannica, Chicago, 1982, Ethical Life, p53

58 Matthew Arnold, *Culture and Anarchy*, (Ed J Dover Wilson), Cambridge, 1932, p70

59 Philip Collins, *Dickens and Crime*, Macmillan, 1965, p13

60 Henry Mayhew, *London Labour and the London Poor*, (Ed John D Rosenberg) Dover Publications, 1968, p2

61 Cesare Lombroso, *L'Uomo Delinquente (Criminal Man according to the Classification of Cesare Lombroso)*, Patterson Smith, 1972 (orig 1911)

62 Gertrude Himmelfarb, *The Idea of Poverty: England in the Early Industrial Age*, Faber & Faber, 1985, p367

63 Henry Mayhew, *London Labour and the London Poor*, (Ed John D Rosenberg) Dover Publications, 1968, p2

64 Eileen Yeo pointed this out when she noted that 'Mayhew was no relativist.' From Eileen Yeo and Edward Thompson (Eds), *The Unknown Mayhew*, Penguin, 1973

65 Emile Durkheim, *Suicide*, Routledge & Kegan Paul, 1970, p255

66 Stewart Clegg and David Dunkerley, *Organisation, Class and Control*, Routledge & Kegan Paul, 1980, p20

67 Emile Durkheim, *The Rules of Sociological Method*, Free Press, 1966, p58

68 Emile Durkheim, *The Rules of Sociological Method*, Free Press, 1966, p56

69 Colin Sumner has given a useful summary of Durkheim:

    'On the one hand, he expressed a nineteenth-century positivism which:

    ● saw criminal statistics as the true indices of the moral state of society
    ● assumed a distanced, elevated, scientific posture towards crime, allegedly free of political commitments
    ● saw law as an accurate index of the collective sentiment rather than sectional interest
    ● was still inclined to judge many individual "criminals" as morally or psychologically pathological.

    On the other hand, he also expressed an early twentieth-century vision of doubt, irony, relativity and depth, which

    ● saw crime as a social category defined by the collective sentiment of the day rather than any universal values

● doubted the ability of societies to exist without crime or moral censure
● appreciated that social deviants can be visionaries or critics pointing the way toward social reform
● recognised the modern contradiction between the relentless search for profit and the need for moral regulation throughout society.'

Colin Sumner, *The Sociology of Deviance: An Obituary,* Open University Press, 1994, pp10-11

70   Colin Sumner, *The Sociology of Deviance: An Obituary,* Open University Press, 1994, p4

71   Gertrude Himmelfarb, 'The de-moralisation of society: from Victorian virtues to modern values', *Institute of Economic Affairs,* 1995. However, Norman Hampson cites the early nineteenth-century German historian Johann Gottfried von Herder as the first to speak of values and cultures in the plural. In highlighting the exceptional character of German culture, Herder was standing out against the dominant idea of universalism and its origins in the French Revolution. Norman Hampson, *The Enlightenment,* Penguin, 1968, p60

72   Israel Zangwill, *The Melting Pot*, a play first performed on Broadway, New York in 1908. Zangwill's title recalls the words of M-G Jean de Crevecoeur: 'Here individuals of all nations are melted into a new race of men', *Letters from an American Farmer,* Fox, Duffield & Co, 1782, pp54-55

73   Gertrude Himmelfarb, 'The de-moralisation of society: from Victorian virtues to modern values', *Institute of Economic Affairs,* 1995, p19

74   Colin Sumner, *The Sociology of Deviance: An Obituary,* Open University Press, 1994, p43

75   David Matza, *Becoming Deviant,* Prentice Hall, 1968, p45

76   Louis Wirth, *On Cities and Social Life,* (Ed AJ Reiss Jr), University of Chicago Press, 1931, pp230-31

77   Louis Wirth, *On Cities and Social Life,* (Ed AJ Reiss Jr), University of Chicago Press, 1931, pp232-33

78   Louis Wirth, *On Cities and Social Life,* (Ed AJ Reiss Jr), University of Chicago Press, 1931, pp232-33

79   Louis Wirth, *On Cities and Social Life,* (Ed AJ Reiss Jr), University of Chicago Press, 1931, p232

80   'the interpenetration of diverse ethnic and cultural groups in the urban world has resulted in the enormous multiplication of value systems, each one of which is binding only upon a segment of the population', Louis Wirth, *On Cities and Social Life,* (Ed AJ Reiss Jr), University of Chicago Press, 1931, p48

81   'a cursory survey reveals that such consensus as does exist in modern Western society when it is not at war is extremely limited, in the sense that those who participate in the consensus constitute only a small portion of the total society', Louis Wirth, *On Cities and Social Life,* (Ed AJ Reiss Jr), University of Chicago Press, 1931, p53

82   Edwin Lemert, 'Some aspects of a general theory of sociopathic behaviour', *Proceedings of the Pacific Sociological Society,* XVI Congress, p25

83   LK Frank, *Society as the Patient: Essays on Culture and Personality,* Rutgers University Press, 1948, p1

84 'So-called social problems and the seeming perversity of individual behaviour become intelligible. They are to be viewed as arising from the frantic efforts of individuals, lacking any sure direction and sanctions or guiding conception of life, to find some ways of protecting themselves or of merely existing on any terms they can manage in a society being remade by scientific research and technology. Having no strong loyalties and no consistent values or realisable ideals to cherish, the individual's behaviour is naturally conflicting, confused, neurotic, and anti-social, if that term has many meaning in the absence of an established purpose and ideal.' LK Frank, *Society as the Patient: Essays on Culture and Personality,* Rutgers University Press, 1948, pp1-2

85 Frank Tannenbaum, *Crime and the Community,* Columbia University Press, 1938, p25

86 Donald Taft, *Criminology,* Macmillan, 1942, p240

87 Frank Tannenbaum, *Crime and the Community,* Columbia University Press, 1938, p20

88 Noel Annan, *Our Age,* Fontana, 1990

89 C Wright Mills, *The Sociological Imagination,* Oxford University Press, 1959, p171

90 'it is a sociology of and for the new welfare state. It is the sociology of young men with friends in Washington. It is a sociology that succeeds in solving the oldest problem in personal politics. How to maintain one's integrity without sacrificing one's career, or how to remain liberal although well-heeled.' Alvin Gouldner, 'The sociologist as partisan: sociology and the welfare state', *American Sociologist,* Vol3 No2, 1968, p110

91 David Matza, *Delinquency and Drift,* Wiley, 1964

92 Howard Becker, *Outsiders: Studies in the Sociology of Deviance,* Free Press, 1969, p9

93 Jock Young, 'Left idealism' in 'Capitalism and the rule of law', *National Deviancy Conference/Conference of Socialist Economists,* Hutchinson, 1979, p12

94 Jock Young, 'Left idealism' in 'Capitalism and the rule of law', *National Deviancy Conference/Conference of Socialist Economists,* Hutchinson, 1979, p12

95 Jock Young, 'Left idealism' in 'Capitalism and the rule of law', *National Deviancy Conference/Conference of Socialist Economists,* Hutchinson, 1979, p16

96 E Schur, *Radical Non-Intervention: Rethinking the Delinquency Problem,* Prentice-Hall, 1973

97 J Kitsuse, *Social Reactions to Deviant Behaviour,* 1962, p253

98 Ian Taylor and Laurie Taylor (Eds), *Politics and Deviance,* Penguin, 1973, p7

99 'the task is to create a society in which the facts of human diversity, whether personal, organic or social, are not subject to the power to criminalise.' Ian Taylor, Paul Walton and Jock Young (Eds), *The New Criminology: For a Social Theory of Deviance,* Routledge & Kegan Paul, 1973, pp281-82

100 David Matza, *Becoming Deviant,* Prentice Hall, 1969, p80

101 KT Erikson, 'Notes on the sociology of deviance', *Social Problems,* Vol9, 1962, p311

102 Stan Cohen and Laurie Taylor, *Escape Attempts,* Penguin, 1978, p2

103 Stuart Hall and Tony Jefferson, *Resistance through Rituals: Youth Sub-Cultures in Postwar Britain,* Hutchinson, 1975

104 Alvin Gouldner, *For Sociology,* Pelican, 1975, pp37-38

105 Roger Graef, *Living Dangerously: Young Offenders in their Own Words,* Harper Collins, 1992, p3

106 Jonathan Alter and Pat Wingert, 'The return of shame', *Newsweek,* 6 February 1992

107 Charles Murray and Richard Herrnstein, *The Bell Curve: Intelligence and Class Structure in American Life,* Free Press, 1994

108 Martha Nussbaum, 'Virtue revived', *Times Literary Supplement,* 3 July 1992

109 John Braithwaite, *Crime, Shame and Reintegration,* Cambridge University Press, 1993, p156

110 John Braithwaite, *Crime, Shame and Reintegration,* Cambridge University Press, 1993, p9

111 Jonathan Alter and Pat Wingert, 'The return of shame', *Newsweek,* 6 February 1992

4
Racial identities: the degradation of human constructions

Suke Wolton

Race has been one of the most important and strategic concepts of the twentieth century. Only 60 years ago, it was seen as common sense to suppose that humanity was made up of naturally discrete groups of people. Today, the idea of a racial hierarchy has been generally discredited. The overt differential treatment of groups on the grounds of their skin colour is now as politically unacceptable as a politician swearing in public. This is not to say that it does not happen, it is just that very few people would admit to it. Today there appears to be more of a consensus than ever before that 'race' is something that exists primarily in the mind. This chapter is a critical look at how the unreality of race is argued and what consequences this has for a humanist challenge to the ideology of race.

The collapse of 'scientific racism' is one obvious feature of the present day.[1] There are very few authors today who attempt to use science to justify a hierarchy or indeed the existence of races.[2] Modern genetics, rather than providing the key to defining race, has shown that the concept of race has no genetic basis.[3] The more that our DNA is investigated, the more that we discover the extent of human individual diversity—and the impossibility of confining difference to one particular characteristic. Individuals of a similar geographical and 'racial' background differ genetically by 85 per cent. National differences account for about five to 10 per cent. The genetic difference between 'races' is about the same as the difference between any two countries (eg, between two countries in Africa). Steve Jones, the University College of London geneticist, summed this up in the *Reith Lectures* as: 'Individuals—not nations and not races—are the main repository of human variation.'[4]

Genetics has a difficulty in defining race because there is simply so much variation from individual to individual that it is impossible to pin down any borderlines in terms of physical features.[5] Geneticists have found few inherited characteristics that can be seen as clear markers—that are either present or not present. The few they have found, such as the ability to roll the tongue or wiggle the ears, are interestingly the least used characteristics for the old ideas of racial traits. Most physical features, such as skin colour, have too much variety to have a clear cut-off point. More importantly, physical characteristics are not associated with each other in any fixed form—hair texture varies independently of skin colour, for example. The key problem facing anyone studying race is not its connection to nature but its association with anything at all. Why should one feature seem to stand out as a definer of people rather than another characteristic? And more importantly, why does the process of classification into groups occur at all? These are the questions that are central to the study of race and racism. It is the assumption of difference that this chapter seeks to investigate, particularly in some more recent theories.

The concept of race was tainted by its association with Nazism during the Second World War. In the 1950s university sociology departments ignored the sensitive methodological question of defining race.[6] Instead sociologists focused on empirical studies of immigrant groups as Nathan Glazer and Daniel Moynihan did in *Beyond the Melting Pot*.[7] These studies were still imbued with racial assumptions about the superiority of whites. At the same time, however, overt racism had become unacceptable. Instead of using the language of racial hierarchy, the sociologists studied immigrant assimilation which indicated the status, in the eyes of the sociologists, of the different ethnicities. In the melting pot of America, the fortunes of immigrant groups were meant to indicate their cultural adaptability and initiative, in other words; their relative worth. It was assumed that the whites were the ideal, the model, for other groups to aspire to. Today, it is the reverse. In contemporary studies the most problematic grouping is seen as the 'white race'. Recent academic studies illustrate a role reversal in terms of the valuation of features. Unlike Newt Gingrich, the new Speaker of the House of Representatives, most cultural studies academics celebrate the music and independence of black youth and see positive values in black culture. What they do not question, however, is the idea that people make up separate ethnic groups.

The first challenge to the empiricism of the sociologists was an attack on the act of categorisation itself from people like French sociologist Michel Foucault and Palestinian literary theorist Edward Said. The judgement required to place people into certain classes involved an assumption of superiority. The ability to categorise and scrutinise indicated a relationship of control and domination. Edward Said criticised the study of the Middle East for being Orientalist where 'Orientalism, then, is knowledge of the Orient that places things Oriental in class, court, prison, or manual for scrutiny, study, judgement, discipline, or governing'.[8] Instead of the empirical standpoint of accepting the idea of many different ethnicities, the new school saw that very classification as the problem, the thing that caused the oppression.

The definition of boundaries was the way of limiting and confining freedom and thus controlling the people so described. Michel Foucault expressed this idea as: 'Discipline is a political anatomy of detail.'[9] Foucault suggested that the authority of knowledge had its origins in political domination.

Stuart Hall, in the late 1970s, used this critique of the oppressive way that definitions work to demystify the stereotype of the black mugger. He convincingly demonstrated in *Policing the Crisis* that mugging was an invented crime, a fictitious scare, to classify young black men as dangerous. The invention of the mythical identity of black muggers was the expression of establishment fears about moral decline in Britain. 'The "mugger" was such a Folk Devil; his form and shape accurately reflected the content of the fears and anxieties of those who first imagined, and then actually discovered him: young, black, bred in, or arising from the "breakdown of social order" in the city.'[10] Stuart Hall criticised pigeon-holing and concluded that the category of the mugger was invented in a conspiracy to blame black youth for the sense of social decline.

The analysis of the construction of stereotypes developed into the invention school in the early 1980s. The term was coined when in 1983 Eric Hobsbawm and Terence Ranger published *The Invention of Tradition*.[11] This book took apart notions of traditional British identity to demonstrate how these were artificial customs invented by the ruling establishment in modern history. Terence Ranger wrote about how the colonial administrators constructed out of their preconceptions 'tribes' and 'traditional' culture in Africa.[12] This book started a fashion for the idea of the invention of cultures and ethnicities. Many academics found the notion useful to challenge the conservative theory of race. The widespread use of the concept of invention allows us to loosely classify it as a school of thought, although there was much variation within this broad church.

The invention of tradition

The 'invention' school challenged the biological explanations with an alternative understanding of the construction of racial identities. This school's viewpoint, that identities are invented, emphasised the fluidity of identities by accentuating their modern origins. So, for Ranger examining Southern African history, the tribes were not primeval as the missionaries had thought, African groups only ossified into tribes after their contact with the missionaries. Ranger explains that ethnic groups were imposed on an African political and economic division of labour. The Zulus were built up into warriors by the British, while the unfortunate Tonga of the Zambezi Valley ended up as the 'Night-Soil' tribe with their god-forsaken task.[13] The physical and mental characteristics of each tribe were invented almost to suit the job. The invention school, unlike the early anthropologists and missionaries whom they sought to criticise, saw identity as something 'constructed and made operative under different historical conditions'.[14] Furthermore, the influence of Foucault and Franz Fanon, the celebrated champion of Algerian independence, encouraged the invention school to see the construction process itself as a means of control. The new school blamed the fragmented and backward identities of oppressed groups on Western elites—who had invented such structures to enhance their domination and authority.

More recently, the methodology of the invention school, called social constructionism, has been applied by some authors to the white working class. The wider application of this analysis is indicative of a change in attitudes towards the white establishment. The social constructionists have questioned the customs of white groups and by doing so sought to deny any privileged status to being white. The white working class is seen as an ethnic group just as much constructed by the establishment as the tribes were created by the colonial administration.

The American labour historian, David Roediger, has concentrated on the development of the white working class in America. Like other social constructionists, he argues that 'race is given meaning through the agency of human beings in concrete historical and social contexts, and is not a biological or natural category'.[15] Roediger's insight is that racial ideas of white superiority enchained the white working class to their bosses as much, if not more so, than it did the black working class. The meaning of race, for Roediger with his background in labour history, is that it becomes the way in which the employers threatened the job security of white workers with 'scab' labour. For the white working class, the black worker is also the symbol of the freedom they have lost in the transition from frontiers man to wage-labourer. Roediger describes the formation of racist images as:

> the white working class, disciplined and made anxious by fear of dependency, began during its formation to construct an image of the Black population as 'other'—as embodying the preindustrial, erotic, careless style of life the white worker hated and longed for.[16]

It is the mixture of fear of unemployment and desire for freedom that constructs the racist attitudes among the white workers.

Through the concerted efforts of the employers, working people are supposed to direct the agony of their lives at another set of workers. Because, in a sense, it is their own misery that they are transposing on to black skin, the workers believe this ugly portrayal to be true. The credibility of the racist project thus depends in large part on the inability of the workers to transcend their own subjugated position. David Roediger illustrates this point when he describes the efforts at the start of the 1877 St Louis general strike against the negative propaganda of the newspaper bosses.[17] When the strike collapsed the courts punished the black workers whereas members of the white strike committee, who had negotiated the sell-out, were barely prosecuted.[18] One strike leader, Albert Currlin, as an afterthought, blamed the failure of the strike on a 'gang of niggers', thus illustrating the association of the political weakness of the working class with the growth of racism.[19]

Roediger gives a contrasting example in another essay. Dan Scully is a fighting union man who learns to be critical of racism. In 1907, Scully, the Irish American head of the Longshoremen's union, testified before the Louisiana legislature:

> You talk about us conspiring with niggers....But let me tell you and your gang, there was a time when I wouldn't even work beside a nigger....You made me work with niggers, eat with niggers, sleep with niggers, drink out of the same water bucket with niggers, and finally got me to the point where if one of them...blubbers something about more pay, I say, 'Come on, nigger, let's go after the white bastards.'[20]

With this example, Roediger demonstrates how the experience of challenging the domination of the capitalist class undermines the racism of the white working class. The spontaneous formation of racist views is weakened in the process of asserting the common interest of the working class against the establishment.

The presumption that Roediger's analysis seems to make is that there is already a separation of the black and white working class that the ruling class can exploit. The employers can ship in black workers to undercut white workers especially when the conflict in industry has spiralled to a deadlock. One clear presentation of this story-line is the film *Matewan* where black scab miners were bussed in and the strikers were forced to confront racism to build the union.[21] Both this film and Roediger's book presume that the segregation of workers was already commonplace so that the blacks were in some way 'outsiders'. Roediger, therefore, tends to assume what needs to be explained: an existing division of black and white workers that can be manipulated from above. Given his construction of the white working class by the people in power, it is as if the ruling class first segregated the working class as a plan to pit them against one another.

Theodore Allen, author of *The Invention of the White Race*, makes this point unequivocally. He writes that he will 'show racial oppression [was] introduced as a deliberate ruling class policy.'[22] Allen details the repression meted out to the Irish by the English and then to the blacks by the Irish-Americans. His analysis draws out the parallels of these occurrences and brings to life their brutality. He argues, the position of authority created racism because the elites (whatever their earlier origins) demonstrated their position of superiority by the scars they inflicted on their subordinates. One problem with this thesis is that the viciousness of the discrimination does not prove the existence of a conspiracy. The ruling class may be in a position of power that enables it to mete out repression to the lower orders but that position alone does not explain why it should differentially oppress different groups of people. In my view, it is not the strength nor power of a ruling class that informs the action of discrimination; rather its actions are a consequence of its sense of weakness. The establishment is not in a position to direct society consciously; its policies are its attempt to react to a society that is out of control and to deal with its inability to determine its surroundings.

The example of the British establishment's role in the development of discrimination in India would seem, at first sight, to support Roediger's and Allen's thesis that racial divisions are imposed from above. But the first emissaries of the East India Company did not start out with a colour bar. In fact, the early clerks of the company were encouraged to take Indian wives, for the climate was thought too extreme for British ladies.[23] When India became a colony of the Crown, the new Empress of India, Queen Victoria, had no intention to divide and rule the Indian people. The onset of the policy of differential treatment of Muslim and Hindu was a response, in the first instance, to the loss of British control in the Indian Mutiny of 1857. Discrimination began as a consequence of a sense of weakness rather than of confidence in their control. After the experience of the 1857 crisis, the British generals looked to the Muslims for loyalty and rationalised their fears by saying that the Punjab contained the 'martial races' of India which could provide good fighting stock.[24]

Even on a local level the action of the administration in creating segregated housing did not involve a conscious policy for future control. For example, when Malcolm Hailey (who became governor of the Punjab and later the United Provinces) worked on the redistribution of people along newly irrigated land in India he segregated Muslim from Hindu. As a youthful Colonisation Officer, Hailey did not see this policy as a conspiracy that would lead to the partition of India and the deaths of five million in the inter-communal violence that followed, although in the Punjab British policy did seem to be designed to foment ethnic conflict. The British distribution of land discriminated between Hindu, Sikh and Muslim.[25] The policy, however, was antecedent to the real basis of the division. The low investment in agriculture meant that there was a shortage of fertile land. The ethnic division only became important because of the scarcity of resources and the need to ration them. The political strength of the colonial administration seems to be measured by its ability to set Sikh against Hindu against Muslim. The need, however, to resort to such tactics speaks of a broader social weakness. The initial problem that the policy addressed arose because of the inability of the Raj to incorporate competing aspirations by systematically developing the region.[26] Hence the British in the Punjab had decided that the allocation of the canal zone should *not* go to the landless as that would 'upset the existing social and economic order'.[27] Hailey helped to parcel out the fertile new fields to prosperous farmers to encourage loyalty and peace. In their fear of instability the colonial administrators began to create a tension which would only subsequently become 'divide and rule'.

The British Raj was not capable of inventing Pakistani nationalism or Sikh separatism as the invention school might be tempted to suggest. The Raj feared the social disruption of the uneven development of capitalism in India and tried to minimise its impact by restraining the Hindu money lenders. It was the instability of the capitalist social system that encouraged the colonial administrators to endorse segregation in a crude attempt at containment. The fashion, therefore, for the idea of invented identities de-emphasises a crucial aspect of social reality; the conditions of the competitive market and the limitations of resources within a particular social system. More importantly, however, as a consequence, the invention school tends to blame a conscious policy (of the ruling class) for racial divisions.

The invention school overestimates the extent to which the ruling class is in control. Seeing the apparatus of domination, the invention school forgets that these tools are a response to an inability to determine the behaviour of the rest of society. The establishment introduces mechanisms of control precisely because it is trying to run an out-of-control system. The elites reap the profits of capitalism but they are unable to design or manipulate relationships in society. Capitalism is not a planned society. The paternalism of the upper classes is a reflection of their desire for that level of control but, in general, it is an anarchic mode of wealth creation that rewards them. As a member of the elite, Lord Hailey could not foresee the factionalism he was engendering in India. Forty years later, after the experience of colonial insurrection in Ireland and India, Lord Hailey was more aware of the dangers of elite insensitivity: 'Where there is inequality of treatment, or undue insistence on colour superiority, one may look to find a growth of resentment which will show itself in political discontent.'[28] Only in the 1930s Lord Hailey saw, too late to save the empire, the danger of explicit white racism for British colonial rule.

My research involves charting Lord Hailey's changing opinion of race and his concern with white prestige which grew out of his rising sense of imperial weakness rather than an inexorable outcome of ruling class ideology. His concern is illustrated by his comment on the repercussions of the Second World War in the British African colonies:

> Historians have seen in the Russo-Japanese War one of the earlier causes for the change in the attitude of the Asiatic peoples, and particularly those of India, towards European rule....It seems certain, however, that the effect of the conflict between European nations, which extended to the soil of Africa itself and involved the use of native troops, must have affected the general prestige of Europeans....It is, of course, too early to judge of the full reactions of the present war on the African outlook, though they cannot fail to be far-reaching.[29]

Lord Hailey, originally a relaxed colonial administrator, had become anxious for the fate of white prestige just as the 'superiority' of white domination was being challenged by the barbarity of war. In the twentieth century, as the ruling classes throughout the globe felt increasingly under pressure from opponents abroad and 'sedition' in the colonies, so the importance of presenting themselves as being in a position of command became a strategic issue.

Ultimately, the flaw of the invention school is their narrow concern with conscious policy; they presume that the upper classes can introduce racism by design, and furthermore that it would be only to their advantage. But like many aspects of society, the effects of real policy are often more contradictory than this schema suggests. Many researchers have now turned away from the invention school—to focus not on the weaknesses of the establishment, but on the strengths of the oppressed. Not only did the invention school grant unlimited authority to the elites, they thereby implied that others believed and obeyed such ruling class conspiracies. But, argue their yet more radical critics, if we look closer at the stories of the oppressed, the tales of the segregated groups, we might find a more complex account. It is this trajectory that many have followed—to recount the histories of the 'others' and to tell the stories of their *imagined* identity.

The imagination of identity

The late 1980s has seen a shift in the theoretical discussion of identity away from the idea that identity is imposed and towards the idea that identity is the self-construction of cultural boundaries. The self-construction process attempts to explain the consensus within an identity. If people create their own group image then it is *their* identity, not one imposed from the top by the elite. The focus on the active role of the group in the production of their own self-image also moves away from seeing them as victims. Black people and people in the colonies are now seen to be imagining their own communal symbols and shaping their cultures. This was important as a statement about the way in which black people were also influential in determining cultural history. This point of view criticised the invention school for seeming to characterise the mass of people as clay to be moulded by the elites. The imagination school reversed this emphasis and looked at the way in which people created a space for themselves and challenged the authority of the establishment. The new generation of writers, like Paul Gilroy, Homi Bhabha, Clive Harris, Winston James, David Goldberg, Peter Jackson, Jan Penrose, Howard Winant, bell hooks and many others, focus on the *self-construction* of ethnicity. They took the term 'imagined' communities from Benedict Anderson who first argued that communities are not fabricated, but imagined. Anderson wrote that: 'Communities are to be distinguished, not by their falsity/genuineness, but by the style in which they are imagined.'[30] In this way he laid the stress on the communal agreement to create the identity.

Through pin-pointing the issue of resistance, Homi Bhabha began to represent identity as a terrain for independence. The anti-colonialist politicians of the fifties and sixties had chosen the battleground of indigenous parliaments and self-rule. The post-colonial theorists, like Homi Bhabha, looked at the self-images of the colonial subject and sought to uncover valuable contributions to the struggle for independence in these (instead of supposing them to be the constructions of the departing imperialists).[31] Bhabha's approach emphasised that the imperialists were not omnipotent: 'The effect of colonial power is seen to be the production of hybridisation rather than the noisy command of colonialist authority or the silent repression of native traditions.'[32] Identity became the product of give and take between the colonialist and the native: the process that Bhabha calls 'hybridisation'. Identity was the expression of the native's resistance; the creation of a cultural space that denied access to colonialism. Robert Young summarises Bhabha's argument in his new book, *Colonial Desire*:

Bakhtin's intentional hybrid has been transformed by Bhabha into an active moment of challenge and resistance against a dominant cultural power. Bhabha then translates this moment into a "hybrid displacing space" which develops in the interaction between the indigenous and colonial culture which has the effect, he suggests, of depriving "the imposed imperialist culture, not only of the authority that it has for so long imposed politically, often through violence, but even of its own claims to authenticity".[33]

Homi Bhabha thus reverses the invention school's viewpoint when he inter-
prets identity as a challenge to imperialist culture rather than the imperialist's
imposition. It is interesting to note that while post-colonial theory is anti-
imperialist in tone, politically this point is rather more moderate. 'Identity'
has become the outcome of a negotiation between oppressed and oppressor.

In our time of increasing disillusionment with the 1960s independence
movements, identity studies have begun to chart out a new arena of debate
between the oppressed and the oppressor. Instead of the sharp dichotomy
between freedom and enslavement, there is the varied and varying dialogue
of identity. Through the discovery of multi-faceted identities the imagina-
tionists hope to create a limited, but wider, area of space for black people. bell
hooks is part of this project and makes this her starting point in her book,
Yearning: 'We have too long had imposed upon us from both the outside and
the inside a narrow, constricting notion of blackness.'[34]

White anti-racists, according to the new generation, see the intellectual
origins of black separatism in white culture. The new school reverses this
arrangement and 'privileges' the role of black people. The agency of black
people in constructing their identity, rather than having it forced upon them
from above, is the central motif of cultural studies today. Paul Gilroy, in his
recent book, *The Black Atlantic,* places black people centre stage of their own
culture in order to challenge the assumption that black culture is only a product of white racism. Gilroy writes that:

> it is the struggle to have blacks perceived as agents, as people with cognitive
> capacities and even with an intellectual history—attributes denied by modern
> racism—that is for me the primary reason for writing this book.[35]

Gilroy's point is understandable as a response to racism, for the purpose of
self-affirmation, but the question left unanswered is whether this is a truer
picture of reality. It is almost as if Gilroy's project is to encourage self-
confidence for the future by uncovering an active role in the past. Through
finding a historical intermixture in black culture, Gilroy seems to suggest that
contemporary identities are just as varied, dynamic and hybrid, and thereby,
contain the potential for further development.

If the purpose of looking at the self-construction of black images is to
boost the status of black communities, then the imagination school has
looked for characteristics that emphasise positive potential. There are certain
key-words which are applied to describe identity, such as 'dynamism',[36]
'hybridity',[37] 'mutation and intermixture'[38] and 'plural'.[39] These words suggest
that the thing under examination is transient and unbounded. Many
researchers are explicit about their preconceptions of the fluidity of identity;

Peter Jackson and Jan Penrose proudly announce that: 'Rather than assuming that identities are fixed and singular, we have shown them to be dynamic and plural.'[40] This conception of identity is so un-fixed that it is difficult to define. As a consequence it is difficult to see how these group images satisfy the criteria of being identities. But, by emphasising their fluidity, these authors seek to demonstrate that black identities are not exclusive, narrow-minded and parochial like those of white identities.

More importantly, in the literature, black culture has become something to be proud of and to celebrate. The identity of black people is presented as dynamic and developing through the activities of black people. The self-construction theory of identity argues that the boundaries are supposed to be built by the people on the inside. For example, Winston James and Clive Harris claim that: 'Afro-Caribbean people in Britain have erected boundaries in relation to those with whom they identify.'[41] Although it is true that young blacks seek their own language of rap to hide their anger in a form inaccessible to their white teachers, the blacks in Stonebridge Park, White City or Broadwater Farm did not 'erect boundaries'; they were coralled into ghettos and policed into seeing 'differences' by the presence of riot vans and early morning 'visits'. To suppose that black people in Britain are responsible for their own isolation and segregation is to turn reality upside down.

It is important that our research does not ignore the real inequality of power in society. To this day, blacks are still the most disadvantaged group in Britain and America. Young black people between 16 and 24 years old are twice as likely to be unemployed as their white counterparts.[42] In Britain, Asian Muslims suffer four times the unemployment rate of whites in the same area.[43] Discrimination in housing and wages is still entrenched in the structure of society. There is one insight in the self-construction analysis but to endorse it as the true picture gives us a distortion of reality.

What the 'imagination' school has successfully captured is that most people rationalise their surroundings. The organisation of discrimination and social difference is an unconscious and spontaneous process in the capitalist social system. We make a conscious appropriation of our circumstances and so appear to have a hand in their creation. The boundaries of our lives are set by constraints outside of our control but the way in which we relate to those boundaries is more of our own making.

An extreme example of this is the development of poor and rich ghettos. In Los Angeles young black people are confined to certain areas by the operation of 'Armed Response' notices of local security firms and what Mike Davis calls 'archisemiotics'—building for the exclusion 'of class war'.[44] It is the harsh division between rich and poor which sets out an underlying conflict. For the gangs of south-central Los Angeles, their own territorial warfare may induce a sensation of commanding the ramparts but their own neighbourhood is conditioned by an exclusion from uptown LA. The arguments to justify the segregation are developed after the division is socially marked. In Rio de Janeiro the wealthy Brazilians live in a compound surrounded by 20-foot high barbed wire fences and patrolled by guards.[45] Those in control of ordering the policing of the walls believe that they are constructing their own boundaries. The white self-image confined in the Brazilian compounds does not see itself as imprisoned, but freed from the fear of the 'underclass'. Even for the affluent, the rationalisation of 'freedom' within walls is the afterthought of a divided society.

The process of conscious appropriation of one's surroundings occurs after the event. It is the *post-festum* nature of consciousness in this social system that means that the construction of identity is a spontaneous and unplanned process.[46] The reproduction of social divisions in ideological manifestations does not mean that the ideology created the real separation. Rather, ideas articulate the consequence of social limits and, in doing so, further entrench those groups of people as discrete formations with distinct cultures.[47]

Paul Gilroy and bell hooks imply that black culture provided a refuge from the exclusion and marginalisation of blacks from white society. On the one hand, they both seem to be uneasy with celebrating black culture un-equivocally; Gilroy challenges a monolithic approach to black diversity, while hooks is not afraid to criticise the products of modern black art such as Spike Lee's film of *Malcolm X*. On the other hand, it is hooks' reasonable disappointment with the civil rights movement that informs her own appreciation of the role of black people in creating their identity. hooks is right to say that desegregation failed, but replies by reinterpreting the project of change. The greater the disappointment in the aftermath of desegregation, the more the hopes of the civil rights movement seem to be a closed book to hooks. As an aside, hooks' negative assessment of the desegregation parallels the renewed interest in the separatist Malcolm X as against the waning popularity of Martin Luther King's integrationist dreams.

hooks romanticises her childhood memories of segregation as if the Jim Crow era was chosen by the black community. She hated the way in which the civil rights actions of the 1950s and 1960s ended up by putting the children in the front line of challenging whites-only schools. The experience of bitter political struggle encouraged a nostalgic view of the past that she wept to lose:

That black world of my growing up began to fundamentally change when the schools were desegregated. What I remember most about that time is a deep sense of loss....I wept and longed for what we had lost and wondered why the grown black folks had acted as though they did not know we would be sur-rendering so much for so little, that we would be leaving behind a history.[48]

In the face of Jim Crow, black communities did develop mechanisms of self-help like black schools and colleges. Current attempts to desegregate Howard University seem to underscore hooks' point that we would be 'surrendering so much for so little'. However, hooks' argument lacks proportion. Networks of self-help arose as a defence against the greater force of white supremacy. But the precondition for the network of resistance is the subjugation of Jim Crow, the poll tax, the literacy test, lynching and the truck system. The one is logically connected to the other. hooks' romanticisation of the community of the past forgets, in her horror of the present, the brutality that forged that sense of togetherness.

hooks' conservative attachment to separate development is only marginally qualified by the concept of 'border-crossing' introduced in her latest work:

> Given that cultural fascism is on the rise, that there is such open demand for separatist politics, embracing notions of inclusion and exclusion, whether based on shared gender, race, or nationality, seriously impedes all progressive effort to create a culture where border crossing enables both the sharing of resources and the production of a culture of communalism and mutuality.[49]

It is a strange reflection on the anti-racist politics of the late twentieth century that it should find its metaphor in passport control. The real weakness of this philosophy is that difference is regarded as primary and connection derivative. Common humanity is thought to be secondary; derived from the presumed prior existence of separate groups.

Howard Winant, the American sociologist, goes much further than bell hooks in assuming racial division. Winant writes in his new book, *Racial Conditions*, that:

> Race is a means of knowing and organising the social world; it is subject to continual contestation and reinterpretation, but it is no more likely to disappear than other forms of human inequality and difference.[50]

Howard Winant reproduces, in a more aggravated form, the methodological limitations of the invention school. Like Roediger and Allen, Winant presupposes what needs to be explained; racial division. Like hooks, Winant is describing how people elaborate racial identities; the various cultural and institutional mechanisms they develop to accommodate the problem of racial division. Given his theoretical assumptions, it is not surprising that Winant explicitly states that racial division is an ever-present human condition.

Interestingly, while the invention school argued that racial division originated with ruling class machinations, the imagination school presents no explanation for the origin of this separation. The conspiracy theory of the invention school misinterprets social limitations for conscious design. The silence on this question from the imagination school, meanwhile, relegates the division of people to the intractable and the inevitable. It is so assumed that it has been normalised; indeed, actively embraced by Howard Winant, who writes: 'The liberation of racial identity is as much part of the struggle against racism as the elimination of racial discrimination and inequality.'[51] The former, the liberation of racial identity, is itself an expression of inequality and discrimination rather than being a counter to it. The real intellectual task facing future theorists of racial identities is to explain the origins of these divisions in social processes.

Marxism

Jerry Cohen explains the roots of Marxism in three great schools of thought: German idealism, French Socialism and British political economy.[52] Marx brought together the best human understanding of society to give a new insight into the process of changing society. Central to Marxism is the importance of a theoretical interpretation of society because, as James Heartfield explains, it provides a means of seeing beneath the surface mediations of the social organism.[53]

Capitalism developed out of feudalism which had been a hierarchical society with God at the centre of the universe. The social ranking of any person in that period was determined at birth by the status of the family. The individual's future was dominated by their origins. The beginnings of capitalism overturned this arrangement. Gradually in Britain, the first capitalist country, and later and more rapidly in France, social mobility became a possibility through the acquisition of wealth from production instead of land. The full development of the new social order encouraged the migration of people—to move to work in the new factories and the new mines. The early proponents of capitalism were full of these new-found freedoms and challenged the old hierarchy, even the position of God. But fears of the consequences of such liberties expressed themselves in parochial concerns. The contradiction of capitalism appeared in its abstract form: the social freedom that was the precondition of capitalism was also a source of instability. The reaction to the French Revolution attempted to limit liberty to certain accredited people. The painful struggle to extend the franchise is testimony to the limitations on freedom within capitalism.

The nineteenth century saw the full development of the working class and, consequently, the full fear of the elites. They were scared of the mob, scared of the great crowds of people, that they had helped to create through their demand for cheap labour as the source of their wealth. The rich establishment used the rationale of 'a certain breeding' to distinguish themselves and control the 'lower classes'. The first reaction of bourgeois thinkers was to naturalise social relations: they presented the organisation of society as a product of nature. They apologised for the poverty of capitalism by attributing the misery to nature. The elites kept their grip on profits and justified their higher living standards with Social Darwinism. This theory, legitimated by some association with Darwin, assumed that ecology was the operation of the competitive market in the jungle and then rediscovered the same nature in man's society. The 'survival of the fittest', the Darwinian explanation for niche development in evolution, was applied to human cultures to give scientific credibility to limiting wealth to those with power.[54]

This rationalisation of unequal wealth through the use of nature culminated in scientific racism where biology justified discrimination. The racism developed in the nineteenth century rested on, in the first instance, the growing gap between rich and poor within Britain and between Britain and the colonies. But the intensity of the fear and hatred of the Other, especially after the Indian Mutiny of 1857 and the Jamaican uprising of 1865, was shaped also by the increasing dependency of Britain on the colonies. The racism of the British establishment was based on both a terror of and a need for those whom it subjugated.

At the heart of capitalist society is a paradox in the relationship of the individual and society. On the one hand, it celebrates the freedom of the individual and, on the other, capitalism is founded on cooperation in the heart of the productive process. Our ability to act as free individuals relies upon others to provide the things which make our lives easier. Simply put, going to the supermarket for a pint of milk is quicker than finding a cow. Our day-to-day activities are shaped by the conditions of production. Free from the pressures of survival, we can develop our individual creativity. Our individuality is made possible through a labour-saving division of labour while, at the same time, competition for jobs and resources pits people against one another. As Marx explained in *Grundrisse*, the notebook for *Capital*:

> Only in the eighteenth century, in 'civil society', do the various forms of social connectedness confront the individual as a mere means towards his private purposes, as external necessity. But the epoch which produces this standpoint, that of the isolated individual, is also precisely that of the hitherto most developed social (from this standpoint, general) relations. The human being is in the most literal sense a political animal, not merely a gregarious animal, but an animal which can individuate itself only in the midst of society.[55]

The breakthrough that Marx made was to understand that the individual in capitalist society meets the social teamwork and division of labour, not in terms of people, but in the shape of commodities; mere things to satisfy our needs, our 'private purposes'. On the other hand, it is the efficiency of such cooperation that frees us from the constant pressure of survival and permits some flowering of individuality. Capitalism thus creates the conditions for individuals but it constrains their creativity and abilities, not only by forcing the mass of people to struggle to survive, but also by making a personality creative only in so far that it is commercially realisable. By mystifying the division of labour into the drive for profits, the framework of such a society distorts every positive impulse into the pursuit of money and selfish ambition. Conversely, however, it also makes selfish desire look to others for its satisfaction.

Both, therefore, on the level of the class and at the level of the individual there is a tension between the need for others and the fear of them. Without the organisation of some social group, the individual is powerless. The fraught relationship of people in such a competitive society, atomised but not truly individualistic, gives identity a key role. There is a constant interplay between asserting difference and negotiating common interests. This also means that identity, being such a fluid and tense social relationship, is a poor methodological tool. It tends to reify the existing arrangement which is often just a particular social coincidence. It is the underlying trends that give rise to such social groupings that are more important to identify.

There is, therefore, a contradiction at the heart of social division. The coming together of an 'identity', for a certain time, to pursue some particular interests or as a defence against further attack, both rejects the wider society and forges its own cooperation and bond within itself. For example, the aspiration to challenge the colonial hegemony of the white Western powers after the Second World War brought together people with a common goal. The framework, however, in which that independence was sought was that of national freedom. The demands for liberation were forced then into national and 'ethnic' competition for resources. Thus today, 50 years on, that framework has degenerated into the destructive cycle of fragmentation as in the allocation of aid in Mogadishu to one or another clan. In America, issues of social and racial equality have been forgotten for debates on quotas, percentages and affirmative action. The competitive society has crippled the aspiration for freedom.

One of the consequences of the antagonism between people and, at the same time, the dependence relationship is expressed in a distorted desire. The school of social constructionism has given us vivid descriptions of the development of racial culture. In its formation, they have shown us, there is a recurring theme of sexual imagery and eroticism. If we return to Roediger's description of the construction of the American white working class cited earlier, he points out that the black population was seen as 'embodying the preindustrial, erotic, careless style of life the white worker hated and longed for'. Recently, more researchers have become aware of this theme and have tried to incorporate the language of sexuality into race studies through the addition of gender politics.[56] But sexuality is *intrinsic* to the issue of identity, from a Marxist perspective, because ever-changing identity is itself based on a relationship of need as well as fear. It is the repressed yearning that expresses the hatred of the 'Other' as an erotic desire for domination. Sexuality and hatred become intimately related personalised categories shaped by the circumstance of a contradictory social system.

The most obvious form of this relationship is the 'forbidden fruit' of the colonial relationship.[57] The illicit nights between the colonial administrator and subordinated 'native' were one thing, but the expression of a loving relationship was quite another. The imperialist drive for colonies encouraged an adoration of the exotic, while at the same time, the district officer repressed his admiration to demand obedience. The exploitation and control of the colonies enforced a relationship that was repressive, destructive and also dependent between the coloniser and the colonised.

Nor is the tension between desire and domination only found in the colonial situation. Just as nineteenth-century racial thinking was first developed by the elites in relation to their own working class, so too the expression of their repressed desire emerged in the taste for 'rough trade'. Émile Zola captured some of the sense of the erotic relationship at the heart of capitalism in his novel *Germinal*. In the midst of the miners' strike the owner tours around the villages 'inspecting the lie of the land' and Zola describes that:

> No stone had ever whistled past [Monsieur Hennebeau's] ears, and all he found was silent men slow to greet him; but more often he came across lovers taking their fill of pleasure in odd corners, heedless of politics. He would trot past on his mare, looking straight ahead so as not to disturb anybody, but his heart ached with unsatisfied longings in the midst of this orgy of free love.[58]

Monsieur Hennebeau was being squeezed by the strike and his mines were filling up with water but his thought was of his desire for carefree sex. The French upper class both longed for the rude caresses and felt disgusted at the promiscuity of the working classes. Zola captures, in the 'longings' of Monsieur Hennebeau, the way in which he was both threatened by the labourers and needed them for his own survival. Sexuality was central to his compromised situation.

Although the themes of repression and domination are recurring elements in the study of identity, capitalism is primarily a dynamic system which means that it tends to overturn every order that it creates. At the same time, there are constraints which operate on every attempt to progress. The capitalist system increasingly creates its own barriers to unlimited development. There is the underlying tendency to crisis in the economy which frames every social question.[59] The irrationalism of the social system is continually expressed in the alienation of resources according to a market logic that values according to profit rather than need and a market unpredictability which wastes produce and effort.

The weakness of capitalism is most clearly expressed in the relationship of class exploitation. There is tension and irrationality implicit in the wage labour/capital social relationship. Where those conflicts break out, the capitalist class hangs on to every semblance of normality and continuity to affirm the reasonableness of its out-of-control system. Conservative thinkers assert the tradition of the social order to try to lend it authority in continuity.[60] At the same time, as old ideas become discredited so the presentation of the past is reworked. In every period the images of stability, normality and respectability are renegotiated as the old identities and arguments become compromised by their association with failure.

Even capitalism's most forthright apologists have had to redesign their banners. The early capitalists could uphold the principle of equality, of equal exchange, as their ideal for capitalism's social order. As they challenged the rule of the aristocrats, they championed the principle of freedom. When, however, they discovered that the working class wanted freedom to mean more than the freedom to be exploited, when the workers demanded the right to vote as free equals, the new establishment became romantic for the old order. In this new era of class conflict, in the mid-nineteenth century, race began to replace class as equal citizens were redefined not by their wealth, but by their origins.[61] The separation of economic freedom from political freedom established a framework which confined freedom to mere principle rather than practice.

The new framework and rationale, however, that confined equality and superiority to the white race did not go unchallenged. Racial ideology was born out of the inability of capitalism to live up to its ideals, and the more that the old order came under threat the more the ruling class tried to reaffirm its status. In the middle of the Second World War, some individuals longed for the certainty of the past and their old authority. The wartime bulldog, prime minister Winston Churchill, desperately cabled General Wavell to hang on to Singapore and white prestige:

There must at this stage be no thought of saving the troops or sparing the population. The battle must be fought to the bitter end at all costs....Commanders and senior officers should die with their troops. The honour of the British Empire and of the British army is at stake. I rely on you to show no mercy to weakness in any form. With the Russians fighting as they are and the Americans so stubborn at Luzon, the whole reputation of our country and our race is involved.[62]

Despite Churchill's urgent message General Wavell surrendered on 15 February 1942 after only two weeks of fighting and less than 10 weeks after Pearl Harbor.[63] The loss of Singapore, the supposed 'Fortress of the East', was humiliating for the British. The experience of the downfall of white superiority in the Far East and the association of racism with Nazism in Europe meant that the war forced a renegotiation of the issue of equality. In America, black people had fought the war under the slogan of a 'double victory' for freedom against tyranny in Europe and the Far East and, more importantly, against segregation at home. At the same time, the war against Japan had challenged white pretensions to unequalled strength.[64] The only way the Allies could assert Western superiority was through the issue of 'morals' and 'humanitarianism'. A new civilising mission was subsequently posed in terms of democracy and human rights. The banners of capitalism were rewritten but the content of Western domination hardly changed. The new language of 'ethnic' and 'minority' rights posed Western nations as the guarantors of freedom. In practice, however, they tended to support and aid those 'minorities' which maintained suitable links with Washington, London and Paris.

In many ways, though, the postwar order seemed to be the recognition of a common humanity by the presentation of a universal ideal. The language of humanitarianism recognised the spirit of humanity and maintained a language of common freedoms and rights. But today, just when the mythology of the Cold War has gone, so the validity of universal aims has been challenged by both left and right. The language of freedom has been replaced by the argument for protection of minorities, the conservation of ethnic division, and the preservation of the status quo. The sense of weakness, the lack of purpose and direction that stems from the stagnant underlying economy, has infected every strata of society. Both conservative ideas and the opposition have reconciled themselves to a confined and limited space. If we are to overturn this order, the first fight is to win the battle of ideas—and most importantly for the principle of universal freedom unconstrained by contradictions in capitalism. Without an argument for a wider solidarity, a sense of common cause, not a narrow paternalism or charity, we cannot overturn this destructive system.

We need to put the case for the importance of ideas, not by implicating ideology in the creation of this degraded society, but by demonstrating the strength of ideas in demystifying our social circumstances. The invention school tended to overemphasise the strength of the ruling class in imposing divide-and-rule identities. Their analysis saw a conspiracy of strength rather than the rationalisation of weakness. The bourgeois thought under criticism was itself a product of compromised circumstances. The imagination school, meanwhile, in questioning the invention school, saw the strength of the oppressed in shaping their identity in the weakness of the oppressor. In the end, they appeared to make the same point as each other. Both schools tended to see the rationalisation of identity as the creator rather than the product of the system. But identity is the consequence of the spontaneous process of the contradictory workings of capitalism. Just as capitalism is not a planned system, so the ideology of its sectional parts does not organise its workings, but attempts to make sense of what has already happened. Only from this point is there a dialectical relationship between ideology and social circumstance. For example, hostility between white and black further entrenches discrimination and establishes segregation on every level of society. The ideology of separate peoples, the concept of race, is essentially an apology for a social system that is unable to deliver the full potential of all humanity, and rests instead upon division.

NOTES

1   The history of this is described in Elazar Barkan, *The Retreat of Scientific Racism*, Oxford University Press, 1992

2   Charles Murray gained few positive reviews for his book which tried to use statistics to justify his case that blacks in America are poorer because they have lower intelligence. Richard J Herrnstein and Charles Murray, *The Bell Curve; Intelligence and Class Structure in American Life*, Free Press, 1994

3   Steven Rose, Leon J Kamin and RC Lewontin, *Not in Our Genes: Biology, Ideology and Human Nature*, Pelican, 1984

4   Dr Steve Jones, *Reith Lectures*, Radio 4, 11 December 1991, reprinted in the *Independent*, 12 December 1991

5   Stephen Jay Gould, *The Mismeasure of Man*, Pelican, 1983

6   This absence encouraged the writing of the late 1970s' Unesco studies on race: 'While descriptive studies were abundant, there was a paucity of analysis.' Marion O'Callaghan, 'Introductory notes' in Unesco, *Sociological Theories: Race and Colonialism*, Paris, 1980, p1

7   Nathan Glazer and Daniel Moynihan, *Beyond the Melting Pot*, MIT Press, 1970 (orig 1963)

8   Edward Said, *Orientalism*, Routledge & Kegan Paul, 1978, p41

9   Michel Foucault, *Discipline and Punish*, Penguin, 1977 (1975), p139

10   Stuart Hall, Chas Critcher, Tony Jefferson, John Clarke, and Brian Roberts, *Policing the Crisis: Mugging, the State and Law and Order*, Macmillan, 1978, p161

11   Eric Hobsbawm and Terence Ranger (Eds), *The Invention of Tradition*, Cambridge University Press, 1983

12   'Since so few connections could be made between British and African political, social and legal systems, British administrators set about inventing African traditions for Africans. Their own respect for "tradition" disposed them to look with favour upon what they took to be traditional in Africa.' Terence Ranger, 'The invention of tradition in colonial Africa', in Eric Hobsbawm and Terence Ranger (Eds), *The Invention of Tradition*, Cambridge University Press, 1983, p212

13   Terence Ranger, 'Tribalisation of Africa, retribalisation of Europe', inaugural 'Tribe, State, Nation' lecture published in *Woodstock Road Editorial*, No16, Hilary 1994, p43

14   Stuart Hall, 'Race, articulation and societies structured in dominance', in *Sociological Theories: Race and Colonialism*, Unesco, 1980, p341

15   David Roediger, *Towards the Abolition of Whiteness*, Verso, 1994, p2

16   David Roediger, *Wages of Whiteness: Race and the Making of the American Working Class*, Verso, 1991, p14

17   David Roediger, *Towards the Abolition of Whiteness*, Verso, 1994, p102

18   'Although rank-and-filers, especially black rank-and-file strikers, often went to the workhouse on convictions for breaching the peace, all nine top leaders went free on a *nolle prosequi* verdict after a brief trial in which the prosecution was denied a vital delay.' David Roediger, *Towards the Abolition of Whiteness*, Verso, 1994, p104

19   David Roediger, *Towards the Abolition of Whiteness*, Verso, 1994, p103

20   David Roediger, *Towards the Abolition of Whiteness*, Verso, 1994, p26

21   *Matewan*, directed by John Sayles, 1987

22   Theodore Allen, *The Invention of the White Race: Vol1, Racial Oppression and Social Control*, Verso, 1994, p23

23   'The initial pattern in all early European empires tended towards intermarriage with local women...the keeping of a mistress in British India became a well-established practice by the later eighteenth century, defended as increasing the knowledge of Indian affairs. Some officers recommended it quite openly, and the pattern was set at the highest level.' Ronald Hyam, *Empire and Sexuality: The British Experience*, Manchester University Press, 1990, p115

24   'Indians pointed out with considerable historical justification that the "martial races" were a British invention of the late nineteenth century and that the Company had conquered India with troops recruited in Bombay, Madras and the United Provinces. Only after the Mutiny had the British turned instead to recruitment from the loyal Punjab. Later they had found it convenient to continue to recruit from this area because it was adjacent to the North-West Frontier, which was the main field of the army's actual operations against tribesmen and of potential operations against Afghanistan and Russia.' Richard Symonds, *The British and their Successors*, Faber & Faber, 1966, p59

25   'On the assumption that colonists would fare better if they settled in primary groups, the government tried to aggregate people from different religions and castes. The Chenab therefore became more segregated than the colonists' original homes.' John W Cell, *Hailey: A Study in British Imperialism, 1872-1969*, Cambridge University Press, 1992, p19

26   'The Chenab was meant to make the predominantly agrarian economy larger and more efficient in degree, but not different in kind. Revenue was not used as capital: projects for secondary industrialisation were few, late, and poorly funded. The Punjab canal colonies, their historian concludes, aimed at expansion but not true development.' John W Cell, *Hailey: A Study in British Imperialism 1872-1969*, Cambridge University Press, 1992, p18

27   Punjab press communiqué, 8 December 1914 cited in John W Cell, *Hailey: A Study in British Imperialism, 1872-1969*, Cambridge University Press, 1992, p18

28   Lord Hailey, 'Nationalism in Africa', *Journal of the Royal African Society*, Vol36 No143, April 1937, p146

29   Lord Hailey, *Native Administration and Political Development in British Tropical Africa*, Confidential Colonial Office Report, 1940-42, (Ed Anthony Kirk-Green, 1970), p10

30   Benedict Anderson, *Imagined Communities: Reflections on the Origin and Spread of Nationalism*, Verso, 1991 (1983), p6

31   Terence Ranger noted this modification in a recent lecture at St Antony's college when he remarked that: 'the tendency of the Africanist literature has increasingly been to move from description of the imperial "invention" of tribes to the subsequent African "imagination" of ethnicity.' Terence Ranger, inaugural 'Tribe, State, Nation' lecture published as 'Tribalisation of Africa, retribalisation of Europe', *Woodstock Road Editorial*, No16, Hilary 1994, p44

32   Homi K Bhabha, 'Signs taken for wonders: questions of ambivalence and authority under a tree outside Delhi, May 1817', *Critical Inquiry*, Vol12 No1, 1985, p154

33 Robert JC Young, *Colonial Desires: Hybridity in Theory, Culture and Race*, Routledge, 1995, p23, citing Homi K Bhabha, 'The post-colonial critic', *Arena*, Vol96, 1991, pp57-58

34 bell hooks, *Yearning: Race, Gender, and Cultural Politics*, Turnaround, 1991, p28

35 Paul Gilroy, *The Black Atlantic: Modernity and Double Consciousness*, Verso, 1993, p6

36 See Peter Jackson and Jan Penrose (Eds), *Constructions of Race, Place and Nation*, UCL Press, 1993

37 See Howard Winant, *Racial Conditions*, University of Minnesota Press, 1994 and Paul Gilroy, *The Black Atlantic: Modernity and Double Consciousness*, Verso, 1993

38 Paul Gilroy, *The Black Atlantic: Modernity and Double Consciousness*, Verso, 1993

39 See Howard Winant, *Racial Conditions*, University of Minnesota Press, 1994 and Peter Jackson and Jan Penrose (Eds), *Constructions of Race, Place and Nation*, UCL Press, 1993

40 Peter Jackson and Jan Penrose (Eds), *Constructions of Race, Place and Nation*, UCL Press, 1993, p207

41 Winston James and Clive Harris (Eds), *Inside Babylon*, Verso, 1993, p266

42 *Guardian*, 20 March 1995

43 *Guardian*, 17 June 1995

44 Mike Davis, *City of Quartz; Excavating the Future of Los Angeles*, Vintage, 1992 (orig Verso 1990), p231

45 *Panorama*, 20 March 1995, BBC1

46 Marx characterises the Hegelian Absolute Spirit as consciousness in retrospect of history in the *Holy Family*: 'His participation in history is reduced to this retrospective consciousness, for the real movement is accomplished by the Absolute Spirit unconsciously, so that the philosopher appears *post festum*.' Cited in Franz Jakubowski, *Ideology and Superstructure in Historical Materialism*, Pluto, 1990, p19

47 'The materialist doctrine that men are products of circumstances and upbringing, and that, therefore, changed men are products of other circumstances and changed upbringing, forgets that men themselves change circumstances and that the educator himself must be educated.' Karl Marx, Thesis 3, *Theses on Feuerbach*, appendix to F Engels, *Ludwig Feuerbach and the End of Classical German Philosophy*, 1888

48 bell hooks, *Yearning; Race, Gender, and Cultural Politics*, Turnaround, 1991, p34

49 bell hooks, *Outlaw Culture: Resisting Representations*, Routledge, 1994, p6

50 Howard Winant, *Racial Conditions*, University of Minnesota Press, 1994, pp*xii-xiii*

51 Howard Winant, *Racial Conditions*, University of Minnesota Press, 1994, p169

52 GA Cohen, 'The three sources and component parts of Marxism', given as a paper in this seminar series and reproduced in this volume.

53 James Heartfield, 'Marxism and social construction', given as a paper in this seminar series and reproduced in this volume.

54 Greta Jones, *Social Darwinism and English Thought: The Interaction between*

Biological and Social Theory, Harvester Press, 1980

55   Karl Marx, *Grundrisse: Foundations of the Critique of Political Economy (Rough Draft)*, Penguin, 1973, p84

56   For example: Vron Ware, *Beyond the Pale*, Verso, 1992; Ronald Hyam, *Empire and Sexuality: The British Experience*, Manchester University Press, 1990; and Robert JC Young, *Colonial Desire: Hybridity in Theory, Culture and Race*, Routledge, 1995. In 1944, Gunnar Myrdal noticed the importance of the idea of intermarriage and sex to white views about the black man in America—see Gunnar Myrdal, *The American Dilemma: The Negro Problem and Modern Democracy*, Harper & Row, 1944

57   Anton Gill, *Ruling Passions: Sex, Race and Empire*, BBC Books, London, 1995

58   Émile Zola, *Germinal*, Penguin translation, 1954 (orig 1885), p258

59   Henryk Grossmann, *The Law of Accumulation and Breakdown of the Capitalist System*, Pluto reprints, 1992 (orig 1937)

60   Frank Füredi, *Mythical Past, Elusive Future: History and Society in an Anxious Age*, Pluto, 1992

61   'In effect, race had replaced class as the boundary defining which American men were to enjoy political freedom.' Eric Foner, *Slavery and Freedom in Nineteenth-Century America*, Clarendon Press, 1994, p9

62   Churchill to Wavell, 10 February 1942 cited in Christopher Hitchens, *Blood, Class and Nostalgia: Anglo-American Ironies*, Farrar, Straus & Girous, 1990, p213

63   General Wavell did not die with his troops, he went on to become Viceroy of India until 1947.

64   Celeste Michelle Condit and John Louis Lucaites, *Crafting Equality: America's Anglo-African Word*, University of Chicago Press, 1993, pp167-79

5
Marxism and feminist theory

Ellie Lee

Questioning old assumptions is central to much feminist thought today. In the past feminism relied on the assumption that all women had something in common. In current feminist literature, by contrast, it is suggested that to talk of 'woman' is problematic. The idea that women can be discussed in general, as a group in society with something in common, is said no longer to hold.

Many commentaries on feminist thought highlight the erosion of past certainties that has taken place. The idea put forward is that categories which might once have been accepted as a true description of groups in society no longer hold. These groups are said to have fragmented and no longer exist in a homogeneous way. The following proposition by Margaret Ferguson is typical:

> The increasing fragmentation of the categories of gender, class, race, sexuality, ethnicity and religion challenges easy co-alitions and the privileging of singular political identities, including that of 'woman' or even 'feminist'.[1]

In this way, the categories of people in units such as gender is questioned. In turn, Ferguson draws out the implication of the apparent collapse of such categories. Political projects, based on group unity, are seen as no longer legitimate. If there are no valid groupings, defined, for example, by gender, then there can be no 'easy coalition' based on such a premise. If gender does not apply in a unified way, if women cannot be said to exist as a whole, then clearly there can be no outlook which claims to represent women's point of view. Feminism cannot exist, at least in the sense that it once claimed to.

This approach takes modern feminism some distance from its premises when it emerged in the late 1960s. Then things did not seem so complex. The assumption of feminists in 1968 was that there was a common experience which forged a common bond between all women.[2] As feminist theory has developed, however, this premise of commonality has been called into question. It seems that the more feminists have tried to specify the basis for women's unity, the more difficult they have found it. In the process of theorising the assumption that women share a fundamental experience, many feminists have uncovered the weakness in that idea.[3]

What they have discovered is differences between women rather than a common ground. In fact as feminist theory has developed further, accounting for these differences has become more and more the focus of theory. Many feminists have become preoccupied with theorising what makes women different, rather than identifying what could unite women. This trajectory within feminism is looked on negatively by some feminists. Judith Grant, a feminist writer critical of the direction feminism has taken writes:

> Somehow we have decided that differences among women are and must be reflected in differences among theories, and that if we did not have many different theories we would be somehow authoritarian.4

This focus on difference is seen as problematic by Grant and some other feminists because of the implications it has for the feminist project. If, in theory, all that can be discovered is the difference between women, then where is the basis for a feminist movement? Such a movement has to start with an assumption of a shared problem. Otherwise what can feminists unite around? The result of the absence of such a theory is bound to be disunity and fragmentation, an outcome identified by the longstanding feminist Lynne Segal. Talking of the 1980s, she writes that: 'This has been a decade of increasing fragmentation within the women's movement, with the emergence of divisions between women and the growth of black feminist perspectives.'5

Despite the recognition of the fragmentation of feminism, little explanation has been advanced. The development has been described by some feminists, but no one has unravelled the process to indicate its causes. This essay contends that the fragmentary direction in feminism was an inevitable product of the particular starting point of feminism. In explaining this point, this essay develops the argument made in an unpublished paper on the development of feminist thought, written by Sara Hinchliffe.6

Feminism starts with the way women experience society. The way women view themselves and their relationship to society is where contemporary feminism begins. The feminist project is to draw political conclusions from this experience. Thus they start with the subjective rather than the objective world. In their informative history of the development of modern feminism, *Sweet Freedom*, Bea Campbell and Anna Coote describe the emergence of feminism in the 1970s as follows:

> They discussed their day-to-day experiences, and their feelings about themselves, their jobs, their husbands, their lovers, their children and their parents.

Of course women had been doing this since language was invented—but what was new was that they were now drawing political conclusions from their personal experiences.[7]

The phrase 'the personal is political', the origins of which are described in Coote and Campbell's book, has come to sum up this outlook on society. The aim of feminism from the beginning was to develop a political perspective based on the experience of women. Their perspective was to provide an explanation which could account for the experiences of women from which political strategy would evolve. Feminist theory has, at its centre, the need to explain why women experience the world in the way they do.

It can be argued that the end result of the fragmentation of feminism is given by this starting point. Since women experience life in different ways, a theory that starts with experience is bound to end up with various conclusions. Middle class, working class, black, lesbian and disabled women all undoubtedly have different experiences of life. The lives of women in the third world and the West are dramatically different. If the particular experience of women as individuals is the beginning, then the theory which comes out will inevitably stress something unique. The proliferation of feminist theories was an inevitable outcome from this origin.

Within feminism, this has frequently been seen as a cause for celebration. The existence of 'many feminisms', all reflecting a different experience is regarded as a strong point in feminism's favour.[8] Such 'diversity' has been portrayed as an expression of the ability of feminism to take account of the experiences of different women. Rather than a strength, however, this can be regarded as a weakness. It expresses an inability to generate a consistent theory of women's oppression. It indicates that the feminist approach lacks the capacity to discover what it is about society that acts to exclude women as a whole. Feminism is therefore unable to articulate what it is that gives women something in common.

The lack of such a theory is damaging. Its absence makes creating a consensus about the problems facing women impossible. Instead a lack of agreement and disunity prevails. The coincidence of disintegration takes place in feminist theory and in the feminist movement.

The main part of this chapter traces the development of this trajectory within feminist theory. When reading the essay, two points need to be taken into account. First, the feminist works referred to in the text have been chosen because the author sees them as clear examples of particular currents of feminist thought. This does not mean, however, that other feminist authors, sometimes placed in the same feminist camp, would argue exactly the same thing. The existence of 'many feminisms' means that there are many variations on a theme. For example, there are many 'radical feminist' authors, but each would see their argument, in some way, as unique. Given this rider, however, it is the contention of this article that there are overriding themes central to feminist thought. Some authors spell out these themes most clearly. Certain texts are therefore chosen because they sum up the approach of a certain type of feminist thought.

Second, this is not a chronological presentation of the development of feminist thought. The reader is cautioned against thinking that the different feminisms discussed in the essay follow each other in historical succession. In fact they develop simultaneously, in relation to each other. They have been separated out to make a distinction between them based on their particular understanding of women's oppression. They are discussed in the order they are because of their political perspective, not the point in time at which they emerged.

The theory of patriarchy

Different feminisms have distinct elements to their understanding of women's oppression. One thing that all feminists seem to agree on, however, is the existence of 'patriarchy'. The term patriarchy is central to the feminist approach. For feminists the term expresses what is said to be the common experience of women—their domination by men. They argue that women experience men exerting control over their lives. The explanation given for this is the structure of 'patriarchy'.

It is a catch-all phrase that describes the dominance by men over women. The foundation for the theory of patriarchy is that male dominance is a fundamental characteristic of society which shapes society extensively. For Kate Millett, one of the most significant writers in the formation of the feminist approach, patriarchy is: 'so deeply embedded as to run through all other political, social, or economic forms, whether of caste or class, feudality or bureaucracy, just as it pervades all major religions, it also exhibits great variety in history and locale.'[9] Millett posits patriarchy as the most crucial determinant in making society what it is. Feminists generally agree on this, and place stress on the need to develop an understanding of society— using the idea of patriarchy—to account for the particular experience of women.

In considering the development of feminism, the argument for the need to theorise this experience, and develop an understanding of 'patriarchy', comes about in a very specific way. It is self-consciously justified by feminists through suggesting that existing social theories fail to provide an explanation of society applicable to women. Feminism's own justification is that other explanations of the tensions and problems of society are inadequate.

In particular, many feminists started by criticising the Marxist approach, and this criticism has shaped the form of feminist theory.[10] Several feminist theories of different types take this as a key to their argument. Feminism, thereby, attempts to discredit Marxism. The latter is portrayed as a narrow theory, which is only relevant to economic questions as they affect men. Hence Marxism is seen as appropriate only for its 'target audience'—the male working class, but of little significance to anyone else.[11] Some feminists have accused Marxism of 'sex blindness'[12]—suggesting that Marxism ignores the experience of women, and therefore is of little use to those who are interested in women's liberation. Heidi Hartmann argued this point in her famous essay entitled 'The unhappy marriage of Marxism and feminism' when she wrote that:

> Moreover, the analytic power of Marxism with respect to capital has obscured its limitations with respect to sexism. We will argue that whilst Marxist analysis provides essential insight into the laws of historical development, and those of capital in particular, the categories of Marxism are sex-blind. Only a specific feminist analysis reveals the systemic character of relations between men and women.[13]

To counter this perceived limitation of Marxism, feminists argued that a theory was needed that applied to women in a way Marxism did not. Early feminists pitched their case against Marxism in a very direct manner. Shulamith Firestone was one of the first feminist theorists. She wrote in 1971 that: 'For feminist revolution we shall need an analysis of the dynamics of sex war as comprehensive as the Marx-Engels analysis of class antagonism was for the economic revolution. More comprehensive.'[14]

Here Firestone argues that feminism needs its own categories which explain the conflict between men and women—the 'sex-war'. These need to be posed as equally central to society as the Marxist categories. Where Marxism divides the world into categories based on economic division, of exploiter and exploited, ruling class and working class, feminism needs to present an alternative. It does this by drawing a line between men and women, and then developing the justification for this distinction. Categories were developed, by feminists, which aim to mirror those suggested by Marxism; between a dominant and a dominated group. This portrayal, it is argued, creates an analysis of society relevant to women, where Marxism fails to reach.

The idea that Marxist categories are of no use in understanding women's oppression is a consistent theme in the writings of feminists.

It is commonplace for feminists to suggest that the way Marxism understands society misses out the processes which shapes women's lives. It is frequently suggested that an analysis which is said to focus on the economic system of capitalism is inappropriate as a starting point for examining women's inequality. In her overview of the development of feminist thought, Maggie Humm sums up the criticism made of Marxism in the following way:

> Classic Marxist theory ignores many kinds of activities traditionally under-taken by women, for example housework and child-rearing. In addition, because reproducing and sustaining capitalism in the home did not produce surplus value, women's work did not count as productive labour.[15]

This criticism of Marxism is misplaced for two reasons. Firstly, it is misplaced to suggest that it is Marxism that makes women's work in the home 'unproductive'. The category 'productive labour' is a term used to describe the kind of labour that produces surplus value. This term therefore describes a relationship that exists between capital and labour. Work which 'does not count as productive labour' such as housework, exists in a different relation-ship to capital—that is, it does not produce surplus value. The distinction between 'productive' and 'unproductive' is therefore made by capitalism. It is capital that has relegated women to work unproductively in the home, not Marx.[16]

It is precisely this analysis of women's unique relationship to capital that makes Marxism useful for those who want to understand women's oppression. Through its account of the way capital accumulation takes place, Marxist theory provides an explanation of the particular role of women in the family and in the home. It is this role in turn that explains the second-class status of women in society.

Secondly it is wide of the mark to criticise Marxism because it 'ignores' women's lives. Certainly there are many issues that Marx and Engels have little to say on. Humm is right to say they write little on housework. There is noth-ing in their writings about feminist concerns such as lesbianism, pornography and child abuse. This is of little moment, however, since Marxism was not developed in order to describe the experience of one particular group in society, such as women.

To criticise Marxism on these grounds ignores a more fundamental issue. That is the difference between the Marxist approach and that of feminism. The real difference between the theories lies in the approach taken to under-stand society. The substantial point at issue is not that Marx failed to take an interest in women's oppression. What is really significant is the contrast in the method of analysis adopted by Marxist theory as compared to feminist theory. Marxist method is *the opposite* of that of feminism.[17]

Feminism starts with the immediate, particular experience of women and develops a general explanation of society ('patriarchy') from this basis. Marxism, in contrast, starts with the formation of society in general and aims to explain how society as a whole is organised. It then situates experience in this context. Marxism claims to be a universal theory—one that can comprehend the dynamics and conflicts of society in their totality.[18] Through its approach, Marxism allows for the particular experience of *any* group to be made comprehensible. Marxism rejects the idea that there needs to be different theories to explain different experiences.

Marxism would therefore claim that its method can be used to explain quite clearly the experience of women (or anyone else for that matter). It would see the particular oppression of women as resulting from the general formation of society as a whole. The experience of women can be elucidated from the broader analysis of the workings of capitalist society. The privatised and isolated experience of women as a result of their responsibility for the home and family, for example, is intimately bound up with their role in the public arena of work.[19] Responsibility for home and family places women in an inferior position in the labour market and vice versa. One part of life can be understood in relation to the other.

The main argument of this essay is that feminism rejects this unified approach of Marxism. It rejects the idea that a critique of capitalism is sufficient to underpin an explanation of women's inequality. The feminist argument rejects the idea that a theory of women's inequality and a theory of society as a whole are one and the same thing. Rather its logic, put forward in the theory of 'patriarchy', is to suggest that women's experience has to be understood separately from a broader critique of society. 'Patriarchy' suggests that there is a dynamic based on male dominance over women that exists independently from other social forces.[20] The theory's foundation rests on understanding the origin of male dominance and looks to biological differences between men and women as its source.

Biological woman—radical feminism

One feminist explanation of women's experience in society stresses the idea of fundamental difference between men and women. This is seen to be the origin of 'patriarchy'. This idea emphasises that biology lies beneath difference. 'Radical feminism' has become the broad term used to describe those who hold to this approach.[21]

The biological difference between men and women (for example, women's capacity to bear children) rather than social organisation is seen as the root of women's oppression. Some other 'radical feminist' variants shy away from such 'biological determinism' of women, and instead posit 'male' aggression and violence as being decisive.[22] The logic of this approach rules out any common ground between men and women.

The formative theorist in this tradition is Shulamith Firestone, the author of *The Dialectic of Sex*. In this work she overtly posits women's second class status in society as resulting from biology. The biological fact that women bear children is seen to be at the core of the problem. Firestone suggests:

> let us first try to develop an analysis in which biology itself—procreation—is at the origin of the dualism. The immediate assumption of the layman that the unequal division of the sexes is 'natural' may be well founded. We need not immediately look beyond this. Unlike economic class, sex class springs directly from a biological reality: men and women were created different, and not equally privileged.[23]

It is at this point that feminist theory is at its most coherent. It is coherent in the sense that it seeks to pose a theory of society that is unitary—it claims to be able to explain society as a whole. Firestone suggests that ultimately everything about the development of society can be explained by biological difference.

This thesis also suggests there is a fundamental commonality between all women. The idea is that all women (for all time) face the same problem. The logic of this analysis underpins a certain confidence about the possibility of action—and the subtitle of Firestone's work is *The Case for Feminist Revolution*. As Juliet Mitchell and Ann Oakley have recognised, it seemed that the possibility of creating a women's movement from this starting point was unproblematic:

> Thus women had a natural unity in their biology and feminism could ally itself safely and by definition with all shapes and forms of validation of, and protest by women. It was self-referring—by women for women.[24]

The dangers in this approach, however, were quickly exposed by other feminists, despite the problems for women's unity posed by the loss of biological coherence. Many other feminists objected to explaining oppression through biology. They reacted against this idea because of its conservative connotations. Biological arguments were too associated with racist views to be harnessed unequivocally for radical purposes. And if the chromosomes really were the source of the problem then, outside the formation of a women-only society, there was little possibility of any significant change in the relationship between men and women.

This conflict of opinion came to a head at the 1978 Women's Liberation conference when radical and socialist feminists came to blows over their disagreements.[25] This was the last national conference ever held, demonstrating that biology was not enough to establish a common political ground between women. In opposition to radical feminism, many feminists pointed out that if the difference between men and women is understood to be biological, then that difference has to be accepted. Supposed differences rooted in nature would be beyond our control. As a result, many women sought to discover a non-biological explanation of women's oppression.[26]

Some feminists however have continued a more 'fundamentalist' if not biological explanation in the radical feminist tradition. The focus for radical feminists has become 'sexual politics' rather than biology. In this school the notion that there is an inherent difference between men and women prevails. It is presented as a product of 'male violence and aggression' which is posited as a part of what it means to be male.[27] Patriarchy thus comes down to a male propensity to be spurred on by a hatred of women, and a desire to be violent towards them. 'The fact is', according to Mary Daly, 'that we live in a profoundly anti-female society, a misogynistic "civilisation" in which men collectively victimise women, attacking us as personifications of their own paranoid fears. Within this society it is men who rape, who sap women's energy who deny women economic and political power'.[28]

The origins of this 'collective victimisation' are never really explained. It can only be assumed that at some point in history, men got together and conspired to dominate women. As a result, relations between men and women are said to be inexorably humiliating for women. There is, supposedly, no possibility of finding common ground between the sexes. The sex act has become, for some feminists, an example of male power. Since it is seen as an act by men and for men, it can only be unpleasant and dangerous for women. In this light, Sheila Jeffreys, prominent critic of the so called 'sexual revolution' of the 1960s writes:

> In Anticlimax, heterosexuality is seen as a political institution through which male dominance is organised and maintained. Sex as we know it, under male supremacy, is the eroticised power difference of heterosexuality.[29]

The conclusion of such an approach brings out the prudish conservatism given in the notion of inherent difference between men and women. The idea that women can enjoy sex (the banner of the early feminists) is rejected in favour of a description of women as passive recipients of a degrading act. Elsewhere Sheila Jeffreys has emphasised this point in writing that:

> We have got to understand that sexual response for women and orgasm for women is not necessarily pleasurable and positive. It can be a very real problem. It can be an accommodation of our oppression. It can be the eroticising of our subordination. We need to appreciate that the word pleasure is often used for what we experience as humiliation and betrayal.[30]

In this portrayal, sexual relations between men and women are deemed to debase the latter. Women who do not think so, who think that sex is fun are, in Jeffreys' eyes, duped into using the word 'pleasure' to describe the experience. Instead, for Jeffreys, the real experience hides the 'betrayal' as men exercise their domination over women.

The notion that men enjoy sex and women suffer it, as a description of the difference between the sexes, informs much radical feminist thinking. The experience which colours their approach is of male domination over subservient women. Men are portrayed as aggressive and assertive, women as passive. Men act and enforce their will, women receive and accept what is given to them. A distinction between the sexes is made on this basis. This description is meant to encompass what is specifically different between men and women.

Taken a stage further, 'feminine' characteristics—passivity, nurturing capacity, a desire to care for others—are turned into positive virtues. But these are the same traits put forward by conservatives to ensure that women continue to wipe children's faces, cook, clean and hold the family together. Some women have tried to celebrate these 'female' characteristics which make women different to men. Womanhood, according to some, is no longer associated with oppression, it has become a virtuous status. The influential critic of radical feminism, Lynne Segal, wrote her book to counter the 'public face of feminism' where: 'The problem of "male psychology" and behaviour is contrasted with a more nurturant, maternal, cooperative and peaceful "female nature".'[31]

The reaction to the radical feminist approach has created another kind of feminism. This approach has tried to find another explanation for gender division without a recourse to biology.

The social construction of woman

An alternative explanation of 'patriarchy' can be broadly described as the idea of 'social construction'. The argument is that male dominance occurs as a result of the construction of society. This view posits the second-class status of women outside of a biological framework and thereby looks to society for an answer.

This position is largely associated with those feminists who would describe themselves as 'socialist feminist' as opposed to 'radical feminist'. Judith Grant, in her recent book *Fundamental Feminism*, explains this difference: 'the socialist feminist notion of patriarchy conceptualises patriarchy as a structure with a material basis, while radical feminists tend to think of it as the idea, or the day-to-day lived reality that men universally oppress women.' And the gender differences emerge historically, Grant continues, because 'The social-ist feminist analysis is historical to the extent that it accepts variation among women across time and cultures, and it is economic in that it attempts to link women's oppression to the modes of production and reproduction.'[32] Throughout this section the term 'socialist feminist' will be used to describe those feminists who tend more towards understanding gender difference as a social construction.

Some important points are raised here about the 'social construction' approach. Firstly, patriarchy is seen as having a 'material basis'. That is, it is not a result of biology, but the workings of society. Secondly, Grant's definition implies some variation through time and between cultures. All women are no longer assumed to be oppressed in the same way. Thirdly, women's oppression is seen as related to the economy. Grant identifies a relationship between women's oppression and the operation of capitalism. Anna Coote and Bea Campbell, famous socialist feminists, describe the opposition to the biological stress of the radical feminists:

> They did not conclude that biology was the root of evil: in their view men oppressed women not by virtue of their biological maleness, but by virtue of their social and economic relations with women....Socialist feminists' politics entailed neither a rejection of men nor a withdrawal from them, but an urgent necessity to fight both in and against male-dominated power relations.[33]

To arrive at this conclusion, socialist feminists try to combine the feminist approach with Marxism. They pose themselves as positively identifying with Marxism. They suggest that the formation of capitalist society has to be taken into account in understanding women's oppression. They aim, however, to combine this with the theory of 'patriarchy', and so maintain the feminist focus. Rosemarie Tong, in her useful overview of feminist theories, refers to this approach as a 'dual-systems theory'.[34] Heidi Hartmann, the socialist feminist, put her case in the following way:

> Both Marxist analysis, particularly its historical and materialist method, and feminist analysis, especially the identification of patriarchy as a social and

historical structure, must be drawn upon if we are to understand the development of Western capitalist societies and the predicament of women within them.[35]

Combining Marxism and feminism appears to be a positive departure from the radical feminist approach. It seems that feminism is finding a way of dealing with the emphasis on biology. This development, however, has other consequences. In attempting to avoid one problem, the socialist feminists introduce a new problem—they lose a unified approach and have to introduce another means by which to measure the balance between the feminist elements and the Marxist ones. This perspective represents a step towards losing a theory of women's oppression altogether.

Women's oppression is explained by socialist feminists as a result of two processes, capitalism and patriarchy. Consequently feminism accepts that unitary theories are not applicable to this dual world—there can be no single theory that can adequately explain women's oppression. Socialist feminists suggest that neither Marxism nor feminism alone can explain everything. Their starting point is that two theories rather than one are necessary. In rejecting both Marxism and patriarchy theory as sufficient in themselves, the socialist feminists forfeit coherence as neither theory presumes the other. In fact, quite the reverse, each theory has as its premise the assumption that it alone explains society.

Socialist feminists refused to abandon the central idea of the theory of 'patriarchy', that women's inequality has been fundamental to all previous and existing societies. Many maintained that the women's oppression is, so far, a constant feature through the ages. They also rejected essentialism, that is; explanations that suggest innate differences between men and women. Their project then entailed finding another explanation for oppression outside of biology or 'maleness'. In attempting this, socialist feminism ran into difficulties. It proved very difficult to explain the eternal oppression of women by men in a non-biological way. Grant explains the problem for socialist feminism as follows:

> In fact socialist feminism was never able to explain why women have been systematically oppressed across cultures and time, nor exactly how this oppression can be materially grounded so that one can comprehend the universal construction of genders in a non-essentialist way.[36]

Socialist feminists found it impossible to provide an explanation for 'oppression across cultures and time' that was non-biological. They tried to use Marxism to provide such an explanation, but were unsuccessful.

They found that Marxism could not be used to explain 'patriarchy'. This was because there is no Marxist equivalent of a biological factor. Marxist categories are specific and relate only to a particular society in a certain time. Marxist concepts, therefore, cannot replace eternal characteristics. There was no other convincing explanation that could account for a timeless inferiority of women. Put another way, the socialist feminists could not provide an explanation for the 'universal' or common experience of women in society without recourse to 'essentialist' explanations which relied on inherent differences between men and women.

This was the case because in fact the project of combining Marxism and feminism was doomed from the start. The Marxist approach stands in direct opposition to the idea of patriarchy. Marxism cannot be used to explain patriarchy because any timeless feature is a concept that Marxism rejects. For Marxism the concept of 'historical specificity' is at the core of understanding society. This means that any phenomenon can only be understood when placed in its specific historical context. Thus the position of women in society can only be made comprehensible when it is seen in the context of an analysis of a particular society at a particular point in time. From this perspective, women's oppression today can only be understood as a part of the present form of capitalist society. The subordination of women, when we could be free, is a product of capitalism. Other societies, with a different division of labour, place women in other relations to the community. Some aspects of the drudgery of survival may be similar but the specific role of women may be entirely different. For Marxism, apart from the specific form of organisation, there are no other determinants in society that explain women's inequality. In this way, Marxist theory challenges the mystification of the social forms that lie behind the idea of an endless 'historical structure' of patriarchy.

The outcome of attempting to merge Marxism and feminism resulted in no explanation of patriarchy at all. The end-product was the disintegration of feminism. This fragmentation was exacerbated by the fact that different feminists took different routes, but in each case the aim was to explain oppression through looking at the development of society rather than biology.[37] Some feminists focused on a study of history, others psychology, others the media or education. Each new attempt defined itself in counterpoint to the last. Each one, in turn, further illustrated the lack of a unifying theory of feminism.

One common way of dealing with the problem of the incommensurable theories was to invoke the historical legacy of the past. The history of women's oppression provided a story and a sense of the importance of women's subordination. The use of history gave an initial sense of unity around a common past, and seemed to provide a clear definition. Juliet Mitchell and Ann Oakley, two influential socialist feminists, justified themselves thus:

Emanating in diverse ways from some type of socialist or Marxist background, women's liberationists were unable to assume a common identity for women along a biological dividing line—we needed a social definition and therefore a history.[38]

History, however, on closer inspection does not provide a 'common identity'. Rather feminist historians discovered a myriad of different experiences of women in history. Juliet Mitchell and Ann Oakley acknowledge this development and the ensuing weakness for feminism when they write that:

> the search for women in history has called into question the very stability of the concept 'women'. Feminism in the sixties and seventies has above all been distinguished from any of its earlier expressions by the deconstruction of any fixed meaning to the notion of 'women'. If woman cannot be fixed as an identity beyond the biological female, neither can feminism have a unified definition.[39]

In the absence of a biological starting point to explain what it means to be a woman, no other generally applicable explanation was found. Feminism could discover no universal 'social construction', as an alternative to biology, which could apply to all women. In fact the more attempts were made to develop an understanding of the 'social construction' of women's oppression, the further feminism moved from being able to project a commonality between women. In attempting to put forward an explanation of women's oppression, feminists discovered that they could no longer sustain the idea that women were subject to a common experience. If women did not have a common history, it was difficult to argue that they also had a common experience of their different histories.

In the end the project of 'social construction' became that of questioning whether 'woman' was a valid concept after all. In finding nothing that could adequately replace biology as a unifying concept, feminism came to accept there could be no such thing. Rosalind Delmar demonstrates this point in her essay, 'What is feminism?';

> The employment of psychoanalysis and critical theory to question the unity of the subject, to emphasise the fragmented subject, is potentially subversive of any view which asserts a 'central' organising principle of social conflict...to deconstruct the subject 'woman', to question whether 'woman' is a coherent identity is also to imply the question of whether 'woman' is a coherent political identity.[40]

The result of rejecting the possibility of a unitary theory that can explain the experience of all women is seen in the proliferation of 'feminisms'. Each takes as its starting point a particular experience. At this point feminism is forced to accept that it is incapable of providing a general explanation of oppression. Rather different theories agree to coexist side by side. The different 'segments' of the women's movement are described by Delmar thus:

> Recently the different feminists have manifested themselves as a sort of sclerosis of the movement, segments of which have become separated from and hardened against each other. Instead of internal dialogue there is a naming of the parts: there are radical feminists, socialist feminists, Marxist feminists, lesbian separatists, women of colour and so on, each group with its own carefully preserved sense of identity.[41]

It is evident in the quote above that concern about this disintegrative process exists. The practical paralysis of feminism has been the recognised result. With so many competing identities, there is no sense of a wider social movement. What has been less appreciated, however, is that this consequence was implied in the social constructionist approach. That methodology left feminism without an anchor for its explanation of women's oppression. It did this when feminists rejected the two possible root causes of oppression. Having dismissed the force of biology, they continued to relegate the social content of capitalist society to a mere factor. Both these forces are, within their own theories, prime movers. Each theory becomes meaningless without the centrality of either biology or capital accumulation. The reduction of these forces to the status of a factor destroyed the explanatory power in the theory. Thus the act of combining these theories dissolved the theoretical foundation of feminism.

What remains tends to be a description of the experience of oppression rather than an explanation of why inequality exists. Ultimately, this is what the focus on history or psychology is reducible to. It is a description of life in a subordinate status, with the focus on many individuals—in history—or on the example of one individual—in psychology. Once feminism reaches this point, there is no other possibility except disintegration. Theory must become untenable when the issue of causes and reasons is abandoned leaving only description. Furthermore, the more that the latter dominates, the more that each woman seems different to any other woman, and feminism splinters.

The politics of difference—postmodern feminism

The difficulty feminism has found in generating a persuasive theory of women's oppression has led to the questioning of such a project altogether.

The inability to develop an explanation in theory of women's oppression has created an argument against theory itself. The dominant focus for feminism today has become finding ways of explaining the futility of theory in the first place.[42]

Sandra Harding is a feminist who has elaborated this outlook. Her case is that theories that pretend to be coherent are false. This must be so, she argues since the world we live in is incoherent. There is no pattern to the way society works, rather it is chaotic. Theory that has as its starting point an assumption of consistency can therefore tell us little. It will always fail to see the complexity of social arrangements. Judith Grant spells this point out in *Fundamental Feminism* when she writes that:

> Coherent theories in an obviously incoherent world are either silly and unin-teresting or oppressive and problematic, depending upon the degree of hege-mony they manage to achieve. Coherent theories in an apparently coherent world are even more dangerous, for the world is always more complex than such unfortunately hegemonious theories can grasp.[43]

The implication is a pessimistic one. Harding is suggesting that the world is too difficult a place for us to understand. Human attempts to grasp the way in which society operates are doomed to failure. Theorising can only ever lead to the enforcement of a particular outlook on to society, which will reflect little about the way in which that society actually works. The implication of this view is that all we can really hope for is a partial insight into or an under-standing of a fragment of human experience. Anything more comprehensive is beyond our grasp.

Some feminists, including Harding, take this argument against theory one stage further. As suggested in the quotation above, attempts to theorise are seen as worse than useless—they are in some way 'oppressive'. They are per-ceived as the imposition of a particular opinion on other people. Universal theories, in this schema, represent an attack on autonomy. Anne Phillips has put forward this perspective, and argues that claims of universality are in fact nothing more than the perspective of those in power. She writes that:

> The pretensions towards a universal truth or universal humanity have been rightly criticised, and the work of many recent feminist theorists has revealed how persistently such abstractions confirm the perspectives of the domi-nant group.[44]

In particular, the idea of the possibility of a single true picture is dismissed as a male concept. It has become accepted in recent feminist studies that there can be no such thing as truth in any meaningful sense. No one person can claim to tell the truth about what is happening in society since no one can overcome the domination of gendered outlooks. Consequently, for the postmodern feminists, all theories up to now which have said they are objective, are really nothing more than the world as described from the point of view of men. Judith Grant, in her useful contribution to the debate about post-modern feminism, has explained the development of this outlook as follows:

> By now this idea that male and female experiences differ, and that those differ-ences have important implications, in particular for theories of knowledge, is clearly the orthodoxy in academic feminism. Knowledge it is held, is appre-hended directly through gendered experience and all knowledge that we have heretofore viewed as 'truth' is really something more like male opinion. That is 'objectivity' is really the misnomer given to the world when it is viewed and experienced from the male perspective.[45]

The result of this approach is the feminist rejection of any need to find some objective reality. Without this, there is less pressure to uncover a convincing explanation of women's oppression. Being definitive, and claiming a certain truth status is seen as unnecessary deference to male academia. It is worse than irrelevant; it is male.

This viewpoint reconciles feminism to its inability to find the cause of women's oppression. The problem of developing theory, and the impasse reached in trying to do so, is portrayed as the inescapable outcome of theorising. The failure of feminist theory is blamed on the nature of theory not the nature of feminism.

The absence of theory has certain implications. Feminism follows through its criticism of 'truth' to its logical conclusion. If rationality, truth and logic are male, then they are undesirable. According to some authors, feminism should abandon 'male standards'. Rather than trying to emulate male qualities, feminism has shifted to centre on a celebration of difference. Some argue for accentuating the differences between women and men rather than abolishing them. This approach is exemplified by the rising popularity of the critique of equality in feminist writing. Sondra Farganis outlines this argument in her helpful summary of the development of feminist thought:

> Although equitable treatment sounds fair, the argument goes, it is always a matter of making women equal to men and men's standards. Rather than glorify liberalism's equity, we need to affirm feminism's emphasis on women's ways of seeing and being in the world; moreover it is not simply that women see the world differently, but that they have certain virtues which stem from

any number of factors—their maternalism, their marginality, their alienation
—that allow them to see and relate to each other in ways that give them both
an epistemological and political edge.[46]

As Farganis shows, 'difference' has become a positive virtue. This result
applauds oppression because what makes women different from men is
women's oppression—their unequal position in society. To glorify this is to
approve of all that is problematic for women. This is shown in the quotation
above. The repressive aspect of women's lives—their sole responsibility for
bearing and rearing children, which excludes them from operating equally
with men—is seen as a cause for celebration. The degradation of 'alienation'
and the 'marginality' of women are no longer reasons to champion women's
rights, but a standpoint that gives us a 'positive edge' in criticising others.
Women have gained the moral high ground to judge others, but we seem to
have lost, in this process, the list of demands that we started fighting for. The
world has been turned on its head. Inequality has been made good and
so justified.

If one result of eschewing the possibility of theorising women's oppression
is its celebration, another is the denial that it can be said to exist at all. This is
the case made by some postmodern feminists. Here feminism comes to terms
with the earlier difficulty in the theory of women's oppression, by suggesting
that trying to find a commonality between women was flawed from the start.

For postmodern feminists, the diversity of women's experience calls into
question the notion that there is something all women have in common.
If experience is the only valid truth, then, it can be argued that, there are many
truths. Feminism, at this point, dovetails with the postmodern rejection of the
idea, as Grant puts it, of 'a primary epistemological discourse that assumes
a knowing and active subject seeking access to objective reality, which, at least
theoretically can be understood in its totality'.[47]

The possibility of understanding objective reality is challenged. For
postmodernism, there is no theory that can comprehend the world in all its
complex arrangements. For postmodern theory this leads to the more limited
project of knowing our individual interpretation of the world and ignoring
the question of its correspondence to an underlying social structure. Grant
argues that the distinction between interpretation and reality, 'wrongly
assumes a reality that exists objectively, apart from interpretation'.[48] The idea
of separating out what we individually experience from what we can
collectively know about the world is dismissed as an invalid project.

In this sense the existence of oppression as a real force in society is called
into question. Only our own particular interpretation can be said to exist.
This and only this can be said to be real. There can be no sense in which

a process in society can be identified which organises oppression, and so affects all women. Postmodernists argue that it is impossible to talk objectively of society in this way. Rather it is understood that only the individual's sensations are valid points of reference. The consequence of such a position is to undermine the concept of oppression. It has become a mere feeling of subjugation and not necessarily one founded in the structure of society.

Postmodern feminism negates, therefore, feminist theory. It destroys the original assumptions of the feminist perspective. The notion of patriarchy as a social force affecting all women is denied by the postmodernist rejection of social forces. If there is nothing that affects all women then there can be no feminist theory. Farganis understands this dilemma for feminism in the questioning of the 'category' woman. She points out that:

> The problem that confronts a feminism in dialogue with postmodernism is one of reconciling the diversity of women's experiences with the unity of female embodiment. For if women are so diverse and might see things differently as a result of that diversity, in what ways could we say that there is a category called 'women' that sees the world in ways that men do not?[49]

Farganis also discerns that in undermining feminist theory, postmodernism also undermines feminist practice. The diversity of experience makes the creation of a united movement impossible. There can be no women's movement if there is no category of woman. Farganis summarises this point when she writes that:

> Scepticism of universalist ideas encourages us to think about how distinct and different people are; but by taking this track, there is the chance that moral indifference and uncertainty will undermine the very basis on which a feminist politics is founded—that is, the shared status of women who want to overcome what they see as oppressive conditions and establish their human authenticity.[50]

If postmodern feminism articulates the fragmentation of the women's movement, it also inaugurates the creation of the men's movement. Ironically it is feminist theory that provides the theoretical underpinnings for masculinity theory by accepting a definition of oppression that is 'felt' and defined by the oppressed. Masculinity theory argues that men, like women, have been trapped and oppressed by gendered relations. Some say men are more oppressed than women because this condition has gone unnoticed. The emergence of this viewpoint has been greeted with hostility by many feminists. Yet the basis of masculinity theory was implicit in the acceptance of a subjective definition of women's oppression. With the demise of the women's movement, it was only a matter of time before this internal logic became apparent.

Masculinity theory presents itself as an attempt to explain the experience of men in the way that feminism has done for women. Like feminism, it takes experience as its starting point. It suggests that a man's life has many obstacles and, in many ways, degrades men. This experience, it is said, has been ignored for too long, as women held centre stage. Neil Lyndon, the infamous masculinist, argues that: 'the focus of reforming light and zeal being directed upon the position of women, a shadow or penumbra of neglect has fallen upon the realities of life for men and upon the social terms and conditions by which men's personal and family lives are extensively defined and limited.'[51]

In pointing to the 'realities of life' as experienced by men, and indicating that this is 'limited', masculinity theory asserts that men are oppressed. It suggests that men's lives are at least as confined as women's. Furthermore, some people argue, it is men that are oppressed, not women, since the former have to face death fighting in wars.[52]

Feminists have reacted strongly to the proposition that men face as many if not more problems than women. Masculinity theory has been described as part of the 'backlash' against feminism, and several books have set out to dispute its claims. Methodologically, however, it is hard for the feminists to challenge masculinity theory as it shares their focus on the subjective. Without an overarching theory of society, then there is no foundation from which to dispute the claim by men that they experience life in a less than ideal way. In fact, one would respond as a Marxist, of course men's lives are not perfect, but, at the same time, men are not relegated to fulfil domestic chores to lubricate the functioning of society for free. Capitalism is a social framework that distorts and deforms all human life but also particularly denies even the promise of freedom to certain sections of society.

Conclusion

The degeneration of feminist theory has consequences wider than simple academic interest. The methodological difficulties of feminism are important as they have practical effects for the women's movement as a whole. Theoretical incoherence has had obvious implications for those who campaign for women's liberation. The absence of a strong foundation for activity has made strategy discussions often very divisive. Each analytical vantage point draws out a different locus for political action. As a result, any debate on demands, stunts, protests and meetings has tended to further shatter the women's movement rather than unite it. Ever since the emergence of contemporary feminism the disintegration of the movement has been accelerating.

The clearest expression of this weakness has been the failure to maintain a women's movement which can fight for liberation. Mirroring the disintegration of feminist thought, has been a disintegration of the Women's Liberation Movement. For many feminists, this has meant a shift away from activism. Campaigning has been sidelined in favour of more passive concerns. This decline was identified early on by some feminist activists. Certainly by the early 1980s, many had become aware that their aspiration to create an active movement had been lost. As early as 1981, Val Coultas wrote in *Feminist Review* that: 'cultural feminism, living a "feminist lifestyle", reading women's literature, attending women's discos, having women friends has become more of the focus for some women as an alternative to the early campaigning approach of modern feminism.'[53]

The retreat from activism has also been expressed in the development of Women's Studies courses. Many feminists have redirected their ambition into finding a niche in the university system. Academic ambition, however, is not the problem. Many would agree that study and developing an understanding is a good thing. But the burgeoning of so many new departments and courses should be situated in its context. Alongside the disappearance of the women's movement, the move to academia represents a retreat away from practical politics. Women's demands have ended up being shaped by their circumstances, like the demand for more women tutors, and have tended to ignore the fundamentals of nursery provision and the vagaries of temporary work. Overall the impact on the women's movement has been to intensify its passive orientation while diminishing the practical enthusiasm it started with.

For those feminists who have maintained an active profile, the focus of campaigning has shifted. The emphasis at the start of the Women's Liberation Movement was on the need to campaign for women's rights. Rights such as abortion on demand, the right to contraception, childcare and equal pay were laid down as the goals. These issues have been scaled down relative to the recent stress on women's 'victimhood'.

Today activists make their case by highlighting the situation of women victimised by violent men. Committed feminists are to be found in campaigns about rape or domestic violence. Lynne Segal has noted the defensive posture of present campaigns. With Mary McIntosh, she attributes the legacy of past failures from which 'feminists were less confidently on the offensive, less able to celebrate women's potential strength, and many were now retreating into a more defensive politics, isolating sexuality and men's violence from other issues of women's equality'.[54]

As Segal notes, certain aspects of women's oppression, such as rape, have been separated from the issue of women's equality. One manifestation of women's second class status has been isolated at the expense of investigating underlying causes. One reason for this shift in feminism has been to justify its own existence. It seems to be easier to talk of the most extreme effects of oppression—rather than the process of oppression itself. To gain wider support, feminists emphasise the most degrading expressions of inequality, rather than inequality itself. In the long run, this strategy will have implications for those who wish to campaign for equality.

The shift away from equal rights to better treatment is articulated in the content of feminist theory. It is only possible to campaign for equal rights for women if there is an identifiable common denial of rights to all women. It has to be shown that the structure of society is denying women as a whole the ability to operate equally with men. Without the framework of a common problem, a campaign for rights make little sense. But if it is meaningless to talk of the category of woman, it is also senseless to campaign for women as a whole. The need for women's rights has been jettisoned in favour of highlighting the worst experiences of some women.

By ignoring women as a whole, the new campaigns on violence mystify women's oppression. Through the focus on rape, for example, a perception of women's inequality is created, as resulting from the actions of violent or aggressive men. The structural aspects of society which create the systematic discrimination against women have been deprioritised. But rape, and other symptoms of women's inequality, are best explained through an examination of social processes. As Ann Bradley, an experienced political activist, has noted:

> Rape is one of the most brutal physical reflections of power relations between men and women in capitalist society. In a world where women are in reality dominated by men and denied equality, power and influence, it is unsurprising that they are physically brutalised. Women's susceptibility to sexual assault is just one extremely brutal aspect of their inferior status.[55]

But the issue of rape has dominated the recent discussion on women's oppression, squeezing out debate on the causes of the women's inferior status.

By emphasising the danger of rape, the media and the remnants of the women's movement have fed into the image of women as victims. This has involved exaggerating the possibility of being raped. What is fortunately a relatively uncommon experience is turned into a day-to-day possibility. The increasing focus on 'date rape' as a cause for concern provides the most obvious example of this trajectory. Some people have labelled this focus as 'victim feminism'. This is summed up in the preoccupation with the dangers of dating. Some feminists have stressed the risk of a pleasurable encounter turning into an unwanted sexual advance. It is suggested that harassment is only a short step away from agreeing to go out for a drink.

This outlook presupposes that women are always at risk from men, whose undeclared intentions are thought always to be sexual. And many argue that women need protection from these advances. New 'codes of conduct' have been introduced in college campuses and many workplaces to regulate behaviour and to provide guidelines for unruly men. Katie Roiphe has made herself famous by voicing her indignation at such a patronising attitude to women. In her book, *The Morning After*, she describes her disgust with victim status:

> This image that emerges from feminist preoccupations with rape and sexual harassment is that of women as victims, offended by a professor's dirty joke, verbally pressured into sex by peers. This image of a delicate woman bears a striking resemblance to that fifties ideal my mother and the other women of her generation fought so hard to get away from. They didn't like her passivity, her wide-eyed innocence. They didn't like the fact that she was perpetually offended by sexual innuendo. They didn't like her excessive need for protection. She represented personal, social, and psychological possibilities collapsed, and they worked and marched, shouted and wrote, to make her irrelevant for their daughters. But here she is again, with her pure intentions and her wide eyes. Only this time it is the feminists themselves who are breathing new life into her.[56]

This is the product of the feminist campaigns of the 1990s. Roiphe correctly notes the resurrection of the old-style helpless victims, with the significant difference that now, through the development of the women's movement, we are supposed to have made this role for ourselves. Campaigns against pornography, sexual harassment and date rape have helped create a modern women who is vulnerable and seemingly proud of it. The starting point for our rejection of such a degraded position in society is the break with the theoretical assumptions that now legitimate the surrounding paternalism. Understanding the way in which feminism came to articulate the return to a time when women have to be chaperoned is a first step towards expressing a new strategy for our time.

NOTES

1   Margaret Ferguson and Jennifer Wicke, *Feminism and Postmodernism,* Duke University Press, 1994, p2

2   Anna Coote and Bea Campbell, *Sweet Freedom: The Struggle for Women's Liberation,* Basil Blackwell, 1987. This book provides a useful history of the women's movement and its political approach.

3   Juliet Mitchell and Ann Oakley, *What is Feminism?* Blackwell, 1986. Essays in this anthology describe the process feminism went through in trying to theorise women's oppression.

4   Judith Grant, *Fundamental Feminism: Contesting the Core Concepts of Feminist Theory,* Routledge, 1993, p3

5   Lynne Segal, *Is the Future Female? Troubled Thoughts on Contemporary Feminism,* Virago Press, 1987, pix

6   Sara Hinchliffe has written extensively on the issue of feminism and its preoccupations in the 1990s for *Living Marxism.*

7   Anna Coote and Bea Campbell, *Sweet Freedom,* Basil Blackwell, 1982, p5

8   Maggie Humm (Ed), *Feminisms: A Reader,* Harvester Wheatsheaf, 1992. This collection of essays provides useful examples of the different feminist approaches. It suggests, however, that such a range of opinion is testament to feminism's power.

9   Kate Millett, *Sexual Politics,* Virago, 1970 cited in Maggie Humm (Ed), *Feminisms: A Reader,* Harvester Wheatsheaf, 1992, p64

10 Sheila Rowbotham, *Women's Liberation and the New Politics,* Spokeswomen pamphlet No17, 1969. In this formative feminist tract, Rowbotham accuses Marxism of having failed to take subjectivity into account when she writes that: 'Unless the internal process of subjugation is understood, unless the language of silence is experienced from the inside and translated into the language of the oppressed communicating themselves, male hegemony will remain. Without such a translation, Marxism will not be really meaningful.' Cited in Anna Coote and Bea Campbell, *Sweet Freedom: The Struggle for Women's Liberation,* Basil Blackwell, 1982, p9

11 Michèle Barrett, *Women's Oppression Today: Problems in Marxist Feminist Analysis,* Verso, 1980

12 Heidi Hartmann, 'The unhappy marriage of Marxism and feminism: towards a more progressive union', cited in Maggie Humm (Ed), *Feminisms: A Reader,* Harvester Wheatsheaf, 1992

13 Heidi Hartmann, 'The unhappy marriage of Marxism and feminism: towards a more progressive union', cited in Maggie Humm (Ed), *Feminisms: A Reader,* Harvester Wheatsheaf, 1992, p105

14 Shulamith Firestone, *The Dialectic of Sex: The Case for Feminist Revolution,* Jonathan Cape, 1971, p2

15 Maggie Humm (Ed), *Feminisms: A Reader,* Harvester Wheatsheaf, 1992, p87

16 Paul Smith, *Domestic Labour and the Marxist Theory of Value,* in Annette Kuhn and Ann Marie Wolpe (Ed), *Feminism and Materialism: Women and Modes of Production,* Routledge & Kegan Paul, 1978. This essay is a useful explanation of the Marxist position on the domestic labour debate.

17 Karen Guldberg, 'Introduction' to F Engels, *The Origins of the Family, Private Property and the State*, Junius, 1995.

18 Frank Füredi, 'Introduction' to Franz Jakubowski, *Ideology and Superstructure in Historical Materialism*, Pluto, 1990

19 Joan Phillips, *Policing the Family*, Junius, 1988

20 Sheila Rowbotham, *Women's Consciousness, Man's World*, Penguin, 1973

21 Valerie Bryson, *Feminist Political Theory: An Introduction*, Macmillan, 1992

22 Lynne Segal, *Is the Future Female? Troubled Thoughts on Contemporary Feminism*, Virago, 1987

23 Shulamith Firestone, *The Dialectic of Sex: The Case for Feminist Revolution*, Jonathan Cape, 1971

24 Juliet Mitchell and Ann Oakley, *What is Feminism?* Basil Blackwell, 1986, p1

25 'Despite the repeated affirmation of 'sisterhood' in slogans and manifestoes, the Women's Liberation Movement was never really united, and, as time went by, an ideological rift between radical and socialist feminists widened, culminating in a bruising confrontation at the 1978 annual conference in Birmingham, the last national conference of the whole of the WLM.' Joni Lovenduski and Vicky Randall, *Contemporary Feminist Politics: Women and Power in Britain*, Oxford University Press, 1993, p4

26 Anna Coote and Bea Campbell, *Sweet Freedom: The Struggle for Women's Liberation*, Basil Blackwell, 1982

27 Andrea Dworkin, *Pornography: Men Possessing Women*, Women's Press, 1981

28 Mary Daly, *Gyn/Ecology: The Metaethics of Radical Feminism*, Women's Press, 1979 cited in Maggie Humm (Ed), *Feminisms : A Reader*, Harvester Wheatsheaf, 1992, p168

29 Sheila Jeffreys, *Anticlimax: A Feminist Perspective on the Sexual Revolution*, Women's Press, 1990, p3

30 Sheila Jeffreys, 'Sexology and anti-feminism', in Dorchen Leidholdt and Janice G Raymond, *The Sexual Liberals and the Attack on Feminism*, Pergamon Press, 1990, p22

31 Lynne Segal, *Is the Future Female? Troubled Thoughts on Contemporary Feminism*, Virago, 1987

32 Judith Grant, *Fundamental Feminism: Contesting the Core Concepts of Feminist Theory*, Routledge, 1993, p51

33 Anna Coote and Bea Campbell, *Sweet Freedom: The Struggle for Women's Liberation*, Basil Blackwell, 1982, p24

34 Rosemarie Tong, *Feminist Thought: A Comprehensive Introduction*, Unwin Hyman, 1989, p179

35 Heidi Hartmann, 'The unhappy marriage of Marxism and feminism: towards a more progressive union', cited in Maggie Humm (Ed.), *Feminisms: A Reader*, Harvester Wheatsheaf, 1992, p105

36 Judith Grant, *Fundamental Feminism*, Routledge, 1993, p46

37 Juliet Mitchell and Ann Oakley (Eds), *What is Feminism?* Basil Blackwell, 1986

38 Juliet Mitchell and Ann Oakley (Eds), *What is Feminism?* Basil Blackwell, 1986, p2

39   Juliet Mitchell and Ann Oakley (Eds), *What is Feminism?* Basil Blackwell, 1986, p2

40   Rosalind Delmar, 'What is feminism?' in Juliet Mitchell and Ann Oakley (Eds), *What is Feminism?* Basil Blackwell, 1986, p28

41   Rosalind Delmar, 'What is feminism?' in Juliet Mitchell and Ann Oakley (Eds), *What is Feminism?* Basil Blackwell, 1986, p9

42   Judith Grant, *Fundamental Feminism*, Routledge, 1993

43   Judith Grant, *Fundamental Feminism*, Routledge, 1993, p147

44   Anne Phillips, *Democracy and Difference*, Polity, 1993, p71

45   Judith Grant, *Fundamental Feminism*, Routledge, 1993, p4

46   Sondra Farganis, *Situating Feminism: From Thought to Action*, Sage, 1994, p24

47   Judith Grant, *Fundamental Feminism*, Routledge, 1993, p132

48   Judith Grant, *Fundamental Feminism*, Routledge, 1993, p134

49   Sondra Farganis, *Situating Feminism: From Thought to Action*, Sage, 1994, p41

50   Sondra Farganis, *Situating Feminism: From Thought to Action*, Sage, 1994, p2

51   Neil Lyndon, *No More Sex War: The Failures of Feminism*, Mandarin, 1994, p6

52   Warren Farrell, *The Myth of Male Power: Why Men Are the Disposable Sex*, Fourth Estate, 1993

53   Val Coultas, 'Feminists must face the future', in *Feminist Review*, No7, 1981, p36

54   Lynne Segal and Mary McIntosh, *Sex Exposed: Sexuality and the Pornography Debate*, Virago, 1992, p4

55   Ann Bradley, 'Rape: reopening the case', in *Living Marxism*, No40, p10

56   Katie Roiphe, *The Morning After: Sex, Fear and Feminism*, Hamish Hamilton, 1993, p6

6
The return of the Sacred

Lynn Revell

'I remember telling a man beside me at supper that I used herbal remedies for my eczema,' recalls film producer Catherine Meader. 'He was aghast. He actually called it witchcraft. Now at the same dinner parties, half the guests are into T'ai Chi or meditation, the other half want the address of my herbalist.'[1]

The latest survey figures show that church attendance is declining. Fewer and fewer people go to church on a Sunday, marry in church, baptise their children or are buried with religious funeral rites.[2] The hours devoted to religious broadcasting, religious education and private worship are peripheral to the lives of most people in Britain. Yet despite the decline of mainstream religion no one could argue that our world is entirely secular. However you wish to define the Sacred—as organised churches, superstition, belief in the supernatural or religious cults and sects—rational thinking and scientific thought have not banished religion to oblivion.

The persistence of religiosity in all its many forms is frequently regarded with some surprise in the industrialised West. Students of religion are often reminded that the first sociologists predicted the decline and eventual disappearance of religion from society but they misjudged its form and perseverance into the twenty-first century.[3] In their attempts to theorise the origins and future of religion, nineteenth-century thinkers like Herbert Spencer and eighteenth-century rationalists like David Hume anticipated the end of religion. Susan Budd describes their view of religion 'as an intellectual error, which the progress of science and rationality would ultimately weaken.'[4] This early prediction of the death of God has been proved overly optimistic not only because religion survives more than 200 years after Hume's *Natural History of Religion* (1757) and 100 years after Spencer's *The Principles of Sociology* (1876-96), but because, in the West, it survives with the most vigour among those groups in society which are the most educated and are the most familiar with the scientific and rational principles that Spencer and Hume thought guaranteed the end of religion.[5]

Similarly many academics re-prophesied the marginalisation of religion in the 1960s with the development of the secularisation thesis—the proposition that religious institutions, symbols and language would gradually diminish. Thirty years later the secularisation thesis remains a disputed and contested theory. Due to the existence of religious fundamentalism, the religious revival in Eastern Europe, new religious movements and the emergence of the New Age, the Sacred, though eroded and fragile in many places, appears to have survived many of the threats posed by the secular forces unleashed in the 1960s.

The many forms of religion existing today do not resemble the power and authority commanded by the churches in the mid-nineteenth century. In comparison with the grip that Christianity once exercised over the accepted values and codes of behaviour in Victorian England, the impact of the modern Anglican church or new-style religions is both unfocused and often unclear. The examination of religiosity, however, remains of interest because the study of religion is also the study of the relationship between man and society.[6] The analysis of a religion's worldview reveals a commentary on the secular world that it exists within. In some cases the wider implications of a particular religion are implicit and in others they are clearly exposed.

Contemporary examples of this interpretation are to be found in some of the many discussions on the significance of fundamentalism. In his analysis of fundamentalism and relativism Kent-based theologian Robin Gill, argues that fundamentalism in both its Protestant and Islamic forms is not merely a particular interpretation of doctrine or practice. He shows that it is not possible to gain a full understanding of the significance of fundamentalism simply by examining the ideas themselves because the ideas are expressive of other trends within society:

> It is not simply a movement, or a series of movements, based upon scriptural absolutism. Fundamentalism is essentially modern in that it is a post-critical reaction. Those who identify themselves as fundamentalists across a number of quite different religious traditions also see themselves as combating key features of modernity.[7]

The deconstruction of religious beliefs or movements to expose a deeper understanding is widely used not only in the sociology of religion, but also by historians and other social scientists. Two classical examples of this method are EP Thompson's *The Making of the English Working Class* and RH Tawney's *Religion and the Rise of Capitalism*. Thompson interpreted Methodism not merely as a Christian denomination, but as a key element in the formation of a disciplined working class. He illustrated how many of the ideas associated with Methodism, such as the elevation of labour as a virtue, were symptomatic of social and economic trends in England at the time.[8] Similarly, in *Religion and the Rise of Capitalism,* Tawney argued that 'the distinctive note of Puritan teaching' was one of the major forces in the creation of capitalism.[9] Again, a particular religion was seen as a factor in the development of society.

The study and interpretation of religious phenomena can give us insights into the evolution of trends in society. The authors mentioned above drew links between the processes of industrialisation and the ideas and beliefs contained in the religion or denomination of the time. They not only recognised a parallel between the concepts used by certain religions and contemporary material and ideological developments, but they also inferred that there was some relationship between the two—that the religious and social changes affected one another. From this point of view, the form and shape of religious beliefs and practices are significant because they are understood to be determining factors in the process of social development.

Of all the many changes in religion since it became the focus of sociological and anthropological enquiry, it is probably the form of the Sacred that has most clearly altered. The earliest studies of religion revealed a plethora of superstitions, conceptions of god(s), after-lives, rituals and structures. Some commanded the loyalty of small groups and others, like the major world religions, commanded the loyalty, token or real, of entire nations. This diversity has continued to flourish to the extent that there are no longer any barriers to the spread of alternative religious beliefs or the knowledge of different religions. In the late twentieth century no religion can secure a monopoly of faith in any area unless it is a monopoly securely imposed and maintained by the government. At least in the cities of Western countries, religious pluralism is a fact of life.

In the 1920s and 1930s anthropologists like Bronislaw Malinowski and Alfred Radcliffe-Brown described a variety of religious practices outside of the Western world. The sociologist Max Weber, before them, also described the machinations of world religions other than Christianity. Diversity was familiar to these social scientists—but it was outside of their own national or cultural barriers. Today, however, there are few areas of the world that can claim to be exclusively Christian or Muslim or Jewish. The inner cities in many Western countries can be divided into component religious parts to an extent that was only hinted at in the past.

The major religions have infiltrated each other's geographical territories and diversified within themselves; adapting and assuming the colours of their new environment. Many of the Muslim, Hindu and Sikh communities in Britain have altered quite dramatically through a generation, becoming a different version of the Hinduism, Islam or Sikhism to that found in their places of origin.

In addition, to the many manifestations of the world religions, we have seen the growth of new denominations and new religious movements. It is no longer the case that religions act on or within whole communities. Instead single communities now boast a multitude of religious groups and ideas.

Religious life has become fragmented in its diversity. In industrialised countries especially, it is no longer possible to speak of a single faith or a single set of religious beliefs. In *Religion in Britain,* Grace Davie refers to the large churches as 'dinosaur' relics from the past that survive in their institutional and structural forms but have been relegated to the margins of the majority's beliefs.[10]

More and more religious beliefs have become individualised; expressing just personal hopes and fears and a personal perception of the Sacred. There are no society-wide rituals that are practised by everyone with the same motivation or intensity. And there seem to be no shared beliefs in God, nor man's relationship to God, nor even a common view of the nature of man himself. Assessments of the new Sacred, as it appears in the 1990s, start from the premise that the individual rather than society is the pivotal point in any relationship between the two.

The nature of religion, its strength or its absence, is often taken as indicative of wider trends in society or as a metaphor for tensions and conflicts which fall outside the definition of religion. The aim of this chapter is not, however, to explain why religion survives nor why nineteenth-century social scientists misjudged its persistence. Nor is it my concern to chart the development of the sociology of religion but, by a straightforward comparison of two periods 100 years apart, I want to illustrate how the self-image of man has been diminished in the expression of the Sacred. The first period is roughly characterised as the classical era of sociological and social thought and the second is the present day. A comparison of the thoughts and ideas of two such different times is bound to be abrupt and a little stark. What this method loses in nuances, however, it gains in seeing clearly the differences in the two periods.

This chapter contrasts the interpretation of religion in its classical understanding with the ideas that are associated with it today. The interpretation of the nature of the Sacred uncovers the contemporary view of the relationship between man and society. On a more intimate level; how man understands his relationship to God is indicative of how he perceives himself in relation to both the Sacred and secular society. It is the changing perception of mankind in relation to the newly defined concept of the Sacred that is my focus.

The Sacred demands some definition before we can begin this comparison. In many respects, as a concept, religion can be used instead of the Sacred, although religion can be too narrow an idea to embrace the most recent manifestations of the Sacred. One of the most prolific of academics on world religions, Professor Ninian Smart indicated some of the difficulties in defining religion in the introduction to his work, *The Religious Experience of Mankind.* He pointed out that both Marxism and humanism in their emphasis on ethics, or certain texts and doctrines, may appear to resemble some of the world religions.[11] He ultimately rejected them as religions because of their 'rejection of the supernatural' and their 'repudiation of revelation and of mystical experience'.[12] Smart's definition of religion is especially wide just so that it can include all those experiences and beliefs which are beyond the rational. Similarly the American sociologist Robert Nisbet favours a definition of religion that concentrates on its form and shape rather than the role it plays. In *The Sociological Tradition*, he defined the 'religio-sacred' as 'the totality of myth, ritual, sacrament, dogma, and the mores in human behaviour; the whole area of individual motivation and social organisation that transcends the utilitarian or rational.'[13] I prefer to use the concept of the Sacred to religion or religio-sacred because today there are some forms of thought and behaviour that emphasise non-rational experiences and are even anti-rational but are not overtly concerned with the supernatural. Though these ideas are not connected to concepts of a God or life or existence beyond death, they do distinguish between experiences and reality that is ordinary, mundane and, as Durkheim surmised, profane and those which are worthy of veneration, are sublime and, to use Durkheim again, Sacred.

The Sacred in the 1990s exists in a variety of forms. So-called religious fundamentalism, especially in its evangelical Christian and Muslim forms, is a powerful example of a religion's ability to express people's anger, political ambitions and hopes. The millions of people who hold folk beliefs or who profess a belief in God while not belonging to any church or group indicate that today's society is still religious even if not actively so.[14] Even if such religious identity has little or no practical effects on the lives of the faithful, its very existence contradicts the idea of a secular society. In a similar vein there are millions of people who see themselves as members of a church but rarely attend services. Moreover, in Britain, 12 per cent of the population is actively committed to a particular Christian church and there are substantial pockets of practising Muslims and Hindus to bear witness to the continuing attraction of religion.[15] Nor can the Anglican or Catholic churches be dismissed as irrelevant. Despite their decline they are 'still by far the largest overall religious tradition in Britain' and both command significant loyalty in the form of the self-identity of millions who feel that they belong to those churches in some way.[16]

Although they are small in comparison with the traditional churches, the activities of cults, sects and new religious movements dramatically illustrate that the Sacred exists in a number of novel forms in the 1990s. The memberships of groups like the Moonies, the Children of God and the Hari Krishna are tiny but they have become household names across Europe. Even more sensationally, the activities of sects like the Order of the Solar Temple which destroyed itself by fire in Switzerland at the end of 1994, or the Branch Davidians cult which was besieged by the FBI at Waco, Texas in April 1993, prove that intense and seemingly irrational beliefs in the supernatural are quite at home in the industrialised countries.

To highlight the comparison with the nineteenth century, I want to consider the most recent manifestation of the Sacred—broadly called the New Age. Of all the variations of the modern Sacred, the New Age is the most ambiguous.[17] In the literature of the sociology of religion, there is no consensus on what the New Age is nor how extensive or dynamic an influence it is. Despite its elusive nature, the New Age is recognised as the latest version of the Sacred in the West and no modern book on the development of religion is complete without some reference to the growth of New Age and its impact on a variety of groups and disciplines within society.

The New Age

The New Age is sometimes defined as a subsection of the new religious movements (NRMs), so it is useful to chart briefly the emergence of the NRMs to put the New Age in context.[18] Some estimates give the number of NRMs in Western countries as around 3000 with about 500 in Britain since 1945. Although this number is large, their memberships are, on the whole, tiny. Not only is each individual group small, but they tend to have a high turnover; members staying for a short while before moving on—sometimes to another group. One study of the motives of individuals who leave religious movements found that 50 per cent of those who left subsequently became affiliated to a different religious group.[19] The total British membership of one of the largest and most infamous of these groups, the Moonies, 'has never risen to 10 000 at any one time'.[20]

Many of these groups emerged in the sixties and, while some of them incorporated elements of major world religions, many were quite exotic with an eclectic mix of a number of traditions. In attempting to understand the phenomena of the NRMs, sociologists have categorised them according to their significance or their origins. In his essay on NRMs Gerald Parsons, from the Religious Studies Department at the Open University, divides them into three groups: those that 'are clearly and straightforwardly derived from the traditional world religions'; those which are related to the mainstream but are less conventional; and lastly the New Age.[21] *In the Elementary Forms of the New Religious Life* Roy Wallis developed three categories for NRMs; world-rejecting; world-affirming and world-accommodating.[22] Similarly professor of sociology, Steve Bruce, prefers to sort these groups not by the 'religious tradition of their roots', but between those which 'rejected the world while some positively affirmed it'.[23]

There are also conflicting analyses of what the NRMs represent. In the 'New religious consciousness and the crisis of modernity' Robert Bellah argues that the NRMs have replaced the protest movements and alternative lifestyles that emerged in the 1960s.[24] Ronald Enroth, in his survey of the attraction for young people of NRMs and cults, concludes that they are a product of the 'identity confusion [that] is commonplace among the children of influence'.[25] The influential American sociologists, Stark and Bainbridge, have maintained that NRMs form as a reaction to the dominance of secular norms and values.[26] While Eileen Baker entertains the possibility that, despite the intense interest of sociologists in NRMs, they are merely 'a highly publicised collection of options selected from the enormous variety already available in modern societies, which celebrate neither belief nor ideology under any single canopy'.[27]

Although the analysis and interpretation of NRMs is frequently contested, one theme that consistently emerges is that, whatever their cause, they are a new development within society and are clearly distinct from traditional mainstream religions. John Hannigan, from Toronto University, believes NRMs are new in the same way as the New Social Movements—in that they offer novel forms of human relationships in the late twentieth century.[28] Although many NRMs do appear to have links with their more traditional counterparts, it is those groups banded together in the New Age which are most removed from mainstream religion.

Many of the groups and ideas associated with the New Age first gained popularity in the 1980s although their roots are more likely to be found in the 1960s. Michael York believes that the New Age was initially popularised by Baba Ram Dass (previously Richard Alpert) who was responsible for conducting psychedelic experiments at Harvard and later travelled to India and studied the Orient.[29] On his return to America he became the first in 'a series of Oriental-based groups—expounding transcendental wisdom'. Whether or not Baba Ram Dass was the originator of the New Age, his personal journey from orthodoxy to guru is a good example of many of the features found in the New Age: a view of wisdom and truthfulness not based on rational, scientific thought, a link to ancient non-Western knowledge and an approach to enlightenment that emphasises the personal.

The New Age is also rooted in the apparently secular movements, books and theories claiming to develop the hidden self that appeared in the 1960s. The Esalen Institute, founded in 1962 in California, was one of the most famous centres of the human potential movement with research into personal-growth techniques. Erhard Seminar Training (EST), founded in 1971, is now a multi-million dollar business that offers training to empower the individual. In his survey of NRMs and their links with business, Paul Heelas describes EST as 'the largest and most influential of movements which utilise processes in the main drawn from the Western psychotherapeutic tradition to effect enlightenment, the experience of self as God'.[30] EST, along with books like *The Games People Play* and *I'm OK—You're OK* laid the foundation for many New Age ideas through the promotion of the worship of the self.[31]

The self is revered not only because it is important and the primary focus of our happiness and pleasure, but because it becomes the source of all power and knowledge. In *Staying OK*, the sequel to *I'm OK—You're OK*, Amy and Thomas Harris explain that the most effective methods of dealing with 'external confusion' are to 'think', 'talk' and 'ask for clarification'.[32] The answers to the questions 'Does the murderer have diminished capacity, or is he responsible?', 'Are interest rates up or down?', 'Shall we sell the silverware or hide it?' and 'Shall we enrol in Weight Watchers or Slim Gym?' are to reorder our personal lives—external confusion is rendered manageable by the self's ability to understand it.[33]

The variety of New Age groups is bewildering. Although academic writings on the New Age are still dwarfed by the immense literature on NRMs, popular literature on the New Age is huge and covers topics from alternative health to new approaches to business management. Popular New Age subjects range from herbalism, Goddess worship, the everyday use of crystals and self-awareness training for businessmen. The New Age may sometimes appear cranky and odd but it would be a mistake to dismiss it as the exclusive preserve of New Age travellers or a few 'hippies'. Many of the ideas and practices associated with the New Age are now accepted as conventional and mainstream.

Women's magazines designed for practical, efficient and glamorous women who run families and careers celebrate aspects of the New Age. *Vogue*, the magazine for women who take fashion seriously, recently published an article examining the growth of New Age thinking among middle class women. Mimi Spencer has charted the middle class and superstar romance with ideas that were once the preserve of the unwashed and anti-fashion counter culture:

Courses at the London College of Massage are over-subscribed; long queues snake outside Chinese herbalists in Covent Garden and Westbourne Grove on a Saturday morning; five years ago, shops selling crystals were unheard of— now you won't see a pop star in interview without a lump of rose quartz around his neck; New Age books are the only sector of the publishing industry that is growing—they now account for 20 per cent of the book-selling market....Acceptance of alternative ideas is not just happening, it's positively hip.

Smog-bound denizens of Hollywood are currently competing for points on the spiritual scale...Richard Branson and Sir Nicholas Greenburg of Marks & Spencers have both had their offices attended to by a Feng Shui expert, who has placed desks, mirrors and word processors in positions that encourage optimum energy flow.[34]

New Age ideas are not only popular with the fashionable, but also with those who are searching for solutions of any kind. Books like *You Can Heal Your Life* by Louise Hay focus on day-to-day activities to release the 'hidden qualities of the everyday woman'.[35] Compared with the chaos and tensions in twentieth-century life, the baffling levels of technology, the sense of belittlement by powers and forces out of control, many New Age ideas seek to strengthen the individual in this modern maze of everyday survival. These are philosophies that can be adapted and integrated into conventional lives with the minimum of disruption but which none the less serve as a way of reordering people's lives in some sense. In an article on the attraction of New Age ideas to Middle England, Professor Claxton, a visiting Professor of Education at Bristol University, explained how his ideas were not extreme or far-fetched, but simply alternative, when he described himself as a 'middle-of-the-road Buddhist' which later became 'a rather left-of-centre Rajneeshi' and has finally settled as a 'middle-class pilgrim'.[36] Many New Age practices like water-dowsing, dream-work, graphology and last year's election, by Leeds university students, of a white witch to be their chaplain, may still seem eccentric to some people. Yet the boom of New Age publications, and the placing, in high street chemists, of homeopathic and holistic medicines on the shelf beside conventional remedies indicate the level of integration of New Age ideas into the mainstream.

Occasionally the New Age is described as a group, sometimes as a loose federation of beliefs. Elsewhere it has been defined as a practice such as acupuncture, water-divining or aromatherapy. What is clear, however, from either of these categorisations is that the New Age has no relationship to mainstream religion. The phenomena investigated by today's sociologist as part of the New Age bear no resemblance to the phenomena that was studied by the earliest generation of social scientists.

The classical interpretation of the Sacred

It is wrong to assume that the earliest social scientists were only interested in the big religions of their time, Judaism and Christianity, and that they located the Sacred only in these religions. Durkheim was one of the most influential sociologists whose ideas still form the backbone to many strands of sociological thinking, especially within the sociology of religion.[37] His major work *The Elementary Forms of the Religious Life* written in 1912 is a study of Australian aboriginal totemism using the field work of Spencer and Gillen.[38] Though he theorised about the nature of religion and the role of religion in society, the focus of his study was the religious practice of the Australian tribes. The aim of his study was, however, to go beyond the parochial limits of his subject matter in order to explain the general function of the Sacred—whatever the religion, whatever the society. As Malcolm Hamilton explains in *The Sociology of Religion*, Durkheim's aim was to discover the dynamics and forces that are present in all religions and that in looking at the 'most primitive form of religion, he is looking for that which is constant and unvarying in religion; its essential features'.[39]

Similarly one of Durkheim's most influential teachers and the first to use the concept of the Sacred 'in the interpretation of social organisation and institutional change', Fustel de Coulange, made the subject of his major work not the predominant religion of his time, Christianity, but a comparison between the ancient city states of Rome and Greece.[40] In *The Ancient City* Fustel de Coulange isolated the source of meaning and social coherence in the ancient world in a 'primitive religion'.[41] Like Durkheim the subject of his study was not the whole aim of his work. Again, like Durkheim, he was intent on drawing wider conclusions in understanding the society of his day from the study of other phenomena. His real subject was secular modern man but the form of his enquiry was the role of religion in the shaping of man's relationship to the family, authority and the state.

Marx, Weber and Freud, who contributed to the classical interpretation of the Sacred, were more conventional in their choice of subject matter in that they studied the major religions of their day. What is noticeable about their work, however, is that they all identified the social consequences of religion as the most important and defining element of the Sacred. In *A Contribution to the Critique of Hegel's Philosophy of Right* Marx locates the existence of religion in man's condition under capitalism.[42] Religion, for Marx, is not a set of false ideas that can be replaced by true ones, but an expression of man's alienated position within society. It is because man is alienated in his real life that his understanding of the world in which he lives is also alienated. The alienation of labour means that human creativity and hard work become the wealth of another, taken away from those who produced it. The separation between inspiration and product is re-expressed in religion when people see God and the sublime as divinely inspired rather than the product of people's imagination. Marx explains this alienation:

The worker therefore feels himself at home only during his leisure whereas at work he feels homeless. His work is not voluntary, but imposed, forced labour. It is not the satisfaction of a need, but only a means for satisfying other needs. Its alien character is clearly shown by the fact that as soon as there is no physical or other compulsion it is avoided....Just as in religion the spontaneous activity of human fantasy, of the human brain and heart, reacts independently as an alien activity of gods or devils upon the individual, so the activity of the worker is not his own spontaneous activity. It is another's activity and a loss of his own spontaneity.[43]

So, for Marx, the alienation of man's creativity into the Sacred arises out of an alienated society.

Weber, like Marx, drew a link between religion and the forces that shaped and conditioned society. Weber isolated *charisma* as the extraordinary quality that certain individuals have which allows them to act as the source of dynamism for other relationships and structures within society. Although charismatic authority is mostly subsumed beneath 'bureaucratic authority', at its height a charismatic leader has the power to lead, inspire and influence all those held in his sway. His powers and ability to move and impact on society come not from his personal being, according to Weber, but because he is touched by the divine. For Weber, charisma in an individual is proof that 'he personally is the genuine master willed by God'.[44] In contrast, Freud located the primary importance of religion 'in directing surplus and unexpressed instinctual energy'.[45] By containing man's feelings of fear and helplessness, religion was meant to act as a source of calm and order within society—without which man's inadequacies and infantile psyche would destroy society.

The Sacred was never seen as an isolated belief in God, the supernatural or just a set of values and norms. Whatever the particular definition of Sacred, it was its relevance to man which was seen as its defining characteristic. The classical understanding of the Sacred rooted its significance in the midst of the conflicts and tensions of society. The understanding of the New Age Sacred, however, suggests an entirely different viewpoint.[46]

The Sacred and the secular

One of the differences between the classical and the New Age outlook is their evaluation of what is true. The New Age groups do not share a common outlook towards the material world. Some embrace the world while others reject it and celebrate the spiritual. There is no common source for New Age traditions or texts; some look to the East and some are based on the occult in their conception of the nature of God or the supernatural. The element that binds the New Age together is precisely that it is undefinable and ambiguous. Steve Bruce argues that one way of characterising this feature of the New Age is to understand it as essentially anti-rational. Traditional Western rationality demands some proof to establish a certain knowledge. In contrast to this, the New Age belief of an individual is true if that belief is acceptable to that person.

> New Agers tend to have little interest in conventional notions of testing. That one or two people assert that a therapy worked for them is enough to establish its efficacy. New paradigms are not 'discovered' by painstakingly trying to explain observations that do not fit with existing well-established theories, but by revelation and by returning to archaic traditions.[47]

The deliberately relativist outlook of New Agers—what is true for one person is another person's falsehood—ensures that it is impossible to define the New Age by its beliefs, its religious dogma, texts or practice. Two New Age groups may have conflicting ideas and practices that oppose one another and yet both can be defined as New Age. It is the inherent relativism of the New Age which sets it apart from the classical awareness of the Sacred. In contrast to the orthodox approach to truth, New Age thinking celebrates the relativisation of truth as an advantage over the restrictions of old-fashioned dogma. The New Age rejects a rationality which rests on objective or collective criteria tested in competition with other theories. In his introduction to David Spangler's *The Rebirth of the Sacred*, self-confessed New Ager Sir George Trevelyan condemns the 'rationalist material worldview' as 'hopelessly inadequate to explain our fantastic universe'. He believes that the only guarantee we have of successfully participating in 'the greatest saga in human history' is for us, like 'Frodo and Sam', to open our minds to new knowledge.[48]

The New Age considers rationalism as an inadequate and untrustworthy tool with which to understand the world. In the 'Nature of nature' Thomas Kelting argues that our search for reality is hindered by science because it fools us into thinking that we have explained something when all that we have really done is to defer the 'questioning to another domain'.[49] This disregard of objective truth is further reinforced by the growing relativism within mainstream thought and even mainstream religion. Ernest Gellner in *Postmodernism, Reason and Religion* notes that relativism has been encouraged by the lack of certainty within the churches themselves. When 'formal doctrine is ignored and participation treated as a celebration of community not conviction' disparate versions of the truth are tolerated even within the one church.[50] Similarly, relativism is also found in many strands of feminist theology.

In a recent article, Richard Grigg explains the trends in much feminist theology which emphasise a relationship between individuals and God that is not fixed by dogma or tradition, but is uniquely interpreted by each individual as it is experienced. In this way God 'is a relation that human beings choose to enact'.[51] God, and the qualities of God, have become, in this theology, determined by the nature of each interaction with Him.

Modern sociologists often point out that the New Age is difficult to categorise because the defining feature of each group or belief is its relevance not to society, the group or the community, but to the individual. It is the individual who chooses the belief and who can reject it with no wider or further ramifications outside the consciousness of that particular individual. Since science and rational thinking have been abandoned, the only reliable guide to truth has become the inner self. New Age literature often stresses its relativity and celebrates its accent on individuality. When Sir George Trevelyan lectured at the recent Festival for Body, Mind and Spirit he championed the elevation of the self:

> This is what things look like to me. If it doesn't seem like that for you, you don't have to accept what I say. Only accept what rings true to your own inner-self.[52]

In contrast, the Sacred, as it was studied and understood by classical sociologists, was defined by its relationship not just to the individual, but to the community. It was not that the Sacred embraced a particular belief in God or type of God which expressed this form of the Sacred. The God discussed by Marx and Freud in their analyses of Christianity was obviously very different from the God that Durkheim considered when he studied the Aboriginal belief system. For Marx and Freud, God was significant in so far as belief in the existence of the supernatural was an expression of a deeper malaise within society itself. For Durkheim, God was meaningful because the collective worship of a God was indicative of the existence of a society working and living together as a functioning unit. Weber, too, was concerned not with the nature of the Sacred in itself, but its relationship with the wider world. In his essay 'Major features of world religions', Weber outlines the effect and importance of each major world religion on the secular world around it. According to Weber; Confucianism provided the ethical basis for 'a Chinese way of life'; beyond the religious, Hinduism generated the basis of a rigid 'status stratification' throughout India; Sufism encouraged the growth of 'petit bourgeois' brotherhoods and Judaism was intertwined with 'an increasingly quasi-proletarian and rationalist petit bourgeois intelligentsia'.[53] The nature of each religion and its particular concept of the Sacred was an important determinant of the society in which it existed. His concern was not merely to isolate the specific nature of each particular religion, but its wider impact on communities and groups.

Just as modern sociologists have noted that New Age thinking gains its legitimacy from its relationship to the individual, the earlier sociologists noted that the Sacred was a social phenomena that was expressed through its interaction and acceptance among a community of people. Fustel de Coulange identified a religion's significance for ancient societies not in its teachings to the individual, but its shaping of family and the community. He believed that there was an important link between 'men's ideas and their social state' and that it was the balance provided by this link which determined whether society was essentially religious or secular.[54]

Durkheim's view of the social importance of the Sacred was more explicit as the Sacred was 'nothing other than the collective force of society over the individual'.[55] Durkheim's emphasis on the role of religion in forging social commitment can be seen with his explanation of suicide. He noted that Protestants, Jews and Catholics had different suicide rates and that Protestants were twice as likely to commit suicide as Catholics or Jews. Durkheim believed religion was the predominant influence in the differential suicide rates of Jews, Catholics and Protestants and that the explanations for the different rates of suicide could be found in the differing dogmas and social organisations of those religions. As Robin Gill explains, Durkheim believed it was the 'strong nature of Catholicism and Judaism as societies or moral communities (and the relative weakness of the Protestant community) which was the causal factor'.[56]

Like Durkheim, Marx thought of religion only within the context of society. Robert Towler explains that for Marx, religion flowed from an 'inverted world order' where everything appeared as its reverse.[57] From a religious worldview God creates man; in reality it is the other way round. The religious worldview is rooted, however, in the real world, and it cannot be dismissed. To overturn religion, first society has to be transformed, only then can religious ideas lose their purchase on the human imagination. For Marx then, religion, whatever faith, was not the product of an individual's misunderstanding or confusion, but a reflection of his confused and alienated position within society. The absurdity of the religious worldview is the product of an absurd reality.

In some ways Freud's understanding of religion appears to be very similar to certain aspects of New Age thinking. His emphasis on the individual's psychological trauma as the origin of man's need for religion suggests that, for him, the primary role of religion was to mediate between abstract ideas and the individual psyche. Religion, for Freud, was a mechanism for the individual to come to terms with childhood agonies. But although Freud located the origins of religion in the individual, as Towler explains, it 'is a process repeated for every human being, not something which is discovered or invented and then handed on to later generations'.[58] Every individual was undergoing the same process, and thereby creating a community of that religion. Since, as Towler describes, most men 'accept uncritically all the absurdities that religious doctrines put before [them]' so the religion expresses a commonality in the way that people believe.[59]

The classical sociologists believed that the Sacred was dynamic because it was a social phenomena. For Durkheim and Weber, religion was not only more significant than the sum of individual beliefs, but it was the force that helped to stimulate and regulate society. Roderick Martin explains that Durkheim and Weber were primarily concerned with the nature of society; Durkheim with the 'effect of industrialisation on community', and Weber that 'the organisational expression of rationality, bureaucracy, would destroy individual autonomy'.[60] Both sociologists attributed the problems of the social order of their day to the decline of religion. Durkheim and Weber acknowledged this themselves with their respective concepts of *anomie* and disenchantment; both of which presumed discontentment.

Durkheim and Weber insisted that religion played a role in the life of man independently of rational thinking and science. Religion, the Sacred, charisma, fulfilled a part of man that had nothing to do with his physical or intellectual needs. With the decline of traditional religion, Durkheim and Weber addressed the dilemma of man's needs in the context of the evident loss of confidence in mainstream religion.

The fear and concern about a society without religion is evident in many of Durkheim's and Weber's writings. Durkheim stressed the need to discover or create new agencies and new methods to cohere and give society meaning. If traditional religion could no longer function, then it was necessary for man to create a new normative order to replace the old.

Weber, too, identified the absence of the Sacred in the modern world as a major cause for concern. He isolated the effects of rationalisation as the central danger to society. Speaking at the University of Munich, 18 months before his death in 1919, he said 'the fate of our times is characterised by the rationalisation and intellectualism and above all by the disenchantment of the world'.[61] Weber interpreted this disenchantment as a disease preventing the healthy regeneration of society. Despite the fact that the spread of rationalism was aided by the spread of Protestantism, Weber feared that man would be unable to live in a world free from bureaucracy because of the continued retreat of religion.

Marx's analysis of the position and retreat of mainstream religion in society differs significantly from Durkheim's and Weber's. Because Marx believed that religion was a product of the way in which wealth is created in society he did not anticipate the decline of religion, nor a world about to 'strip off its mystical veil', until man himself had changed society.[62] For Marx, the decline of the mainstream religions was not indicative of the absolute decline of the Sacred—merely the diminishing of one particular expression of it. As society changed, the form and shape that man's alienation assumes also changes. The Sacred persists as an expression of man's position in society but takes on shapes and structures that are suggestive of new times and new faces. The source of religiosity persists but manifests itself in new guises.

The individual and the sacred

The two opposing interpretations, modern and classical, of the Sacred assume a particular relationship between the individual and the Sacred. In the New Age, that relationship is between the self-defined Sacred and the inner self. For the classical sociologists the relationship is between the individual and society as it is represented or expressed in the Sacred—whether that society is a tribe or industrial society. Underlying these two different relationships are two contrasting versions of the self. It is in the two opposing concepts of the self that we can see the most profound difference.

Since accepted 'values' in the modern world are, according to the LSE sociologist Eileen Barker, 'novelty and individualism' then 'it is perhaps not surprising that these individuals should pursue different worldviews, different meanings and different lifestyles'.[63] Although it is unsurprising, it does suggest that such a widespread preoccupation with the self is indicative of something new. Writing about post-Christian feminism Linda Woodhead identifies a common conception in this version of the Sacred: a self that is elevated above all else. She identifies feminist spirituality movements as eclectic, saying that 'myths, rituals, gods and goddesses are apparently plucked at random from available sources' with, whatever the source, the believer herself as the dominant partner in the relationship:

> All believe that each woman must trust her own experience above all else, and that there is some basic spiritual experience which all women know when in tune with their real selves.[64]

Women who adhere to this new Sacred have replaced the traditional transcendental, omnipotent God of orthodox theology, with a 'My Self' that 'is master of all it surveys' which rejects all other truths and knowledge as an invasion.[65] For a true enlightenment, the inherently true self, they say, must be rediscovered and rescued from the dictatorship of all externally imposed truths. The assumption that the individual is God is a recurring theme throughout New Age thinking. There is no process of developing new understanding and new knowledge—instead there is the elevation and celebration of what already exists. It is not involvement or engagement with society which enriches the self, but the championing of the self above society that the new Sacred embraces.

In common with the post-Christian feminists, William Bloom of the New Age team of St James, Piccadilly, believes that it is the 'inner reality' which is primary.[66] From this worldview, the individual is already perfect and there is no need to reach beyond our own individuality to try to overcome our own limitations. As David Spangler, the founder of the Lorian Association, has explained in his book on the New Age, traditional religion was all about 'the process of honouring, supplicating, or pleasing an external deity'.[67] The relationship was one of subservience before a greater and more perfect reality; religion showed us how 'we are different from God and dependent upon the divine presence for our very existence'.[68] In contrast, contemporary mysticism evens out the relationship between the perfect divinity and the imperfect man, so that we are 'one with God and co-participants with divinity in the enfoldenment of creation'.[69] In the New Age, perfectibility is a matter of bringing 'into full manifestation' what is already there. In his critique of the New Age, Paul Heelas refers to this as 'self-religiosity', where all that is good in life 'is the self'.[70] What distinguishes the New Age Sacred is not merely the emphasis on the self, but the rejection of virtues and perfection outside of the self as an illusion.

The traditional Sacred related to the individual with quite different implications. The major world religions laid down laws and codes of behaviour for the individual: the individual was expected to behave in a certain way, to perform certain rituals and duties and to embrace a certain interpretation of the world. However, as Durkheim stressed in his work on the significance of totems, the Sacred was not merely the belief of the individual or the physical act of worship, but the process by which man created and maintained society. The totem was understood to be the symbol of man's collective experience; its formation and continuation was meant to be vital for the sense of community.[71] Durkheim's central point was that without the Sacred man was incapable of working and cooperating with other men. There could be no shared experiences and no communities without the Sacred because the Sacred was the means by which a common framework was addressed. On his own man is simply an individual, whereas bound together with other men he could develop the potential to become more than himself. The expression of the expansion of opportunity by cooperation is seen in the idea that the source and impetus to greatness lies not in the inner soul, but in the striving towards the outer perfectibility as it is expressed in the divine. As Durkheim explains in the *Elementary Forms of Religious Life*, it is the Sacred that transforms man into a social animal:

> For our definition of the Sacred is that it is something added to above the real; now the ideal answers to this same definition; we cannot explain one without explaining the other. In fact we have seen that if collective life awakens religious thought on reaching a certain degree of intensity. It is because it brings about a state of effervescence which changes the conditions of psychic activity. Vital energies are over-excited, passions more active, sensations stronger, there are some which produced only at this moment.[72]

Durkheim not only sanctioned society and the advantages of the community, but he believed that the individual, the self, was impoverished without such a relationship to the group. In this way the relationship between the self and the Sacred is an enriching one because it is the Sacred which facilitates not the inward revelation of the self, but its outward interaction with the rest of society.

Marx did not believe that the individual was enhanced by the existence of the Sacred or that it was a necessary feature of human relationships. Nisbet interpreted this as Marx's 'hatred of religion'.[73] Budd construed Marx's view of religion as true in 'a world which was wrong' and Towler summed up this view of religion as a 'social disease, which at the same time symptomises an underlying disorder and also sustains and aggravates it'.[74] Marx clearly despised religion but there is, however, a certain ambiguity in his critique.

Marx was a materialist and he believed that 'man makes religion, religion does not make man'.[75] Marx conceived of religion as a myth created by man, not deliberately or consciously, but grown from man's imperfect grasp and understanding of the world around him. From his confusion, man recreates his own image in the form of God and deifies it. It is in the collective deification of his own image that Marx identifies the positive kernel within the religious mythology. Towler points this out when he comments that: 'Marx gave to [religion] the highest interpretation possible for a materialist. He regarded it as a comprehensive framework within which men had seen and understood their relationship to the world about them.'[76] This interpretation of the Sacred may have expressed man's alienation from the world but, at the same time, it centred on man's *collective* alienation.

Like Marx, Durkheim argued that there was no such thing as an individual's relationship to God because that relationship had already been established by society. According to Marx, the material social world is the cause of man's alienation. But, in his alienated state, man projects an ideal image of humanity and himself into the heavens which he then worships. When he prays before the exemplary figures of Christ or Mohammed he worships what he struggles to be. The supernatural beings he creates are really 'only his own reflection'. It is these fantastic versions of humanity that man struggles to emulate, reaching outwards towards a perfection that he does not realise he has formed in his own unconscious experiences. This is a view where the self is at once exhorted to become better, greater, more than it is, but is limited by man's failure to recognise the product of his collective alienation. Religion thus glorifies what the self can achieve but diminishes the credit man takes for his own achievements.

Conclusion

As society changes so does religion. Even those religions which have maintained the continuity of their name over many centuries are not the same institutions today that they were at their origins. The many shapes and faces of Christianity: early sect; national church; voice of discontent and opposition; liberation theology and Tory Party at prayer are familiar examples of how fluid a single religion can be. Changes in the shape and form of religions are inevitably a part of changes in the environment in which their believers live and work.

The relativisation of the Sacred assumes the existence of tolerance. As we respect each other's cultures we are also meant to respect our neighbour's religion or personal beliefs. The contemporary culture of relativisation has had several consequences. The first is that, despite the language of tolerance, respect is not equally attributed to all forms of the Sacred. As Ernest Gellner explains in *Religion, Fundamentalism and Postmodernity*, not only are some beliefs more tolerated than others, but not all forms of the Sacred exist peacefully side by side. Relativisation has not been followed by mutual respect, but by suspicion of every other belief that is not one's own.

Secondly, the relativisation of belief has signalled the end of beliefs and ideas that can move the whole of society. Postmodernism alleges that there are no more single histories and no universal values. It is the attack on universals that is the most significant conclusion of relativism because it implies the end of man's grand projects developed as part of a forward-reaching humanity. The fragmentation of the Sacred is symptomatic of the fragmentation of human possibilities. The denial of human possibilities symbolises the end of progress. When there is no common view of humanity, merely the empowered individual, then there is an absence of shared ambitions. The visions and after-lives projected by the classical Sacred expressed a collective vision of the present and inspired a collective vision of the future. This was an integral part of society's ability to plan its future as a society. Today our utopias are small. Not only do they lack the grandeur and ambition of the past, but they also lack the promise of a common and shared enlightenment.

The new Sacred is not only a diminishing of the old, but a retreat from past designs. It is not merely that the individual and the self are elevated above the collective or the group, but that the individual itself is also diminished. The fulfilment of the self becomes the beginning and the end of truth, and the self, isolated from all other humanity, becomes the final guarantor of right and wrong. There is no liberation in freeing ourselves from the authority of an omnipotent God if the only task of that freedom is to turn inwards, seeking personal meaning and individual answers. This is not so much a new liberation as a prison constructed out of self-centred whims with the concomitant destruction of knowledge and achievements gained through shared experiences.

The changing perception of the Sacred is part of a changing perception of the individual. While the Sacred was once external and more perfect than man, it was a perfectibility that was shared by all. Men shared their vision and their inspiration from the Sacred and in this way the Sacred articulated an aspiration to the universal. For Durkheim this sharing was the cement binding society and for Marx it was the transposed self-glory of a debased society. In the partnership between the Sacred and the individual, the individual was subservient and yet striving to be greater. This was also an understanding of the individual in which he is enhanced by his interaction with other people. It was this external and perfect Sacred that enabled man to become more than the individual.

The new Sacred is no longer external to the individual and no longer shared with other people. In the past, people may have worked or worshipped in isolation but they still shared a common inspiration and aim, whereas today people may be physically together in the same room, read the same book and use the same crystals, but in each case their experience of the Sacred is in isolation from each other. In the partnership of the individual and the Sacred there is more equality but it has occurred at the cost of degrading the individual. There is no longer any possibility of the individual's enhancement in the process of interaction with the rest of the world. The scientific and rational world has apparently lost its capacity to be a trusted guide. The voices and visions of other people are not your visions and not your voice. The self may have become God but it is an isolated and lonely self, limited by the fragmentary nature of its own parochial experiences and dreams, and impoverished by its inability to communicate with any other soul than its own.

NOTES

1   Quoted in Mimi Spencer, 'Beyond the fringe', *Vogue*, January 1995

2   Peter Brierley, *Christian Europe: What the English Church Census Reveals*, MARC Europe, 1991

3   Roland Robertson (Ed), *Sociology of Religion*, Penguin, 1969, p11

4   Susan Budd, *Sociologists and Religion*, Macmillan, 1973, p1

5   *British Social Attitudes Survey*, HMSO, 1991

6   Man is used interchangeably with the term individual in this chapter to give variety rather than imply any peculiarly male relationship with God.

7   Robin Gill, *Competing Convictions*, SCM Press, 1989, p131

8   EP Thompson, *The Making of the English Working Class*, Pelican, 1963, Ch11 'The transforming power of the cross'

9   RH Tawney, *Religion and the Rise of Capitalism*, Penguin, 1926, p270

10 Grace Davie, *Religion in Britain since 1945: Believing without Belonging*, Blackwell, 1994, p62

11 Ninian Smart, *The Religious Experience of Mankind*, Collins, 1969, p19

12 Ninian Smart, *The Religious Experience of Mankind*, Collins, 1969, p15

13 Robert A Nisbet, *The Sociological Tradition*, Heinemann, 1966, p221

14 Grace Davie, *Religion in Britain since 1945: Believing without Belonging*, Blackwell, 1994, p8

15 Peter Brierley, *A Century of British Christianity: Historical Statistics 1900-85*, MARC Europe, 1989

16 Gerald Parsons, 'Contrasts and continuities: the traditional Christian churches in Britain since 1945', in Gerald Parsons (Ed), *The Growth of Religious Diversity*, Routledge, 1993, p88

17 Grace Davie, *Religion in Britain since 1945: Believing without Belonging*, Blackwell, 1994, p41

18 Gerald Parsons, 'Expounding the religious spectrum: NRMs in modern Britain', in Gerald Parsons (Ed), *The Growth of Religious Diversity*, Routledge, 1993, p283

19 Jacobs, 'Deconversion from religious movements: an analysis of charismatic bonding and spiritual commitment', *Journal for the Scientific Study of Religion (JSSR)*, Vol26, 1987, pp294-308

20 Eileen Barker, 'NRM: another great awakening?', in Philip E Hammond (Ed), *The Sacred in a Secular World*, University of California, 1985, p41

21 Gerald Parsons, 'Expounding the religious spectrum: NRMs in modern Britain', in Gerald Parsons (Ed), *The Growth of Religious Diversity*, Routledge, 1993, p280

22 Roy Wallis, *The Elementary Forms of Religious Life*, Routledge, 1984

23 Steve Bruce, *Religion in Modern Britain*, Oxford University Press, 1995, p96

24 Robert Bellah, 'New religious consciousness and the crisis of modernity', in C Glock and RN Bellah, *The Consciousness Reformation*, University of California, 1976

25 Ronald Enroth, *Youth Brainwashing and the Extremist Cults*, Paternoster Press, 1977, p151

26 R Stark and W Bainbridge, *A Theory of Religion*, Lang, 1987

27 Eileen Barker, 'NRM: another great awakening?', in Philip E Hammond (Ed), *The Sacred in a Secular World*, University of California, 1985, p47

28 John A Hannigan, 'New Social Movement theory and the sociology of religion', in WH Swatos Jnr (Ed), *A Future for Religion*, Sage, 1993

29 Michael York, 'The New Age in Britain', in *Religion Today*, Vol9 No3, Summer 1994, p14

30 Paul Heelas, 'Cults for capitalism, self-religions, magic and the empowerment of business', in Peter Gee and John Fulton (Eds), *Religion and Power: Decline and Growth*, Chameleon Press, 1991, p28

31 Eric Berne, *Games People Play*, Pan Books, 1964, and Thomas Harris, *I'm OK— You're OK*, Pan Books, 1968

32 Amy Harris and Thomas Harris, *Staying OK*, Pan Books, 1985, p102

33 Amy Harris and Thomas Harris, *Staying OK*, Pan Books, 1985, p92

34 Mimi Spencer, 'Beyond the fringe', *Vogue*, January 1995

35 Louise L Hay, *You Can Heal Your Life*, Eden Grove, 1988

36 Quoted in Jonathan Margolis, 'Looking for enlightenment', *Sunday Times*, 9 April 1995

37 Anthony Giddens, *Sociology*, Polity, 1993 (1989), p459

38 Emile Durkheim, *The Elementary Forms of the Religious Life*, Allen & Unwin, 1912

39 Malcolm B Hamilton, *The Sociology of Religion*, Routledge, 1995, p98

40 See Robert A Nisbet, *The Sociological Tradition*, Heinemann, 1966, p238

41 Fustel de Coulange, *The Ancient City: A Study on the Religion, Laws and Institutions of Greece and Rome*, 1864, cited in Robert A Nisbet, *The Sociological Tradition*, Heinemann, 1966, p240

42 Karl Marx, *A Contribution to the Critique of Hegel's Philosophy of Right*, in *Marx: Early Writings*, (Quintin Hoare, Ed) Pelican, 1975

43 Karl Marx, *Economic and Philosophical Manuscripts*, in Thomas B Bottomore and Maximilien Rubel (Eds), *Selected Writings in Sociology and Social Philosophy*, Penguin, 1956, p177

44 Max Weber, 'Wirtschaft und Gesellschaft', in *Selections in Translation*, WG Runciman (Ed), Cambridge University Press, 1978, p229

45 Sigmund Freud, *The Future of an Illusion*, Penguin Collected Works, Vol12, Penguin, 1962, p231

46 Paul Heelas, 'The New Age in cultural context: the pre-modern, the modern and the postmodern', *Religion*, Vol23 No2, April 1993

47 Steve Bruce, *Religion in Britain*, Oxford University Press, 1995, p107

48 David Spangler, *The Rebirth of the Sacred*, Gateway Books, 1984, pxii

49 Thomas Kelting, 'The Nature of nature', *Parabola*, Vol20 No1, February 1995

50 Ernest Gellner, *Postmodernism, Reason and Religion*, Routledge, 1994, p5

51 Richard Grigg, 'Enacting the divine: feminist theology and the being of God', *Journal of Religion*, Vol74 No4, October 1994, p807

52 Quoted in Paul Heelas, 'The New Age in cultural context: the pre-modern, the modern and the postmodern', *Religion*, Vol23 No2, April 1993, p16

53 Max Weber, 'Major features of world religions', 1946, reprinted in Roland Robertson, *Sociology of Religion*, Penguin, 1969, p21

54 Fustel de Coulange, *The Ancient City: A Study on the Religion, Laws and Institutions of Greece and Rome*, 1864, cited in Robert A Nisbet, *The Sociological Tradition*, Heinemann, 1966, p241

55 Malcolm B Hamilton, *The Sociology of Religion*, Routledge, 1995, p102

56 Robin Gill (Ed), *Theology and Sociology*, Geoffrey Chapman, 1987, p47

57 Robert Towler, *Homo Religiosus*, Constable, 1974, p34

58 Robert Towler, *Homo Religiosus*, Constable, 1974, p28

59 Robert Towler, *Homo Religiosus*, Constable, 1974, p29

60 Roderick Martin, 'Sociology and theology: alienation and original sin', in Robin Gill (Ed), *Theology and Sociology: A Reader*, Geoffrey Chapman, 1987, p102

61 Quoted by Roderick Martin, 'Sociology and theology: alienation and original sin', in Robin Gill, *Theology and Sociology: A Reader*, Geoffrey Chapman, 1987, p105

62 Karl Marx, *Capital*, Vol1, Lawrence & Wishart, 1983, p84

63 Eileen Barker, 'NRM: another great awakening?', in Philip E Hammond (Ed), *The Sacred in a Secular World*, University of California, 1985, p46

64 Linda Woodhead, 'Post-Christian spiritualities', *Religion*, Vol23 No2, April 1993, p170

65 Linda Woodhead, 'Post-Christian spiritualities', *Religion*, Vol23 No2, April 1993, p175

66 Cited in Paul Heelas, 'Cults for capitalism, self religions, magic and the empowerment of business', in Peter Gee and John Fulton (Eds), *Religion and Power: Decline and Growth*, Chameleon Press, 1991, p16

67 David Spangler, *The Rebirth of the Sacred*, Gateway Books, 1984, p19

68 David Spangler, *The Rebirth of the Sacred*, Gateway Books, 1984, p144

69 David Spangler, *The Rebirth of the Sacred*, Gateway Books, 1984, p144

70 Paul Heelas, 'Cults for capitalism, self-religions, magic and the empowerment of business', in Peter Gee and John Fulton (Eds), *Religion and Power: Decline and Growth*, Chameleon Press, 1991, p17

71 Susan Budd, *Sociologists and Religion*, Macmillan, 1973, p39

72 Emile Durkheim, *Elementary Forms of Religious Life*, printed in Roland Robertson (Ed), *Sociology of Religion*, Penguin, 1969, p51

73 Robert A Nisbet, *The Sociological Tradition*, Heinemann, 1966, p225

74 Susan Budd, *Sociologists and Religion*, Macmillan, 1973, p54, and Robert Towler, *Homo Religiosus*, Constable, 1974, p35

75 Marx-Engels, *Gesamtausgabe,* Section 1, Vol1, p403 cited in Thomas
    B Bottomore and Maximilien Rubel, *Karl Marx: Selected Writings in Sociology
    and Social Philosophy,* Penguin, 1956, p41

76 Robert Towler, *Homo Religiosus,* Constable, 1974, p33

7
Determined to be different: social constructionism and homosexuality

Peter Ray

'Lesbians and gay men go to bed with each other all the time in our group.'

During the first half of the 1990s there has been a striking change in the public profile of lesbians and gay men and the attitude of public opinion towards homosexuality. From Hollywood to Channel 4 gay characters and themes have invaded popular culture. From the 'queer' tactic of outing public figures to the political campaigns around the age of consent in Britain or the right to serve in the US military, the issue of sexual identity has moved into the mainstream of public life. One American writer has characterised this period as the 'gay moment' and a leading British campaigner felt confident enough to open a recent anthology celebrating 25 years of gay liberation with the decidedly upbeat observation that 'lesbians and gay men are the one social group for whom life seems to be getting better'.[1]

These changes indicate a significant shift in the understanding of sexuality in Western society. The remark quoted above, made to me recently by a student member of a university lesbian and gay society, is not exceptional, but symptomatic of the fact that the meaning of the gay identity itself is also changing as the relationship of homosexuality to the wider society changes, most markedly in the hothouse environments of college campuses and metropolitan social scenes.

To explain these changes in the status and meaning of homosexuality is a fascinating theoretical problem. However before this can be tackled, it is first necessary to take a step back and assess the approach of historians and sociologists to homosexuality and the way in which its meaning has changed in our century. That is the purpose of this chapter.

Two ways of thinking have predominated in the study of homosexuality over the past century or so. The first view sought the origins of human sexual desire, and the forms that it takes, in the biological or psychological constitution of individuals. Whether, like the pioneers of sexology, sexual desire was thought to be rooted in mental functions or hormonal differences or, like the psychoanalytic approach of Freudians, in the resolution of infantile sexual conflicts, the categories homosexual and heterosexual tended to be assumed as given. In the second approach, developed by sociologists and historians, these categories themselves have been questioned.

Over the past 20 years the perspectives of the sociological approach loosely called social constructionism or deconstruction, have become the orthodoxy in the academic study of homosexuality in Britain and America, displacing the earlier domination of the disciplines of psychology and sexology. From the constructionist standpoint, the theoretical problem posed by homosexuality is not to fathom the 'cause' of an individual's sexual desires, but to expose the category 'homosexual' as a convention established by historical and cultural processes.

According to the social constructionist perspective, sexuality is not a 'thing'; the meaning of sexual activities and desires, and the sexual 'identities' adopted by people, are not the self-evident consequence of some fixed 'essence' determined by genetic or physiological mechanisms. Such a view is described as 'essentialism' by constructionist writers. The radical Freudian version of 'essentialism' propounded by writers like Wilhelm Reich and Herbert Marcuse was that sexual desire was an innate human drive that had been constrained and distorted by the institutions of modern civilisation. In his *History of Sexuality* Michel Foucault attacked this idea as 'the repressive hypothesis'.[2] On the contrary, Foucault argued, contemporary sexuality was not simply a question of the repression or permission of natural drives, but a modern invention, precisely a consequence of the new ways of defining sexual activity that developed in the nineteenth century.

Social constructionism is far from a monolithic school of thought with different writers drawing their methods and outlooks from Anglo-American sociology, Lacanian Freudianism and French post-structuralism. However for present purposes I will deal with what Carole Vance has described as the mainstream constructionist approach:

> At minimum, all social construction approaches adopt the view that physically identical sexual acts may have varying social significance and subjective meaning depending on how they are defined and understood in different cultures and historical periods.[3]

I want to look at a central theoretical problem in social constructionist theory, that of determination, and suggest how it might shine some light on contemporary developments around the contested idea of the gay identity.[4] In what follows, I tend to focus on the work of the British social historian Jeffrey Weeks because his work exemplifies the dominant understanding of the gay identity and has been highly influential for that reason. This view of modern homosexuality needs a brief introduction before going on to investigate some of its problems.

Constructing the homosexual[5]

The starting point of the constructionist analysis is to distinguish between homosexual *behaviour* and homosexual *identity* or 'the homosexual'. The former is found in all human societies but the latter is specific to modern urban industrialised societies. 'Sex has no history', declares David Halperin, 'It is a natural fact'; it is sexuality that has a history.[6] Halperin goes on to illustrate this distinction by explaining the significance of the celebrated same-sex love practised by the citizens of ancient Athens.

To Athenian society, sexual relations were an expression of the social status of the participants. A free-born Athenian male might have sex with a woman, a slave or a free-born boy but nobody would have considered the citizen and the male slave as sharing an identity or as in any way similar. Halperin explains that the sexual roles adopted by the participants involved precisely the erotic expression of their social difference. Athenian society severely disapproved of male citizens having sex with other male citizens. In ancient Greece 'identical physical acts' to those which take place today had very different meanings. The past is indeed another country where they did things differently, even when on the surface they appear to be the same. There may have been a great deal of same-sex intercourse in ancient Athens but there were no homosexuals, nor heterosexuals.

The more or less agreed understanding of the modern homosexual established through the work of Weeks and Foucault is that such a person emerged in Europe in the mid to late nineteenth century.[7] (The term homosexual was not coined until 1869.) Before that period sexual acts and sexual crimes were understood only in religious terms. The crime of sodomy referred not just to anal sex, but to a whole series of non-procreative sexual acts including those between men and women and bestiality. These acts were sinful, but could potentially be committed by anyone. It was not until the late nineteenth century that the idea that different sexual acts were associated with different types of person, with particular sexual constitutions or orientations, emerged, through a process which Weeks terms the 'moral, legal and medical regulation' of sex.[8]

In the second half of the nineteenth century, sexologists and psychiatrists sought to explain the origins of homosexual behaviour in the biological or psychological make-up of the people who practised it. Richard von Krafft-Ebing

saw homosexuality as a mental illness, 'a functional sign of degeneracy' which
was mostly determined by heredity.[9] To Magnus Hirschfeld homosexuals
formed a 'third sex', intermediate between men and women, with innate
differences in their physiological constitution. Havelock Ellis' theory of sexual
'inversion' was backed up by the idea that congenital hormonal development
was the cause. To the Freudian psychologists (though not to Freud himself)
homosexuality was a pathological consequence of abnormal childhood
development.[10] At least until the 1960s, such 'essentialist' views of sexuality were
accepted by more or less everyone including homosexuals themselves. It was
thought that the homosexual was, in one way or another, differently constituted as an individual from the heterosexual: that homosexuals shared some
characteristic traits that marked them out as a distinct minority in society.

Weeks argues that much of this scientific work was addressed to the legal
profession to provide concepts that it could use in relation to sexual offences.
Only in the late nineteenth century did the courts start to recognise the idea
of homosexuality, and the physical expression of homosexual desire was not
specifically outlawed in Britain until the 'Labouchère amendment' of 1885.
It was only with the sensational trials of Oscar Wilde in 1895 that 'the homosexual' became firmly lodged in the wider public consciousness.

But changes in the scientific conception of sexual desire and the legal regulation of its expression were closely related to wider developments. Family
forms in all classes were subject to change in the nineteenth century and from
the 1830s onwards doctors, social reformers and politicians started to intervene in the sexual and domestic lives of the population, and developed
theories to support their efforts for social reform. Weeks and others have provided detailed accounts of these campaigns and ideas. They emphasise that
these ideas did not develop in a linear fashion, but were frequently in conflict
with each other.

In particular the criminalisation of homosexuality was a direct result,
according to the constructionist view, of a moral panic stimulated by one
group of reformers which was focused on abolishing laws that were related to
earlier reforms. The Labouchère amendment came in the wake of the Social
Purity movement's campaign against the Contagious Diseases Acts. The acts
were draconian laws under which prostitutes could be forcibly detained and
tested for venereal disease. They were based on what Frank Mort calls the
'sanitary principles' of mid-nineteenth century preventative medicine which
had linked the spread of disease and moral contagion.[11] This medical outlook
was itself the outcome of an earlier period of moral panic about the living
conditions of the urban masses.

The Social Purity movement was an alliance of religious non-conformists,
missionary groups and early feminists. They focused their efforts against the

double standard in the Contagious Diseases Acts, under which women were blamed for the problems of sexual immorality while men went unpunished. By contrast, the Social Purity movement campaigned against 'male lust', blaming it for problems like prostitution. Male homosexuality also became a target of the campaign, which led to its criminalisation in 1885.

The Social Purity movement mixed feminist demands for women's equality with religious ideas of chastity and the sanctity of marriage. Weeks points out that its concerns chimed with the growing imperialist fears about the strength of the British race and nation at a time when the British Empire was facing stiff competition from Germany and other powers. The family was seen as the bedrock of the nation and sections of the ruling class supported the reforms while other more traditional elements resisted Social Purity's demands for more than a decade. At the same time Social Purity had wide-spread support among working class people angry at the conditions endured by working class women.[12]

Two aspects about the constructionist account need to be emphasised. The first is that the different ideas and campaigns that informed the nineteenth-century attitude to sexuality had different sources and their proponents different motivations. The middle class evangelists might have been most prominent but they were far from monolithic in their views. At the same time, the working class, frequently the focus of moral panics about disease and morality, were not simply passive recipients of philanthropy and sermons, but active participants; and their own outlook was not merely reactive, but an expression of 'a distinctive social experience'. The sexual categories that emerged were a consequence of the interaction of moral and religious ideas with new scientific discourses in medicine, biology and psychology. Weeks argues for 'the importance of locating sexual categorisation within a complex of discourses and practices'.[13] The eventual emergence of the idea of the homosexual and his criminalisation was just one outcome of this complex. In other words, for Weeks, there can be no single explanation of the categories of sexuality.

The second important feature of the constructionist perspective, is that it was this very shift in the way that society understood, regulated, celebrated and stigmatised different sexual behaviours—the shift in their meaning—that produced modern sexual identities. Constructionist writers argue that the homosexual is a contingent product of the discourses which regulate sexual behaviour. In the jargon, the discourses of sexuality are constitutive of the phenomena. One sympathetic observer noted that the furore surrounding the trials of Oscar Wilde in 1895 'appears to have generally contributed to give definiteness and self-consciousness to the manifestations of homosexuality, and have aroused inverts to take up a definite stand'.[14] Indeed those most sympathetic to 'the love that dare not speak its name' were unsurprisingly enthusiastic proponents of the ideas of sexual 'inversion', the 'third sex' and other *names* and causal definitions for homosexual behaviour. It was the very discussion of the problem of homosexuality, and the stigma and criminal status attached to it, that seemed to produce a consciousness among those who engaged in homosexual behaviour that they formed a distinct social group, that they were homosexuals.[15]

Weeks was one of the first to tell the story of the homosexual transformation from a repressed outcast minority to the self-confident communities of today. In his seminal *Coming Out* he divides the development of homosexuality in the twentieth century into four phases. As they were categorised and defined, homosexuals formed first a semi-secret sub-culture, then various faltering campaigns for reform before bursting 'out of the closet' in the gay liberation movement of the 1970s to eventually form the gay community of the eighties and nineties.[16]

It is the attitude of mainstream constructionism to the reinvention of homosexuals as lesbians and gay men, taking the stigmatised definition as a mark of pride in their identity, an attitude exemplified by Weeks, that reveals a problem with this theoretical approach.

The 'paradox of gay liberation'

There is an apparent inconsistency in the attitude of social constructionism to the modern gay identity which the Marxist historian Bryan Palmer has pointed out. Palmer contrasts Weeks' constructionist theory, sketched above, with his loyalty to the gay movement, arguing that his writing:

> oscillates uneasily between its theoretical fixation on sexuality as discourse...and its political acknowledgement...that those subjected to the categories and definitions of discourses of sexuality "have taken and used the definition for their own purposes".[17]

Palmer argues that Weeks 'is sufficiently embedded in the politics of gay activism to privilege gay identity'.[18] By 'privileging' the gay identity, Palmer means that Weeks assigns to lesbians and gay men as a group, as a community, a unique insight and virtue which endows them with a capacity to change society for the better.[19]

For Palmer, this privileging combines 'uneasily' with Weeks' theory that homosexuality is basically an invention of discourse, of legal, medical and scientific thought. Palmer's point is that it is theoretically inconsistent to argue that sexuality is not an instinctive and innate drive, but a question of the individual's relationship to discourse and then to 'privilege' one particular identity that is so produced. If all sexualities are merely conventions, why does one convention have any more importance than another? What gives one 'social fiction' more insight than another?

Weeks argues that his deep commitment to the gay identity is that its very contingency gives it 'critical importance in challenging the imposition of arbitrary sexual norms'.[20] And Weeks believes that the assertion of the gay identity can do the whole of society a service in leading to the 'possibility for all of different ways of living sexuality'. But why are lesbians and gay men able to do this? What permitted them to 'come out' and why, if there is a strong degree of contingency, do lesbians and gay men continue to exist at all?

Weeks himself has acknowledged that if sexuality is such a contingent matter, the constructionist approach implies 'endless possibilities of sexualisation', and yet contemporary society is dominated by a rather limited set of sexual types, in which the homo/hetero division has remained central.[21] The problem for theory must be to explain, rather than to assume, the persistent centrality of the heterosexual/homosexual distinction in the production of sexual subjects. In assigning special characteristics to the gay identity, it seems that Weeks is in danger of falling into the very essentialism he set out to criticise.

This privileging of the gay identity is one expression of a problem that is as old as the gay liberation movement; a problem that Kenneth Plummer has called the 'paradox of gay liberation'.[22] The gay liberation movement of the early seventies recognised that the division between homosexuals and heterosexuals was a product not of biology, but of the oppressive and unequal treatment of same-sex desire. In her slogan 'We will never go straight, until you go gay', the Radicalesbian activist, Martha Shelly, summed up the gay liberationists' belief that same-sex desire was a potential in everyone and that the artificial categories of sexuality could be overcome.[23] But this insight immediately posed a problem. In 1971, in one of the earliest theoretical works associated with the gay liberation movement, Dennis Altman asked: 'If we finally transcend the divide between heterosexuality and homosexuality do we also lose our identity?'[24] Plummer summed up the paradox for social construction theory in his introduction to *The Making of the Modern Homosexual*:

> This book...persistently strains to debunk the category of "homosexual", to show its relativity, its historical sources, its changing meaning and—overwhelmingly— its damaging impact on human experience. Yet at the current moment it also tacitly finds it hard to believe that "liberated, joyful homosexuals" could ever have attained their "liberation" without that label. It is a theme which haunts this book and will probably haunt inquiries to come.[25]

The new orthodoxy of social constructionism holds that the homosexual is an effect of Victorian society's discourse on sexuality. Individuals were classified, and classed themselves, according to this discourse and adopted the behaviour patterns that 'society' mapped out for them. The gay identity, on the other hand, emerged as the individuals categorised and stigmatised as homosexual adopted the category and then positively embraced it, redefining it as 'gay' and openly asserting it in new ways, as a lifestyle to be proud of. In Michel Foucault's formulation homosexuals engaged in a 'reverse' discourse, changing the meaning of the categories.[26] While the homosexual is defined by society, in the construction story, the lesbian or gay man voluntaristically redefines her or himself. This is an analysis that provides considerable insight into the changing possibilities for individuals in different periods but, strangely, for a school of thought which insists on the *socially* constructed character of sexual identity, it is unable to account for social trends. Why are these possibilities the ones before us? Moreover how do these social conventions come to life in the experience of individuals, so much so that those individuals can spontaneously believe that they are eternal, biologically given differences? And why did their meaning change in one time and place and not another?

Constructionism is hard put to answer these questions because while it points to sexuality's historical character, it focuses in David Halperin's words, on 'the ideological dimension—the purely conventional and arbitrary character— of our own social and sexual experiences'.[27] If our social and sexual experiences really are *purely* conventional and arbitrary then these questions cannot be answered. But there is more to society than ideology, and ideology is not simply 'arbitrary'.

Social constructionism starts from the insight that there is no biologically given essence in the homosexual individual, that sexuality and sexual identities are ideological phenomena. The constructionists may intend to deny that there are naturally given sexual desires which are either repressed or permitted by society, and to emphasise that modern society is productive of different sexualities, but they go much further than this, denying that there is any spontaneous element at all in human sexual relations. For most constructionists there is nothing about society that can be known for certain behind the conscious 'discourses' of science, law and politics through which the institutional arrangements of society are organised.

The social constructionist perspective has produced sophisticated and detailed histories of the changing forms of sexual relations. Weeks and others have opened up a whole area of human experience to historical analysis. Their method, however, rules out of bounds any investigation of society that goes beyond the actions and beliefs of its conscious actors to look at social relations that are established spontaneously and, so to speak, 'behind their backs'.

Social constructionists decry such investigation as 'essentialist' but without going beyond appearances sexual categories are hard to explain. Weeks himself has noted this problem and Californian gay activist Steve Epstein has summed it up concisely as: 'constructionism is unable to theorise the issue of determination.'[28]

This chapter is not an attempt at a rewrite of the history of modern homosexuality. It aims to identify a logical structure in that history and to suggest that this logical structure can help to explain the paradox of gay liberation and the contemporary character of the 'gay identity'.

The family and sexuality

One social constructionist writer who has tried to go beyond the surface appearances of the history of sexuality is John D'Emilio. In introducing his ground-breaking essay 'Capitalism and the gay identity', D'Emilio points out that Jeffrey Weeks and Michel Foucault 'had each argued that "the homosexual" was a creation of the nineteenth century, but without convincingly specifying how or why this came to be.'[29] D'Emilio himself identified the necessary preconditions for the homosexual as a distinct type of person in the emergence of the free market and capitalist production which transformed the character of family life and personal relations. It was the market that provided the material basis for the emergence of modern sexualities.

In pre-capitalist society production was based on the 'household economy'. Peasant households were economically self-sufficient units which produced the goods their members needed to survive and to reproduce themselves. The land and equipment required to do this was either owned by the household or controlled by traditional rules and conventions. Only production that was surplus to the household's requirements was sold on the market in an *ad hoc* fashion.

In an economy dominated by self-sufficient households, a family was the organising unit of production. Family arrangements determined access to the means of production and children were needed as a source of labour in a society which lacked the modern developed sense of childhood that we are familiar with.[30] Domestic work like cooking, cleaning and child-rearing was primarily undertaken by women but it was not separated out from the production of goods for the rest of the family. Equally, sexual relations were necessarily connected with marriage and reproduction. While it was possible for people to enjoy the odd sexual act outside of wedlock and child-bearing, they could not organise their lives in any way on the basis of such activities. The family was necessary for the individual's survival.

The capitalist mode of production, on the other hand, is organised through the exchange of commodities in the market. The key to capitalist production is that the worker is free from the traditional economy. Marx called this freedom in a 'double sense': 'that, as a free man he can dispose of his labour-power as his own commodity, and that on the other hand he has no other commodity for sale'.[31] The worker who is freed both from traditional duties to landlord or community is also freed from ownership of the means of production. He can, but he also must, sell his capacity to work in order to live. The owners of the means of production (capitalist firms) can then purchase the workers' only commodity, their capacity to labour (labour-power) at a price (wages). The price of labour-power, like that of all commodities, is determined by the value of the commodities required to reproduce it (food, clothing, fuel, housing etc), which the worker buys with his wages on a private basis. Production is separated from the private sphere of consumption in a way previously unknown.

The nineteenth century witnessed the generalisation of capitalist production relations in Britain, the USA and Western Europe. Earlier forms of production based on the self-sufficient household were destroyed and the economically active population became increasingly dependent on wages and on market relations generally. This process transformed the basis of sexual relations.

Freedom from traditional production relations, and dependence on the market, weakened the necessary connection between sex and marriage and between sex and reproduction that had held previously. In capitalist society people relate to each other as individual owners of commodities. Their survival depends immediately on selling their commodity at a price. For the bulk of the population that commodity is their labour-power. In principle market relations recognise no *particular* domestic arrangements, as people confront society as individuals (although, as we shall see, the family production unit is transformed in capitalist society through a new division of labour between domestic self-reproduction and public value-production).

In contrast to earlier societies, the capitalist market presents a cosmopolitan potential for people's sexual lives. The great cities of industrial capitalist society offer endless possibilities for sexual relations freed from traditional constraints. This is the social basis and the necessary condition for the appearance of different sexual identities which were inconceivable prior to the universalisation of market relations. As D'Emilio concludes: 'Capitalism has created the material conditions for homosexual desire to express itself as a central component of some individuals' lives.'[32]

However, while market relations offer the potential for cosmopolitan sexual relations, the capitalist mode of production also limits the capacity to realise that potential. Marx comments that the sphere of market relations 'within whose boundaries the sale and purchase of labour-power goes on is in fact a very Eden of the rights of man'.[33] Formal equality exists in the market place, the public sphere, but not in the private, domestic sphere.

Capitalist firms employ labour-power in order to make a profit. The profit stems from the difference between the value of the commodities required to reproduce the labour-power in a given period of time and the value of the commodities that a worker can produce for the firm in the same period. This surplus value is accumulated and reinvested in search of more profit.

Capitalist production needs a constant supply of labour-power if it is to continue to make profits and accumulate capital. The labour-power that is consumed in a day must be replenished; the worker must be fed, washed and rested to work again, and a new generation of workers must be reared and trained. The reproduction of the working class involves a whole battery of chores. This domestic work is necessary for the accumulation of capital, but itself produces no surplus value and capitalist firms have no direct interest in paying for it. On the other hand, the worker must organise this domestic work if he is to have a decent life. Marx put it like this:

> The maintenance and reproduction of the working class is, and must ever be, a necessary condition to the reproduction of capital. But the capitalist may safely leave its fulfilment to the labourer's instincts of self-preservation and propagation.[34]

The capitalist mode of production presupposes some sort of family to look after the worker and raise children as a condition of its existence.[35] But where in pre-capitalist society individual consumption and social production were not separated into different spheres, by contrast, in capitalist society 'the reproduction of labour-power takes place *outside* the capitalist mode of production...although in a manner determined by it'.[36]

This is the key point. The modern family while necessary to the capitalist economy is not an integral part of its productive mechanism. All social classes have an interest in the maintenance and reproduction of labour-power, but the work required to do this does not enter into the creation of surplus value. The individual capitalist firm need take no interest in the private circumstances of the workers. It is this tension between the necessity of the family to capitalist production and its being 'external' to that mode of production which conditions the whole history of the modern family and the consequent moral panics and discourses of sexuality that preoccupied the Victorians in particular.

From the passing of the first Factory Acts in the 1830s, the reformers struggled to improve the social conditions of the newly forged working class.

The low wages, long hours and desperate living conditions endured by men, women and children reduced great masses of urban workers to a degraded condition that alarmed the growing professional middle classes. By outlawing the employment of women in heavy industry and of children from the labour market altogether, they helped to generalise a sexual division of labour which was already established among the middle classes and at the same time was appropriate to the needs of the capital/wage labour relationship: domestic work performed by women, as wives and mothers, while men went out and earned the wages. As Marx points out in *Capital*, the reformers' efforts were bitterly resisted by the capitalist manufacturers themselves. The employers saw these restrictions on a free labour market as a threat to their profits. The institutionalisation of the working class family involved the payment of a 'family wage' which included the value of commodities required to support wives and children. It was the establishment of the modern state to oversee the general interest of capital that made this possible by overcoming the petty concerns of individual capitalists, and asserting the limitations on women and children's labour in the interest of capital as a whole.

From this standpoint it is possible to point to the underlying logic in the variety of discourses confronted by the social constructionists in their attempts to provide a social basis for sexual relations. The relationship between discourse and its social determinants can be seen in the construction of sexuality under capitalism.

The new division of labour entrenched a new sexual division. As Edward Shorter has argued, in a market society where the immediate connection between procreation and the household economy is severed, marriage was no longer based on kinship, old property considerations and naturally determined procreative sexual roles, but on the romantic and sentimental attachment of the partners.[37] This 'bourgeois' marriage and family based on 'emotional egotism' and the new division of labour forms the basis of the dominant ideas of gender and (hetero)sexuality.

In the new division of labour the public realm of work was male dominated and by the middle of the nineteenth century male sexuality had been 'defined as an instinctual force...as a powerful expression of basic physiological processes'. The home and family were regarded as women's proper sphere, and women's sexuality was generally 'defined in terms of the norm of asexuality and the absence of sexual desire'.[38] Motherhood, marriage and domesticity were thought to be basic female instincts. Naturalising gender and sexuality in this way was reinforced by the prejudices of nineteenth-century medicine, as Frank Mort demonstrates, but it made sense and was sustained by the broad social consensus in favour of the sexual division of labour in the family. The middle classes, working class and the elite were all, in different ways, well-disposed by their material interests to its success. The family filled a gap in the social structure of capitalism.

Nineteenth-century reformers and campaigners made their case in terms of the available ideas of the time which, as the constructionist writers have shown, were varied and not necessarily harmonious. Mort's account demonstrates how the authority of the medical men gave way in the 1870s to the combination of religious and feminist ideas in the Social Purity campaigns. However much the real basis of the family was changing, the marriage bond itself continued to be sanctioned in traditional religious terms as a sacrament. Marriage was for life, extra-marital sex was taboo and at that time there was little questioning of the religious prohibition of divorce. At the same time, the limitation of women in all classes to domestic tasks and the lack of economic independence for women meant that the marital relationship was weighted decidedly in men's favour. As a result, marriage in the nineteenth century rested on inequality. The law passed legal control of a woman's property to her husband. Where one act of adultery was sufficient grounds for a man to sue for divorce, a women had to prove that a husband's adultery was 'aggravated'.

Just as the dominant notion of gender was established so the reaction to the double standard implicit in the sexual division of labour took off in the struggle against the Contagious Diseases Acts. The leader of the Social Purity campaign, Josephine Butler, targeted 'male lust' which she argued exploited 'fallen women' as prostitutes and then condemned them. Butler's stated aim was 'male chastity' and she celebrated a religious conception of marriage and the feminine domestic virtues.[39]

Inevitably homosexual behaviour also became a target of the Social Purity campaign against male lust. It is no accident that, as Weeks has observed, homosexuality and prostitution were normally considered together and as a problem of public order in the English law.[40] They were both by definition sexual relations that occurred outside the proper, private domestic sphere of emotional and sexual relations. Homosexual behaviour could be no more tolerable than males' indulgence in prostitution and needed to be controlled if morality and the family were to be protected. Indeed homosexual indulgence was thought to be far more dangerous than prostitution. The overriding perception of homosexuals as 'corrupters of youth' stemmed from the fact that male homosexuals were seen as 'the archetypal sexed being, a person whose sexuality pervaded him in his very existence, threatened to corrupt all around him, particularly the young'.[41]

Having established the norm of the married heterosexual state and its concordant gender roles, homosexual behaviour was nothing short of the antithesis of the gender relations appropriate to the family and its responsibilities. Although it had not been named as such, monogamous heterosexuality had *in reality* been established as the 'norm'. In 1871 almost 90 per cent of English women aged between 45 and 49 were married.[42]

Mary McIntosh has suggested that the homosexual 'role', once established, had the effect of regulating the sexual behaviour of everyone. Firstly it 'helps to provide a clear-cut, publicised and recognisable threshold between permissible and impermissible behaviour', making it unlikely that anyone would 'drift' into homosexual behaviour for fear of the stigma. And, secondly, it segregated those who engage in the forbidden relations 'within a relatively narrow group' away from the rest of society.[43] To act on homosexual desire an individual had to cast himself into a secret world, which could be embraced and relished in the manner of Oscar Wilde or remain a guilty secret as was much more common, but there could be no question of the extreme moral distinction between homosexual and heterosexual desire. This was the determinate historical basis of the homosexual as a particular type of person.

The idea that homosexuals were 'inverts', female minds in male bodies, or mentally degenerate, psychiatric cases, or a 'third sex', was an immediate product of the dominant intellectual outlook of the time. The nineteenth century, with its zeal for scientific classification and its belief in a natural order in human society, favoured the biological. The twentieth century with its emphasis on the role of environment in influencing the individual has, until recently, favoured the psychoanalytic explanation. But all insisted that homosexual individuals were fundamentally different in their biological or psychological constitution. This idea only made sense, however, and entered popular consciousness in the context of the domination of society by the heterosexual family, and the sharp moral distinction established between heterosexual and homosexual behaviour. Social relations established by the market determined that any expression of homosexual desire was beyond the pale. Homosexuals really were different, not as a result of their biology or psychology, but of their relationship to society.

Weeks has argued that it is reductionist to concentrate in this way on the family's essential role in capitalist social relations as the key factor in the development of sexual categories. To do so is to take no notice of the fact that the 'meanings we give to sexuality in general...are socially organised, but contradictory, sustained by a variety of languages'. David Evans is surely correct when he replies to Weeks that:

> whilst fully accepting that we are likely to encounter different sets of sexual instructions, and that a common ideological theme built in to them all is that no pattern exists, not only may such patterns be discerned so may their structural origins, their means of promulgation and their effects.[44]

Weeks is not wrong to identify a 'variety of languages'—moral, religious, legal, scientific and so on—which 'sustain' the meaning of our sexual practices for us, but he is wrong to rule out any logical structure encompassing these 'languages' and the way they are deployed by the institutions of the capitalist state and society.

The 'complex of discourses and practices' arises because there was no simple, self-evident solution to the problem posed by market relations. Precisely because the family is both necessary to and undermined by capitalist production, the sexual and procreative relations of the population had to be regulated by state intervention. Different interests had differing and even conflicting legal, scientific and moral interpretations of the problem as the social historians have shown. But the really interesting aspect of all the various reform campaigns, conflicting discourses and particular experiences is not so much their variety, but that they did coalesce to produce some fairly stable sexual categories. This was the outcome because, despite their conflicts, they were a response to the spontaneous laws of capitalist production. They provided the *external* influence required to ensure a private domestic sphere for the successful reproduction of labour-power. Whatever the particular experiences and tensions, these discourses and legal reforms were responding to a truly *social* necessity.

It was the capitalist market that made it possible to have a personal life based on sexual attraction, by weakening the former socially determined connection between sex, marriage and procreation. But it was the construction of the particular gender relations of the heterosexual family through the restriction of women to the domestic sphere which shaped the expression of that potential, and made the 'homosexual' a criminalised social marker. For a man to desire another man was the antithesis of a 'normality' implicit in capitalist social relations.

The 'camp of freedom'

It is important to recognise that the hostile attitude to homosexuality was not a mere prejudice on the part of the radical nineteenth-century moralists. From the point of view of its more socially privileged participants, the developing homosexual sub-culture represented a sphere of independence from the uptight Edwardian family. Many educated and middle class men, writing about their homosexuality during the decades of forceful repression, have told of their desire for sexual encounters and relationships with working class men. On the one hand, there was 'rough trade'; Wilde enjoyed 'feasting with panthers' and JR Ackerley searched for an 'animal man' as his 'ideal friend'.

On the other, socialist homosexuals believed in the Utopian possibilities through the propagation of what Edward Carpenter, who lived openly with his working class lover George Merrill, called Uranian love.[45]

Breaking free from the suffocating and provincial values of a domesticated sexual life is a clear theme in the early homosexual literature. The first important English novel with a homosexual theme, EM Forster's *Maurice*, ends deliriously with his hero vanishing from the stuffy world of the Edwardian upper classes in the arms of his best friend's gardener. In *Towards Democracy* Carpenter, inspired by Walt Whitman, praises the 'love of men for each other' as the 'Flag of the camp of freedom'.[46]

Homosexual desire was associated with the refusal of the procreative and domestic responsibilities demanded by the family. Male homosexuality offered the fullest available expression of the cosmopolitan and potentially limitless sexual possibilities for the individual *implicit* in a society freed from traditional constraints on personal relations. It was this that lay beneath the horror which homosexuality provoked in nineteenth-century opinion, both committed to and dependent on the success of the family for the moral regeneration and stability of the nation through the promotion of domestic responsibility.

The homosexual underworld created by the criminalisation of same-sex desire existed for more than half a century in an uneasy and often violently repressive relation to wider society. But its mere existence was ironic testimony to the artificial character of heterosexuality. And this irony was not lost on homosexuals themselves. The adoption of camp and the art of the drag queen characteristic of the mid-century gay style played on the idea of gender transgression. Camping it up was immediately a defiant statement of a person's homosexuality in a society that was reluctant to admit to the existence of such people. But camp gave an acute expression to the fact that masculinity and femininity are contrived artifices, lacking any basis in nature. The drag queen, with her aggressive caricature of femininity, mocked the conventional world for what it was—conventional. The pornography of Tom of Finland was even more subversive since, in his pictures, the macho man, once he was tied to his motorbike, ceased to fit in any unambiguous gender role at all.

No doubt the men who made up the gay world of that time, when they expressed an opinion, for the most part accepted the medical model of homosexuality or argued that they could not help what they did. Nevertheless the style adopted by many homosexuals gave the lie to the idea that there was a necessary relation between biology and heterosexual gender roles. At the same time, camp indicated the degree to which the homosexual world was a reaction to the heterosexual one. The parody of heterosexuality expressed the fact that, for all their contrivance, those roles and the social relations that

sustained them really were the 'norm'. A regular complaint among gay liberationists of the seventies was that 'for straights it is male-female, master-
mistress. For gays it is butch-femme, aggressive-passive'.[47] While the mores
and manners of the homosexual world were subversive of respectable heterosexual values and postures, they were also defined by them.

Morality and lifestyle

If the 'homosexual identity' was a reaction to the particular form of the development of heterosexuality then it is possible to see why constructionists like
Weeks privilege the gay identity and how that tends to mystify the contemporary meaning of homosexuality. It is an inescapable fact that the 'gay identity'
has 'come out', reversing the discourse of the sick, secretive, ashamed homosexual, at precisely the time when the heterosexual family is widely perceived
to be in crisis. Neither the gay community nor gay sociology have developed
in isolation from the disintegration of the heterosexual family ideal.

The problems of the 'nuclear' family have become a preoccupation, not to
say an obsession, of contemporary social commentaries. The rising rate of
divorce and single motherhood, the declining birth rate among professional
women, the perceived deficit in parenting skills, and the concern about child
abuse and domestic violence, have all led to demands for official intervention.
Moral panics about the family have reappeared accompanied by a mountain
of literature. There is a sense of the collapse of the defining features of the
family. That is not to say that real families have ceased to be a major influence
in the lives of the population, but that the status of family life has fundamentally altered as has the relationship to it of the professionals and the authorities.

The contemporary crisis of 'family values' has many immediate causes but
I suggest that the analysis developed here is useful in getting to grips with the
social forces determining them. As we have seen the connections between sex,
procreation and marriage are inherently weakened in a capitalist society.
The family is a private domestic sphere for consumption rather than a unit of
production, and so it is possible to live outside the family. The capitalist
system creates the conditions for the family but not its particular form. The
repression and poverty of life in capitalist society places the family under systematic stress as the private sphere is forced to compensate for the agonies of
work—and no work. Furthermore, in the twentieth century, the drive towards
a more flexible and part-time workforce has undercut the view of work as a male
preserve with the woman's place in the home. The tendency, with greater overall unemployment, to employ women as a source of cheap labour has undermined the sexual division of labour established in the nineteenth century.

As John Costello and John D'Emilio have argued, although changing attitudes and values regarding sex and the family only became the subject of widespread public debate in the seventies, the underlying changes in women's and homosexuals' experience of the labour market, sex and marriage occurred during and after the Second World War as women entered the workplace.[48]

The changes in heterosexual relationships are well-known and undeniable. The postwar period has seen a transformation in attitudes to heterosexual sex, with the taboos against adultery, premarital sex and single motherhood disappearing. The provision of effective contraceptives and the legalisation of abortion have reflected these changes. The public discussion and celebration of sex has become the major motif of popular culture, particularly among the young. This culminated in the so-called sexual revolution of the 1960s.

The most important development has been the changing status of marriage. In Britain in the decade between 1961 and 1971 the divorce rate trebled (reflecting the easing of the divorce laws in 1969, but indicative of the demand) and the remarriage rate climbed steeply in the early seventies indicating the new trend towards 'serial monogamy'. Where in the early sixties 86 per cent of marriages were first marriages, this had declined to 65 per cent by the mid-eighties. Similarly more people started to cohabit outside of marriage. Live births outside marriage increased by 25 per cent in the sixties.[49] And these tendencies have continued to the present day. The figures for illegitimate births show the reduced status of marriage today. In 1992 a full 31 per cent of births were to unmarried mothers. While the number of sole mothers has increased only slightly since the 1960s, the number of 'illegitimate' children registered under a joint name has roughly quadrupled.[50]

It is not that people have stopped getting married, rather that they have stopped believing that marriage and a family are necessarily for life. The changing attitudes towards the family in Britain have been mirrored in the changing relationship to the church.[51] Religion had been an important factor in the claimed moral superiority of heterosexuality over homosexuality, since religious sanction gave the married state an absolute moral status out of the reach of homosexual relationships however 'responsible' they were in other respects.

Today the tendency towards serial monogamy and a much more provisional coupling is unmistakable. The sacred character of marriage has given way to what Anthony Giddens terms the 'pure relationship'. Two people may or may not be married but the relationship 'is entered into for its own sake, for what can be derived by each person from a sustained association with another; and which is continued only in so far as it is thought by both parties to deliver enough satisfactions for each individual to stay within it'.[52] When heterosexual relationships can be characterised in this way, the contrast with the late nineteenth century could not be more striking.

In these circumstances, when marriage is no longer assumed to be for life and heterosexual relations are regarded as contingent and dependent solely on immediate desires, then the heterosexual family can no longer claim to be either the natural form of sexual relations nor even the moral norm. Once serial monogamy among heterosexuals is regarded as an acceptable way of life, the moral basis for the stigma attached to homosexual relationships is fatally weakened. The idea that homosexuals are the 'archetypal sexed being' or that gay men are 'corrupters of youth' becomes increasingly indefensible when every teenager is obsessed with their sex life and the problems of heterosexual 'immorality' are the constant diet of public and political life. Old-fashioned hysteria about homosexuals is now widely regarded as sheer prejudice, because it increasingly has the character of mere prejudice, as homosexual and heterosexual lives become increasingly similar. By the early 1970s it had become possible for people openly to declare their homosexuality and get by, even prosper. They still experienced widespread and vicious discrimination, but the ideological basis of stigma was already in decline.

The insight of social constructionism is that the heterosexual family was artificial and contingent, and so was homosexuality. However, by avoiding the question of the determination of sexualities, social constructionists have missed the reactive character of the homosexual identity and therefore the significance of heterosexuality's contemporary transformation in the rise of the gay identity. *The gay movement emerged at a time when the absolute moral status of the family had already been compromised.*

Moreover that compromise had long been anticipated by the authorities in relation to homosexuality. Aware in the forties and fifties of the weak grip of the old moral certainties and prohibitions, sections of the establishment attempted to deal with the problem through reform. It was apparent that thousands of homosexual men were put outside the law by what was at that time widely considered to be a mental illness. In 1957 the Wolfenden Committee on Homosexual Offences and Prostitution was to recommend that the old gross indecency law criminalising all homosexual acts be changed. Wolfenden proposed this change on the basis that:

> Unless a deliberate attempt is to be made by society, acting through the agency of the law, to equate the sphere of crime with that of sin, there must remain a realm of private morality and immorality which is not the law's business.[53]

Society might be agreed that homosexuality was always wrong, but in a democracy, private sexual behaviour had to be left up to the individual. After 10 years of rearguard resistance by the crustier sections of the British establishment, the argument was eventually conceded. The partial decriminalisation of male homosexual acts in private took place in the Sexual Offences Act of 1967. Of course the parliamentarians who saw through the 1967 law reform did not anticipate today's assertive gay community. In fact, as Lord Arran, one of the act's supporters, famously declared in parliament: 'I ask those who have as it were been in bondage and for whom the prison doors are now open to show their thanks by comporting themselves quietly and with dignity.' But by the late sixties it was to prove very difficult to prevent a lot of noisy queers coming out of the closet and demanding their place in the sun. A few years later, emboldened by the reforms of the sixties, the gay liberation movement started to shout from the rooftops what the establishment had hoped would be accepted 'quietly and with dignity'—that the authorities had tacitly abandoned their insistence on the absolute moral supremacy of the family: they had relativised sexual morality.

Foucault's idea of a 'reverse' discourse is apposite because gay liberation enthusiastically reversed the moral terms. Where previously homosexuals had been thought of as diseased, by 1972 American therapist George Weinberg had coined the now popular term homophobia, suggesting that it was heterosexual bigots who had a psychological problem since they were unable to accept the real diversity of human desire.[54] But in reversing the moral terms, the emergent gay communities implicitly accepted the moral framework. The toleration of diversity was not a new idea; more than a decade before the Gay Liberation Front donned a nun's habit or zapped a psychiatry conference, the British authorities seriously started to consider tolerating a bit of sexual diversity and this toleration had been codified in law three years before the appearance of an 'out' gay movement. The toleration of diversity based on Wolfenden's distinctions between public and private set the terms on which gays came out of the closet, the parameters which have shaped the gay identity.

The gay scene which emerged in the wake of gay liberation in the early seventies was to prove the enduring product of that reform. Out homosexuals moved to set up clubs, manage pubs, found newspapers, stores and self-help groups which today are known as the gay community. The pink economy and its attendant 'identity' remained ghettoised, developing within the spirit if not within the letter of the 1967 Act. The arena in which homosexuals were free to express their desires remained restricted to selected venues, holiday resorts, the privacy of their own homes or, more recently, a few central districts of larger cities. More precisely, homosexuality was increasingly redefined as a lifestyle, a pattern of private consumption choices organised around sexuality, in what Evans has referred to as 'secondary, discrete and "private" (in the sense of hidden from public view) markets, consumable identities, lifestyles and communities, justified on the grounds of natural disqualification or moral threat, but exploitable...all the same'.[55]

This is not to suggest that homosexuals played no part in the changes that have occurred. Activists undoubtedly played an important role in the reform of the law in Britain. The Homosexual Law Reform Society spent years discreetly lobbying politicians and experts in the wake of the Wolfenden report. The contrasting confrontational style and assertiveness of the gay liberationists also had a major impact. But the relativisation of sexual morality that permitted the reform and conditioned the forming of the gay community has tended to be obscured. It was a process rooted not in the lives of homosexuals, but in the declining moral authority of the 'family values' of heterosexual monogamy.

Most social constructionists have been aware of the way in which the terms of reform have maintained the difference between homosexual and heterosexual by segregating the gay lifestyle into a discrete social space created for homosexual desire. But they have taken little interest in the fact that as the married state ceased to be regarded as a sacred institution, the *sine qua non* of respectability, and became a question of lifestyle, so homosexuality ceased to be a profanity, a disease, or a subversive expression of cosmopolitan desire defined in opposition to respectability.[56]

Privileging the gay identity

The paradox of gay liberation and the privileging of the gay identity by social constructionists can be understood in this context. By the 1970s it had become hard to deny the artificial character of sexual categories. The relativisation of sexual morality exposed the contingency of these identities and opened them up to renegotiation. This process permitted the transformation in the meaning of the category homosexual from a stigma to a proudly asserted identity. Lesbians and gay men experienced this transformation in their own lives, providing compelling evidence for the idea that the categories of sexuality are not grounded in nature. Gay thinkers were drawn to the constructionist insights of Anglo-American sociology or French post-structuralism.

To the social constructionists, it appears that it was the claims of the lesbian and gay community that demolished the supremacy of the family. The experience, however, of 'coming out', while compelling in itself, formed a narrow basis for understanding the transformation of homosexuality's social significance. From the standpoint of the gay experience, it appeared that by making their own use of the arbitrary definitions of sexual discourse and challenging the sexual absolutism of the heterosexual family, the former 'deviants' were clearing the way for a plural sexual order. The wider social transformation in which the moral authority of the family was in severe decline has not been probed to the same extent by gay constructionists. Reviewing the debate between essentialist and constructionist positions Weeks argues that:

> The 'sexual outlaws' of old have constructed a way of life, or more accurately ways of life, which have reversed the expectations of sexology. They have disrupted the categorisations of received texts and have become thinking, acting, living subjects in the historical process.[57]

But homosexuals have not changed the terms of society's moral order, nor have they voluntaristically made up their own community as they went along. On the contrary, it is the way in which society as a whole has retreated from its former moral absolutes which has 'conditioned' the emergent gay 'identity'. The expectations of sexology have been reversed by the inability of the heterosexual gender relations of the bourgeois family to reproduce themselves as the socially accepted norm. The actions of homosexuals have helped to give form to this failure and exhaustion of the old order in a way that has radically altered the lives of many who identify as lesbian or gay. For conservatives the rise of the gay community, the confident assertion of gay demands, is the most striking manifestation of the lost authority of their family values. For this reason the struggle around gay rights was a central aspect of the failed right-wing backlash of the 1980s. But the changing forms of homosexual identity exist only in relation to the predominant forms of heterosexuality.

Social constructionism is the orthodoxy in the study of sexuality for good reason. The social significance and meaning of the categories of sexuality and homosexuality in particular have indeed been transformed since the 1960s. Social constructionism is the reflection of that change in thought.

With the exhaustion of the Reagan/Thatcher backlash of the 1980s in the 'Back to basics' fiasco in Britain and the debacle over abortion policy on the American right, the defenders of the old determining moral framework have finally thrown in the towel. Today even the established church can no longer sustain the idea that it is necessary for heterosexuals to be married nor can it uphold the concept of 'living in sin'. The moral predominance of the bourgeois family norm is in danger of giving way entirely to an uncertain plurality of possible lifestyles.

In these circumstances it is not surprising that the gay identity seems to be prospering in the 1990s. But the more that the gay identity is celebrated, the more that its old meaning and coherence are dissipating in reality. Precisely because the homosexual was a reaction to heterosexual monogamy, the change in heterosexual relations has transformed but also undermined the basis for the gay identity. This may appear counter-intuitive when there is a thriving gay community made up of many diverse homosexualities, from the leather queens of provincial clubs to the fashionable queers of Soho's coffee bars. But along with the proliferation of gay lifestyles, the collapse of the moral authority of the old order has had ironic consequences.

There is a marked tendency in the 1990s for gay identity and gay rights to appear less as a question of sexual practices and more as one of moral worth. This development is clear in both the radical 'queer' wing of gay thought and the more moderate advocates of the 'gay community'.

In his concise introduction to queer theory, Moe Meyer explains that queer is about denying any social identity; it is a celebration of surfaces and the 'performance' through which any identity is manifested. For Meyer, 'postures, costume and dress, and speech acts become the elements that constitute both the identity and the identity performance'. What about sex? Queer identity according to Meyer 'is no longer based and does not have to be, upon material sexual practices'.[58] Similarly Michael Signorile, the American queer activist who pioneered the tactic of 'outing' public figures argues that 'by outing we do not discuss anyone's sex life. We only say that they're gay'.[59] Despite their many differences, on this point, the conservative Andrew Sullivan, gay editor of *New Republic*, agrees with Signorile:

> There's increasingly no reason to infer that because someone says she is a lesbian, she is actually engaging in any sexual activity...there's no reason to infer anything about the actual state of her love life, her sexual practices, or her predisposition towards this or that private activity.[60]

Sullivan supports the conclusion that sexual activity is now marginal to gay 'identity' when he points out that: 'No longer is the gay debate framed in terms of promiscuity, sexual practices, discretion and revolt.'[61]

In parallel with the declining importance of sex in the presentation of the gay identity, gay activists have reacted to the collapse of the old moral order by seizing the moral high ground. This is an explicit aspect of the 'outing' campaigns. Michael Signorile in the USA and Peter Tatchell in Britain, in outing or threatening to out politicians, state officials or religious leaders, have castigated establishment hypocrisy and demanded that the rich and powerful live up to *gay* standards of honesty and personal integrity by coming out.[62] Tatchell has taken this idea furthest by suggesting that gay men's identity and behaviour are simply morally superior to the violent, loutish masculinity of straight men.[63]

The more moderate wing of gay politics eschews the radically moralistic stance of the outers, preferring instead to present its case in the terms of traditional conservatism. Andrew Sullivan sums this up concisely in the wake of the campaign for the right to serve in the US military:

The gay rights movements should be renamed. From now on call it the gay responsibilities movement. Homosexuals are demanding...the responsibility of conducting our emotional and sexual lives on the same basis as heterosexuals; the responsibility of serving our country honourably and openly in the military; the responsibility of committing ourselves to one other person in perpetuity in marriage.[64]

Whether in a radical or a moderate form, when gay activism presents its case as a demand for social responsibility, the outlaw sexuality has turned full circle.

It seems the protracted decline of the miserable moralistic absolutism of compulsory lifelong heterosexual monogamy has robbed the gay 'identity' of the subversive and cosmopolitan implications that once set it apart: it is becoming another lifestyle among many. When compared to past struggles against oppression, the assertion of this lifestyle today already involves very different, often conservative, arguments, with very different, often elitist, implications. These changes in the character and meaning of homosexuality could have a significant impact on society. To understand them it will be necessary to recognise the limitations of social construction theory which is itself a product of the same social changes that are transforming sexual relations.

NOTES

1   Angela Mason, *Stonewall 25*, Virago, 1994, p3

2   Michel Foucault, *History of Sexuality*, Vol1, Allan Lane, 1979, pp15-51

3   Carole S Vance 'Social construction theory: problems in the history of sexuality', in Dennis Altman *et al*, *Homosexuality, Which Homosexuality?*, Gay Men's Press, 1989, p18

4   I am indebted to ideas and suggestions from James Heartfield and Frank Füredi during the preparation of this chapter.

5   My argument here is based on the development of male homosexuality. The development of lesbianism has its own specific elements which I do not deal with here.

6   David M Halperin, 'Is there a history of sexuality?', *History and Theory*, Vol28, 1989, quoted in Henry Abelove, Michèle Aina Barale, David M Halperin (Eds), *The Lesbian and Gay Studies Reader*, Routledge, 1993, pp416-31

7   See Jeffrey Weeks, *Coming Out*, Quartet Books, 1990, pp11-32

8   Jeffrey Weeks, *Sex, Politics and Society*, Longman, 1989, p99

9   Richard von Krafft-Ebing, *Psychopathia Sexualis: Sexual Aberration*, 1965, p318

10 Freud himself was both ambivalent towards the idea that homosexuality was inborn and to the assumption that it was necessarily a sickness. Freud's own conception of 'polymorphous perversity' and the absence of a clear distinction between the different components of sexual desire has been influential in undermining the idea that homosexuality is a fixed condition. See Sigmund Freud, *On Sexuality: Three Essays on the Theory of Sexuality and Other Works*, (Angela Richards Ed) Penguin, 1977, especially pp56-58. American Freudian psychotherapy, on the other hand, was notorious for its attempts to 'cure' homosexuals.

11 Frank Mort, *Dangerous Sexualities: Medico-Moral Politics in England since 1830*, Routledge & Kegan Paul, 1987

12 Jeffrey Weeks, *Coming Out*, Quartet Books, 1990; see also M Ramelson, 'The fight against the Contagious Diseases Act', *Marxism Today*, June 1964.

13 Jeffrey Weeks, 'Discourse, desire and sexual deviance', in Jeffrey Weeks, *Against Nature: Essays in History, Sexuality and Identity*, Rivers Oram Press, 1991, p41

14 Havelock Ellis cited in Jeffrey Weeks, *Coming Out*, Quartet Books, 1990, p22

15 This insight is derived from the interactionist school of sociology which is one of social constructionism's major influences. See for example Kenneth Plummer, *Sexual Stigma: An Interactionist Account*, Routledge & Kegan Paul, 1975

16 Jeffrey Weeks, *Coming Out*, Quartet Books, 1990, p6

17 Bryan Palmer, *Descent into Discourse: The Reification of Language and the Writing of Social History*, Temple University Press, 1990, p169

18 Bryan Palmer, *Descent into Discourse: The Reification of Language and the Writing of Social History*, Temple University Press, 1990, p169

19 For an example of Weeks 'privileging' the gay identity: 'It is [the gay] community, in all its diversity and complexity, rather than a narrowly political movement...which has become the real actor on the stage of history.' Jeffrey Weeks, *Coming Out*, Quartet Books, 1990, p*xiii*

20 Jeffrey Weeks, 'Against nature', in Jeffrey Weeks, *Against Nature: Essays in History, Sexuality and Identity*, Rivers Oram Press, 1991, pp94-95

21 Jeffrey Weeks, 'Discourse, desire and sexual deviance' in Jeffrey Weeks, *Against Nature: Essays in History, Sexuality and Identity*, Rivers Oram Press, 1991

22 Kenneth Plummer (Ed), *Modern Homosexualities: Fragments of Lesbian and Gay Experience*, Routledge, 1992, p7

23 Martha Shelly, 'Gay is good', reprinted in Karla Jay and Allen Young (Eds), *Out of the Closet: Voices of Gay Liberation*, Gay Men's Press, 1992, p34

24 Dennis Altman, *Homosexual Oppression and Liberation*, Allan Lane, 1974, p247

25 Kenneth Plummer (Ed), *The Making of the Modern Homosexual*, Hutchinson, 1981, p29

26 Michel Foucault, *History of Sexuality*, Vol1, Allen Lane, 1979, p101

27 David M Halperin, 'Is there a history of sexuality?', *History and Theory*, Vol28, 1989, quoted in Henry Abelove, Michèle Aina Barale, David M Halperin (Eds), *The Lesbian and Gay Studies Reader*, Routledge, 1993, p417

28 Steve Epstein, 'Gay politics, ethnic identity: the limits of social construction' in *Unfinished Business: 20 Years of Socialist Review*, Verso, 1991, p78

29 John D'Emilio, 'Capitalism and the gay identity', in John D'Emilio, *Making Trouble: Essays on Gay History, Politics and the University*, Routledge, 1992, p3

30 See Philippe Aries, *Centuries of Childhood*, Penguin, 1973

31 Karl Marx, *Capital*, Vol1, Lawrence & Wishart, 1974, p166

32 John D'Emilio, 'Capitalism and the gay identity' in John D'Emilio, *Making Trouble: Essays on Gay History, Politics and the University*, Routledge, 1992, p12

33 Karl Marx, *Capital*, Vol1, Lawrence & Wishart, 1974, p172

34 Karl Marx, *Capital*, Vol1, Lawrence & Wishart, 1974, p537

35 For a more detailed discussion of the connection between capitalist production and domestic work see Paul Smith, 'Domestic labour and Marx's theory of value', in Annette Kuhn and Ann-Marie Wolpe, *Feminism and Materialism: Women and Modes of Production*, Routledge & Kegan Paul, 1978, and 'Women's oppression under capitalism', *Revolutionary Communist Papers*, No5, 1976, pp7-9.

36 (Emphasis added) Paul Smith, 'Domestic labour and Marx's theory of value', in Annette Kuhn and Ann-Marie Wolpe, *Feminism and Materialism: Women and Modes of Production*, Routledge & Kegan Paul, 1978, p214

37 Edward Shorter, *The Making of the Modern Family*, Collins, 1976, p15

38 Frank Mort, *Dangerous Sexualities: Medico-Moral Politics in England since 1830*, Routledge & Kegan Paul, 1987, p78

39 See L Hay Cooper, *Josephine Butler and Her Work for Social Purity*, SPCK, 1922

40 Jeffrey Weeks, *Sex, Politics and Society: The Regulation of Sexuality since 1800*, Longman, 1989, p106

41 Jeffrey Weeks, *Sex, Politics and Society: The Regulation of Sexuality since 1800*, Longman, 1989, p107

42 Jane Lewis, *Women in England 1870-1950: Sexual Division and Social Change*, Wheatsheaf, 1984, p3

43 Mary McIntosh, 'The homosexual role', in Kenneth Plummer (Ed), *The Making of the Modern Homosexual,* Hutchinson, 1981, p32

44 David T Evans, *Sexual Citizenship: the Material Construction of Sexualities,* Routledge, 1993, p32

45 See JR Ackerley, *My Father and Myself,* Pimlico, 1968 or Christopher Isherwood, *Christopher and his Kind 1929-39,* Eyre Methuen, 1977

46 Edward Carpenter, *Selected Writings: Vol1, Sex,* Gay Men's Press, 1984, p61

47 NA Diaman, 'On sex roles and equality', in Karla Jay and Allen Young (Eds), *Out of the Closets: Voices of Gay Liberation,* Gay Men's Press, 1992, p262

48 See John Costello, *Love, Sex and War: Changing Values 1939-45,* Collins, 1985, and John D'Emilio, *Sexual Politics, Sexual Communities: The Making of a Homosexual Minority in the United States, 1940-70,* University of Chicago Press, 1983

49 See *Social Trends,* HMSO, 1986, pp38-41

50 See *Social Trends,* HMSO, 1994, p40

51 See *Social Trends,* HMSO, 1986, p175

52 Anthony Giddens, *The Transformation of Intimacy: Sexuality, Love and Eroticism in Modern Societies,* Polity, 1992, p58

53 Report of the Wolfenden Committee

54 George Weinberg, *Society and the Healthy Homosexual,* Collin Smythe, 1975

55 David Evans, '(Homo)sexual citizenship: a queer kind of justice', in Angelia Wilson (Ed), *A Simple Matter of Justice: Theorising Lesbian and Gay Politics,* Cassell, 1995, p122

56 I am not suggesting that, as homosexuality becomes a question of lifestyle, lesbians and gay men will necessarily be granted full legal, let alone social, equality. In fact, as I have argued elsewhere, the 1967 compromise, still the legal framework for the gay scene in Britain, specifically precludes equality. See Peter Ray, 'A private affair', *Living Marxism,* No65, March 1994

57 Jeffrey Weeks, *Sexuality and Its Discontents: Meanings, Myths and Modern Sexualities,* Routledge & Kegan Paul, 1985, pp200-201

58 Moe Meyer (Ed), *The Politics and Poetics of Camp,* Routledge, 1994, p4

59 Michael Signorile, *Queer in America,* Abacus, 1994, p80

60 Andrew Sullivan, *Virtually Normal: An Argument about Homosexuality,* Picador, 1995

61 Andrew Sullivan, *The Independent,* 8 June 1995

62 See Peter Ray, 'Out with the old', *Living Marxism,* No79, May 1995

63 'Can any socially aware person doubt that our society would be an infinitely more pleasant, cultured place to live with fewer heterosexual men around? There'd be vastly less racial violence, gang warfare, wife-beating, and late-night brawling. With an increased proportion of gay men, society would be a lot more calm and peaceful, not to mention caring and creative. This homosexualisation of male culture is, quite obviously, in the public interest.' Peter Tatchell, *We Don't Want to March Straight: Masculinity, Queers and the Military,* Cassell, 1995, p16

64 Andrew Sullivan, *The Independent,* 8 June 1995

8
Political Internet? What a Wondrous Web we weave

Keith Teare

A human life is relatively short, let's say 100 years to be optimistic. As one generation follows another, each has unique experiences that together shape its view of the world. Each decade gives rise to moods and opinions that are in many ways quite different to those of earlier times. Historians are familiar with this process and seek to give labels to each era in human development. The Renaissance, the Dark Ages, the war years, the slump, the postwar boom, the years of revolution, and so on. These labels are readily available tags through which we sum up our overview of the world at a particular moment. They are one-dimensional and for those who look in more detail they are no doubt such sweeping generalisations that they become highly inaccurate. Nonetheless, these generalisations survive because they speak to the real experiences of people who lived through the era itself.

In summing up the present decade, there are already any number of labels available to choose from: the knowledge society, the information age, post-Fordism (the end of mass industrial society), the postmodern age and so on. Historians, journalists, politicians and large institutions are all examining the changing patterns of the society we jointly inhabit and are seeking to coin terms adequate to sum up those patterns, and adequate enough to survive as descriptions. The Internet figures prominently in almost every discussion of the contemporary world.

The explosion of interest in the Internet has given rise to considerable political interest in it. The net is said to embody a culture of optimism and defiance that stands in contrast to the ideas of the 1970s and 1980s, and to some extent represents a challenge to them. It is unlikely that there has ever been a technology that has been the focus for so much political discussion.

Technology and change

One of the great contributions to rational post-enlightenment thought was Marx's *Preface to a Contribution to a Critique of Political Economy* written in 1859:

> At a certain stage of development, the material productive forces of society come into conflict with the existing relations of production or—this merely expresses the same thing in legal terms—with the property relations within the framework of which they have operated hitherto. From forms of development of the productive forces these relations turn into their fetters. Then begins an era of social revolution. The changes in the economic foundation lead sooner or later to the transformation of the whole immense superstructure.[1]

Although brief, and highly concentrated, this little passage retains all of its validity in highlighting the connection between changes in technology and in human organisation (the material productive forces) and the need for social change.

Innovative technical development that benefits the human race is unambiguously welcomed, even when its implementation is partial, or even non-existent. In fact the point is more aggressive than this. In so far as the society is *incapable* of delivering the potential of innovation, it is a *fetter* on progress, there lies the main argument for social change.

There is no hint of the cynic in these remarks. I have no intention to deride the potential of technology nor underestimate its possible impact. The sole conclusion is that if the benefits of technology are hindered by social structure, then the social structure needs replacing in order for technical progress to occur.

Unfortunately many modern commentators are unable to avoid either blind faith in technology or a dour pessimism about its ability to deliver progress. Richard Hoggart, writing in the *New Statesman and Society*, tries very hard to avoid sounding like a Luddite, but ends up complaining that the Internet:

> can now be seen as the latest form of weightless progressivism fixated on an ever-receding future, which is yet felt to be going to produce its own meaning. If only we pursue it far enough, some sort of meaning will emerge from it without pain on our part. We can entirely retire from making those painful choices with which life presents us; the Internet will do it for us. The ultimate leveller becomes the ultimate lowerer.[2]

Hoggart's contention is that humanity is losing its ability to speak and use language. The Internet, along with the telephone, television and probably conversation (I jest) are held responsible for a lowering of literary standards. The *mechanism* of communication is blamed for the poverty of its quality.

James Woudhuysen, writing for *Demos*, makes the same point in stating that it is by no means clear that dreams about superhighways are worth dreaming:

Such dreams can speak of narrow horizons—of a vision which, expansive though it is in rhetoric, is fundamentally cramped. Sometimes nightmarish, frequently myopic, dreams about superhighways forget the old computer adage: Rubbish in, rubbish out. It is human beings and human inputs, not inanimate highways, which will determine the fate of the Earth.[3]

The latter sentence contains a truth that is certainly pertinent. However the two sentences preceding it are essentially identical to Hoggart's sentiments. There is an expectation that a means of communication ought to contain an imperative towards excellence in its content. The technology is blamed for the dearth of quality. This is akin to blaming the cathode ray tube for *Coronation Street* and Bruce Forsyth. In truth the cultural decline of the last century has little to do with medium and everything to do with stasis in society. The Internet, acting as a catalyst for a discussion that questions the society we live in, ought considerably to liven up content too. Whether it does or does not has more to do with people than the Internet.

The real problem with the Internet isn't poor content. Nor is it over-ambitious claims by its advocates. Rather, it is the lack of real investment going into developing it. To be fair, Woudhuysen makes this point very well in his largely excellent *Demos* article. Talk about an information superhighway is in stark contrast to reality. The Internet is largely held together with cabling systems that are entirely inadequate to deliver its promise. While a surgeon in a leading London hospital can use the Internet to see an operation being performed in Belfast, and to assist in its outcome, this is exceptional. Most Internet users would be unable to receive adequate sound or video along the Internet. Many more don't have access to the Internet at all. If the Internet is ever to be more than a pipe-dream then significant investment in infrastructure needs to take place.

The second problem concerns the market in information. While there are high-quality communications across the world, we are also seeing a growth in the purchase of information providers by large companies. The likely outcome is that those who use the Internet will be expected to pay for the information it delivers. The information age will reach only those who can afford it, and will bypass those—the majority—who cannot.

What does the Internet represent?

The Internet is significant. Technical inventions and social change go hand-in-hand, although not always in harmony. The developments like the printing press and the telescope enabled new understandings, new ways of producing things and so challenged the old order. Bertolt Brecht summed this up in his play *Life of Galileo*. When Galileo invented the telescope and said the celestial spheres don't exist, the Pope's inquisitor feared the abolition of 'top and bottom' in the social world too.[4] And social change was necessary for the full potential of these inventions to be realised. With the new social arrangements the pace of technical change could increase. A new society which was more fluid and mobile could develop concepts like energy flows and then harness them for further development. Social change unleashes the power of new technology. Such social change can be readily seen as beneficial by those who yearn for the new.

So what about the Internet? Should we be optimistic about it? Does it demand social change in order to have its potential realised?

Let us begin by asserting that the Internet contains much that would benefit the globe. At its heart it is a model for communication that would allow every individual on the planet to be in touch with any other. The forms of this communication are not limited to voice or text or still and moving images—it can encompass them all. Its adoption on any scale would have the potential to make a remarkable and beneficial impact on many aspects of the way we live.

The Internet could also have a dramatic impact on our experience of the world. Already the fact that it is a global system means that it introduces its users to a less parochial environment. The fact that its early adopters are critical of the established means of communication, commerce and decision-making means that it is intellectually vibrant and refreshingly adventurous. The fact that it is, on the whole, free from government control makes it attractive to those with a libertarian outlook. Opposition to censorship forms one of the driving instincts of Internet people.

It is also true that various vested interests feel threatened by the Internet. Governments, which have no jurisdiction over material originating outside of their borders, are nervously looking for legal remedies to global information flows. Banks and treasuries which print local currencies are worried that global forms of exchange, outside of their control, might be used on a growing scale, threatening national economic strategies. Newspapers and TV stations are concerned that the ease with which individuals can become publishers to a global audience may undermine their media empires. Educational institutions are concerned at the ease with which education might be delivered without them. The key question in many of Britain's board and committee rooms is fast becoming, 'What is our Internet strategy?'.

Internet optimism meets nineties cynicism

It almost doesn't matter whether the Internet is likely to deliver on the hopes that many people invest in it, as, for the time being, it focuses on the aspirations of millions. The optimism among Internet users contrasts starkly with the general pessimism in society.

The last optimistic US president was probably John F Kennedy, the last optimistic UK prime minister was Harold Wilson, both 1960s phenomena. Since then the watchword of most governments has been economic caution, cutbacks in government spending and aggression in foreign policy.

Those born during the 1960s and entering their teens towards the end of the seventies became the cynical generation. Their attitudes are summed up in the songs of the Smiths or in the suicide of Kurt Cobain. Society gave them little to celebrate and in turn they rejected society, albeit in a very private way. To this generation 'big ideas' were simply boring—because they were unbelievable. The 'isms' of the 1960s—Marxism, Leninism, Anarchism, Situationism—no longer have the power to motivate they once had. They have given way to a more individual, private yearning for something better. Politics gave way to therapy as the best way to deal with an unfriendly world.

The Internet has become a focus for the new young. The new young are to be found in all age groups. At the *Cyberia* café in London's Whitfield Street we run a senior cybernauts programme for the over 60s and the demand is such that we can't fit them all in. The new young are those from all generations who remain inspired by the prospects for the future. The Internet inspires the romantic and the dreamer. It speaks to the things we would like to be able to do and it even makes some of them possible.

The catalyst for this explosion is the World Wide Web. By its sheer scope and its simplicity it delivers the type of applications that fulfil the promise that the Internet has long contained.

Inside each of us there is a conservative and an adventurous side. Even the most inward-looking, cynical and insecure of us carries a secret desire to be confident, and optimistic. For 20 years or more there has been no readily available means for the adventurer in each of us to come out. Everything happening in society confirmed the sense in being cynical. The Internet has cut through the cynicism—although there is still much of it about—and has given a real world reason for being optimistic. There is something to feel good about. It is rather like the moon landing and its impact a quarter of a century ago. Now we can all be a bit more adventurous. We can get on-line and experience it for ourselves.

The desire for a better world, the need to be optimistic and confident is very strong. It goes right to the heart of what we are about as human beings.

That is why the Internet bandwagon is so unstoppable. It represents a means of self-fulfilment for millions. In short, it is a rebellion against mediocrity and low expectations taking place in the very heart of modern society. It is people, grabbing the opportunity to extend themselves, and expressing the desire to experience something bigger and better than they had before.

The wonders of the Web

The World Wide Web is a pretty good acronym to describe the Internet as a whole. A series of cables and satellite links covering the planet which, like a real spiders web, is relatively invulnerable to failure. There is always a way to travel from point A to point B even if one part of the web is temporarily out of order, or needs rebuilding. The traffic (*aka* the spider) can always take another route.

Beyond this, the Web brings to the Internet a front door through which everybody can walk. It is the Internet's equivalent of the Venus fly trap. Like the fly, we are lured in and seduced into going further. The availability of knowledge in a readily accessible and clearly presented form is irresistible. Unlike the fly trap there is no sting in the tail. The World Wide Web proves to be a sheer delight. It delivers its promise of a truly global and instant means of receiving and sending information. Like an interactive newspaper, everyone can read and see each others' films, words and even sounds, and then instantly add to the letters pages and pin their reviews on electronic noticeboards. Everyone, from the Zapatista guerrillas to the US government can be on-line—and the Zapatista's newspaper is instantly available all over the world, not just in Mexico.

We are probably at the very start of the development of the Internet. The Web is similar to that period in the history of television when it was still in monochrome. I remember my parents telling me how, despite the fact that the picture was pretty poor, and the programmes were disastrous, they would sit and look at the box in the corner for hours on end. Why? Because they were stunned that anything at all came out of the box. The Internet and the Web in particular are at that early stage.

Most of the people who come to *Cyberia* are first time users of the Internet. Indeed that is why we have a *Cyberia*—to make the net accessible to all in a welcoming surrounding. The one thing they all say, usually when the first page is delivered to them instantly from Japan or the USA or Brazil, is an expression of wonderment that information from so far away is here 'now!'. The very fact that we have this global connection with governments, libraries, hobbyists, political parties and politicians, companies, information services, campaign groups and many others, instantly available, is itself a thing to be astounded by.

But watch this space, as they say, there is more and better to come. How long will it be until it is normal to have your own personal newsletter on the web, available instantly worldwide? How long until that is the main way we speak to each other? One thing is certain—it won't be very long. It is already possible to replace the telephone with an Internet connection and by so doing conduct long-distance telephone calls for the cost of a local call.

In *Cyberia* we are developing on-line services that are providing useful tools for the users of the Web. For example, we have an interactive job centre and also an interactive dating agency. These are free services. These are already used by people all over the world.

The Web is at the heart of the Internet explosion because it is truly amazing while being effective and useful. But more than that it is also perceived as a threat by many vested interests. The Web threatens to replace traditional methods of delivering information—bulletin boards, newspapers, perhaps even radio and TV. The Web also threatens the banking and finance communities. Its promise to deliver global trading and possibly an international currency sends a shiver down the spine of your average bank executive. The fact that there are no national borders on the Internet and no laws capable of regulating it is a worry to governments which, consequently, feel threatened by its growth. Its ability to give the individual access to global information means that local tyrants are unable to control who knows what. Both the British and US governments have participated in a G7 summit specifically intended to examine ways of controlling the Internet and the Web.

These threats to traditional institutions are wonderful. The new generations discovering the world through the Web are pretty unimpressed with those institutions in the first place. They are a cosmopolitan lot. Their experiences of travel and literature already make them suspicious of a narrow national outlook. The Web allows users to meet people from across the globe, and romance them, or do business with them, or simply exchange ideas with them. Who needs national governments, media tycoons, banks and regulatory bodies getting in the way? The Web is a vehicle for ambitious ideas about a different world, one in which the individual has real power to influence events. Of course, the Web cannot deliver these things by itself, that needs people questioning, and rejecting, authority more widely. But it is a way of seeing a world without borders here and now. As such it allows us to imagine the future, or at least a preferred version of it.

What should we make of it all?

Any successful new phenomenon tends to produce an extreme response in society. The Internet is no exception.

On the one hand there are the pessimists who perceive the entire system as a fad, and predict that it will never be more than a hobbyist's dream. Impending doom is forecast, where the traffic flowing down the Internet begins to mirror that on the infamous M25 motorway around London—that is to say, at a standstill. We are also told that the Internet will become a highway into our homes for all kinds of outrageous material that we would universally disapprove of, or perhaps even a super-snooper network through which governments can gain knowledge about us and our habits.

On the other hand, there are the optimists who encourage the belief that the Internet will change the world, that governments will fall and give way to an Internet-style global democracy. We will all be voting by Internet within a matter of months, and it won't be too soon until every home is wired up to a new information superhighway. The soothsayers and the dreamers, we might call them.

The Internet often gets a bad press: porn shocks, paedophile rings, bomb-making advice and so on. Indeed, I would say that well over 70 per cent of all the TV, radio and newspaper interviews I have done in the past year focus on these types of 'stories'. With the vast range of interests that are threatened by the growth of the Web it isn't surprising that many are prepared to go on the record to condemn the whole thing. But there is a wider reason behind the pessimism.

One of the most striking things about the society of the late 1990s is that we are all bombarded daily with messages implying that we are at risk from each other. The greatest focus for this impression is the discussion of crime but there are also many others. We are persuaded that the very act of walking down the street may lead to an unpleasant experience at the hands of a mugger. Even a pleasant experience like sex is now closely associated with risk. We are told that casual relationships may lead to disastrous personal consequences. That very nice person could actually be carrying a killer disease, so look out. Food is often portrayed as a danger—cholesterol can kill—so don't eat too much rich food. Almost any new phenomenon is greeted with a frightened response.

The pessimists give the Internet this treatment too. The 1970s and 1980s generations are imposing their cynicism into the nineties and looking for the downside. There are many intent on destroying the idea before it is really born. Of course this effort cannot succeed. They will increasingly resemble one of those religious sects who parade up and down Piccadilly Circus with banners declaring 'The end is nigh'. I have seen the same man doing this for 20 years now and he is still convinced that the end of the world is around the corner. He does nobody any harm, and in truth, nobody takes any real notice of him. The gains to society from the World Wide Web, and the momentum now gathered in its favour, are turning the critics into unsuccessful party poopers. They begin to look like a very sad bunch of losers...thank goodness!

As with all things there is some truth behind the cynical reactions. The information superhighway has not been built. In the midst of a world recession it is probably too much to expect any progress at all in building it. Ultimately, the technical investment needed to deliver a global information system will not happen. In its place we will most likely have an Internet that reflects the imbalances of the existing social structures—the rich will get it and others will not. These things are not, however, reasons for being cynical, they are reasons for social change. When the world we inhabit is incapable of delivering the future it is, surely, time to change the world...not to abandon the future!

The Internet optimists are also worrying. There are many who look at the Internet through political spectacles. The UK launch issue of *Wired* magazine featured Thomas Paine on the front cover and an in-depth article inside. The implication was clear—that the Internet is a modern form of revolution. The impact that the Internet can have on society is such that it is bound to encourage bold political statements on its likely impact. However, unlike the French Revolution, or the American one which inspired it, the Internet can never be an instrument of social change. Certainly it can alter our behaviour and improve our ability to communicate, but it cannot by itself challenge the entrenched social divisions—both global and local—which make up the current world order. Governments will not topple and be replaced by supranational institutions simply due to the existence of a global computer network. The optimists are, in this sense, complacent. They can be accused of conjuring up a rosy picture that is entirely unjustified by reality.

Where the Internet lobby is correct is in the proposition that there is much wrong with our world. From a purely human, as opposed to a narrowly national, point of view, we organise the world in a ridiculous way. The amount of time, energy, and human life, that is wasted in the perpetuation of nation states is absurd. These nineteenth-century institutions are not adequate to managing a world that is now capable of being perceived as one entity. In the same way that the pre-nineteenth century city states and principalities were outdated in their time, and replaced by nation states, so too are nation states now long past their sell-by-date.

In the late twentieth century we still have to deal with the absurdities of an Earth divided by national borders. The uneven distribution of wealth between the agricultural third world and a service economy First World, and the readiness of nations in Europe and America to go to war, all result from a world with no centre, no common purpose. A world in which national competitive advantage has become more important than human progress. It is true that, by its global and open nature, the Internet gives us an example of what life could be like if freed from the domination of national governments and the vested interests they represent.

To conclude from the above, however, that a *virtual* global community can be created on the Internet is ridiculous. A borderless world must be real, not merely *virtual*. It is not possible to turn a blind eye to the real world and seek to build a different one alongside it. The point is to change the real world. And while the Internet may be an aid to that process it cannot be a replacement for it.

Ultimately both the optimists and the pessimists are wrong. The optimists, while wanting innovation and change, invest too much hope in technology, and underestimate the extent to which change needs to be made by people. The pessimists, on the other hand, while perceiving the limits to change through technology alone, fail to be enthusiastic about the technology or the need for change.

A strategy for the future

The limited implementation of technical developments possible in our society is a compelling argument towards a modern critique of capitalism. The market can only innovate in a partial and uneven manner, thus depriving humanity of benefits that are technically feasible. As a global system of production, it is incapable of utilising the benefits afforded by science. It is, in that sense, a system out of date.

One of the aims of those of us who launched *Cyberia* in August 1994 was to provide a mechanism where the culture of open and critical discussion available on the Internet can be brought to have a bearing in our lives. We are looking to bring together those who are prepared to challenge established practices and authorities, and to champion causes. To bring the spirit of the Internet into the real world.

One of *Cyberia's* earliest decisions was to provide free space on its World Wide Web computer for campaign groups. We also decided to champion the cause of women—who due to the imbalances in our society are often denied access to technology on equal terms with men. The Worldwrite campaign, launched by a group called the Campaign Against Militarism has been one of our early successes. It has involved school children from around the world,

172   *Marxism, Mysticism and Modern Theory*

but particularly from the UK and Japan, opening on-line correspondence about the bombing of Hiroshima and Nagasaki during World War Two. This was set to coincide with a year of activities leading up to the British and US governments' VJ-Day celebrations in August 1995.

Cyberia took the stance that these celebrations were, in effect, a celebration of the melting of tens of thousands of human beings and the mutilation of many tens of thousands more. We wanted no part in them. The Worldwrite campaign was able, as a result, to get to an audience of millions. Before the Internet this would have taken resources beyond the means of the campaign. We were proud to help.

We hope that Worldwrite will be a model for the use of the Internet in a manner consistent with the promise it contains. We certainly intend to do our bit to ensure it is.

This is a real use of a global technology and one that provides a short-term model for the Internet users out there. At the very least the Internet can be useful as a vehicle for questioning the ideas and institutions that hold us back. In doing so it can be one means of developing a critical awareness that can open up the future to real change. There can be little doubt that real change is needed!

NOTES

1   Karl Marx, *A Contribution to the Critique of Political Economy*, Lawrence & Wishart, 1971 (orig 1859), p21

2   Richard Hoggart, 'The uses of computeracy', *The New Statesman and Society*, 5 May 1995, p23

3   James Woudhuysen, 'Before we rush to declare a new era', *Demos*, No4, 1994, p10

4   Bertolt Brecht, *Life of Galileo*, Eyre Methuen, 1980, p92

9
Afterword:
on the problem of
anti-humanism

Suke Wolton

In conclusion I want to draw on some of the ideas developed in earlier chapters to emphasise the problem of anti-humanism today. All too often what seem to be the most radical critiques of social problems prove to be a kind of apologetic, whose end point is to abstract these problems out of the capitalist society that gives rise to them, situating them instead in a denatured 'society'. To analyse the question of anti-humanism today, I start with a logical presentation of the issue. Since this is rather an abstract discussion, I then want to illustrate my argument using some of the more historical material from identity studies.

My argument is that modern social theories both react to previous theories about society and also reflect the modern conditions of society. In doing so they fail to explain contemporary society but do epitomise the current of anti-humanism. By making a rough contrast with the beginning of this century I aim to illustrate some of the key changes underlying their apologetics. Although a contrast can seem a bit crude at times, I think it serves to emphasise how much has changed in the way that people look at society.

It is remarkable that contemporary social theory is scathing in its criticism of such bourgeois institutions as the family, white supremacy and moral norms. But, at the same time, those institutions are, while shaky, in practical terms, unopposed. One of the key questions we need to answer is how could there be so many criticisms of such institutions today and yet they have so little consequence? This deradicalisation of complaint is what I aim to address.

Let me present the logical form of my argument. At the turn of this century, it was considered radical to argue that society was a human product. This idea was in direct contrast to the overriding belief that society was a natural organism. With the development of Darwin's theory of evolution many people perceived the same natural forces in the social environment, making out that competition in the market operated like the Darwinian concept of 'survival of the fittest'. At the time of the expansion of British capitalism, in the middle part of the nineteenth century, the idea that the market was as natural as the birds and bees simply made sense.

The questioning of the social order that was associated with the arrival of the working class in political life and the upheaval of the First World War forced a re-evaluation of just how natural the social order was. In this context, the idea that social organisation was the product of people rather than of biology was the creed of a radical challenge to the status quo. This should not be overstated but, at the same time, the impact of human intervention in the economy and political sphere reinforced a new view of society. The role that people were seen to play in creating society indicated the potential of human intervention and posed society itself as something subject to human influence. This was not the dominant outlook, but among a minority there was a definite radicalisation associated with the idea that society was a human creation.

In contrast today, when critical social theory is commonplace, society is often acknowledged to be a human product. Society is perceived as a creation that is out of control, that has dynamic qualities that have become destructive in their development which demonstrates the 'unanticipated consequences' of a society shaped by human intervention.[1] The apparent prevalence of ethnic conflict, welfare dependency and urban blight serves to reinforce the idea that the process of changing or planning society is a chancy one. The political projects are seen to have incalculable effects as the policies seem to go beyond their stated aim to stir up tensions and disruption. The sense of instability appears to demonstrate that the intractability of the social world is an indictment of human intervention. Even the project of scientific understanding has become tarred with the brush of Nazi medical experiments and other such Frankenstein horrors. In sum, there seems to be no point in trying to change society as it could only have disastrous consequences.

The main assumption underlying this view is that there is no alternative to the market. In fact, market relations have been placed beyond any rational investigation as the unstated assumption of all current social theory. So much is this the case that there is no attempt to theorise the essence of social relations under capitalism. Without any conception of social relations and their consequent social forces, there can only be the appearance of surface relations between individuals.

Consider contemporary social theories. They lack any sense of the collective. The old institutions that expressed and mediated collective interests have become discredited and marginal. Individuals and their actions appear to dominate developments in the world. Even the old allegation that a specific social group, like trade unions, might be responsible for inflation would be too specific for today's generalised slump fatalism. The economic crisis is itself not questioned, only its symptoms and after-effects have become a topic for theory.

Current indicators of decay in society are not perceived as the reflection of something deeper, but as the problem itself. Poverty is presented as a cultural phenomenon, so is crime, teenage pregnancy, violence and sleaze. As Andrew Calcutt has demonstrated, these problems are seen as a problem of behaviour, codes and specific issues concerning only that particular phenomenon.[2]

The problems of society are apparent only at the level of interpersonal relations. Society is full of individuals with different behaviours and different cultural traits, individuals who act with different reasons and ideas. Therefore, people assume, that it is those reasons, intentions and past collective actions of human beings that have brought society to the current point of disorganisation and decay. Even the pursuit of knowledge seems dangerous.

As a consequence of this outlook, human agency stands discredited and degraded. I am not saying that there is no sense of change, but rather that the idea that one should attempt to influence the direction of society seems meaningless and possibly dangerous. And this idea reflects the existing conditions. Without an understanding of the social forces beneath the surface phenomena, our lives are understood as if they were left to chance. The abandonment of the project of changing society means that the given social order is free to dominate our lives and determine our outlook. This individuated, disaggregated society really does pose more risks as the individual bows to the demands of the laws of the market. Contemporary attempts to theorise society are an expression of reality, but an expression that is itself out of control and made mystical.

Since this argument is very compact in this abstract form let's look at this development through the issue of identity politics.

In the prewar period, race was generally understood in terms of a natural hierarchy. Like the evolution of a species, the white race was seen to have developed further and faster than the savage and primitive black people of Africa. Since this development was seen as a product of the race of whites, it was thought that the equivalent development of blacks could only take place over thousands of years, if at all. The difference between the races was assumed to be on the level of different species, and some people asserted that, like the product of horses and donkeys, the offspring of a mixed union would be infertile. Even in the Second World War, the blood of people was assumed to be so different that the Red Cross had to segregate blood reserves.

Developments in the interwar period and during the Second World War itself made this position increasingly untenable. Among other things, the ability of Japan to challenge white superiority in the Far East, and easily defeat the British in Malaya, Burma and Singapore, raised the spectre of racial equality. Combined with the carnage in Europe, the racially motivated barbarism of the German government, and the challenge of the Soviet Union, the moral authority of the European powers could no longer be associated directly with white prestige. What these changes exemplified was the collapse at the heart of the old imperialist club. Although America re-established the authority of the capitalist free market system at the end of the Second World War, it was not able simply to assume political authority over the colonies and spheres of influence vacated by the defeated Axis powers as Britain had been able to do to Germany at the end of the First World War. Churchill had even challenged Germany with wanting to 'transfer native peoples like cattle' at the outbreak of the war—indicating just how much the prestige of colonialism had been undermined.[3] The reconstruction, after and during the end of the war, of the moral legitimacy of the European powers, occurred through a compromise on the issue of self-determination.

What the idea of self-determination recognised was that 'backward peoples' could arrive at development through their own efforts. Although many people anticipated a continuing educative role for the British colonialists, increasingly people put the case that development was self-development, independent of the interference of the imperialist powers. At the same time the argument developed that race was not a valid category. Ruth Benedict published her book *Race: Science and Politics* in 1943. In it she attacked the concept of race and introduced, instead, the idea of culture. Different people were different because they had a different culture, education and a different way of life. By emphasising the way that humans made their social environment, the cultural anthropologists and anti-racists sought to argue that racial identity was not something based in an immutable human nature, but was something more fluid and malleable.

Although we can see today how the arguments of that time did not quite pose the issue of egalitarianism, their attempts to say that different cultures were equally valid and simply different ways of human self-organisation had then a radical element. They challenged the idea that society was a static and natural arrangement, replacing it with the view that human behaviour, rather than being, was the determining factor in making a particular society.

Subsequently, the cultural explanation of race has gained ground in the postwar period. The anti-imperialist struggles after the war took on the view that ethnic divisions were a human conceit and blamed the departing imperialists for sowing these conflicts. The radicals of the 1970s blamed the ruling class for the legacy of racial difference and sought to show how the ruling class had conspired to divide indigenous peoples by inventing ethnic identities and differences. The theories of race-as-culture were part of the heady mix of radical ideas associated with the New Left and as such retained their character of critical and oppositional ideas. Today, however, without the sense of alternative possibilities and outside the context of oppositional movements, this outlook ends up blaming the conscious manipulation of ethnicity for ethnic tension and conflict.

In today's depoliticised climate, the sense of the social has been undermined and so has any critique of the market. The structure of society goes unquestioned and, in so far as society is conceptualised, it is conceptualised from the standpoint of the individual. Identity theory now conflates the spontaneous effects of capitalism which cannot systematically develop society with the impact of conscious intervention upon that society. Without any theory to explain the changing relationships in society, without any theory to say that people are framed by their position in society, the movements of society appear as the consequence of the actions of individuals informed by their own ideas.

Recently, identity theory has gone much further along the road of focusing on the individual. In the 1990s the lack of an alternative to the market has been confirmed in the popular consciousness by the collapse of the Soviet Union. The absence of a collective point of view dominates day-to-day politics. Not only have the collective institutions such as trade unions become marginal to politics, but even the social movements of the 1960s have fragmented, dwindled and disintegrated. There are a few outspoken individuals left, but little social pressure on the powers that be.

The new writers of identity studies do not just concentrate on cultural phenomena, they emphasise the role of the individual in creating and changing particular cultures. The key words of today are things like: fluidity, dynamism, hybridity, intermixture, mutation and plurality. Cultures are evaluated by their variation and change while more static identities are vilified. In seeking to emphasise the fluidity of black culture to show its positive qualities, the fashionable authors latch on to the influences of the individual to show the rapid change in identity. The ideas of migration and diaspora serve to reinforce the sense of change and the role of individuals in effecting that change.

The anti-essentialism described in James Heartfield's chapter is the outlook that matches this disaggregated, individuated social world.[4] The focus on surface effects sees only many individuals as society. Every phenomena is perceived as an effect of consensus and convention. Take the issue of race. The phrase that 'race is a social construction or convention' is no longer confined to obscure academic polemics. Nor is it only the necessary foreword to any discussion about race in a book—it now prefaces the discussion in the quality press as well. For example, *Newsweek,* in its special issue on race relations, argues that: 'lumping these six distinct populations into three groups of two serves no biological purpose, only a social convention. The larger grouping may reflect how society views humankind's diversity, but does not explain it.'[5] *Newsweek* goes further, to stress the social nature of difference, by arguing that some biological characteristics have their roots in the 'social' environment of racial attitudes:

'A social construct can have biological effects, says epidemiologist Robert Hahn of the US Centers for Disease Control and Prevention. Consider hypertension among African-Americans. Roughly 34 per cent have high blood pressure, compared with about 16 per cent of whites. But William Dressler finds the greatest incidence of hypertension among blacks who are upwardly mobile achievers. "That's probably because in mundane interactions, from the bank to the grocery store, they are treated in ways that do not coincide with their self-image as respectable achievers", says Dressler, an anthropologist at the University of Alabama.'[6]

Thus university academics and popular journalism agree today that a sense of racial difference originates with the prejudiced attitudes of white people which subsequently have an effect on the body. It is important to note that the term 'social' used here by *Newsweek* is very much defined at the level of attitudes and ideology, explained in the following way: 'The bottom line, to most scientists working in these fields, is that race is a mere "social construct"— a gamy mixture of prejudice, superstition and myth.'[7]

This is a clear example of the prevalence of the idea that race is simply a social convention. The common view is that cultural differences are just what they appear to be. Social practices, rituals, language, customs are the constituents of a racial identity. Furthermore, it is suggested, the separation of lifestyles into different identities is often encouraged, and sometimes caused by, racial prejudice.

Recently Metropolitan Police Commissioner Sir Paul Condon remarked on the disproportionate numbers of black muggers. While it is true that the Commissioner enjoyed the support of his Home Secretary, many newspapers have highlighted 'social' and environmental explanations of black crime. For example, Polly Toynbee, a liberal but hardly a radical journalist for the *Independent* and the social affairs correspondent of the BBC *Nine O'Clock News*, wrote that:

'Mary Tuck, criminologist and ex-head of the Home Office Research Department, said young blacks are pushed into robbery by the racism of the criminal underworld...blacks find they are offered a fraction of the price their white counterparts receive for stolen goods. So they turn instead to the easiest crime for them, mugging. The image of the black mugger is self-perpetuating and actually assists them in the crime. It is suggested that people are so frightened of young blacks that it is very easy for them to take money off passers-by in the street.'[8]

This example illustrates the role given to ideological consensus in creating the idea of an 'easy crime'. Race is redefined to mean an attitude problem—on both sides of the divide. 'Mugging' becomes a simple behavioural response to mitigate poverty in an article that headlines the quote: 'If people steal, it is because they are poor.' People are thought to act in this way—because they have a *reason* to act thus.

Now here we have the conundrum as it presents itself: on the one hand everyone talks of the importance of 'the social' and, on the other hand, the real sense of the social is more elusive than ever. There appears to be a contradiction between the currency of 'social' theories and the popular rejection of big ideas. But this is not the case if we consider the prevalent understanding of the word 'social' as explained in Heartfield's chapter.

As Heartfield demonstrates the anti-essentialist standpoint of contemporary sociology renders 'society' as its surface appearance—the interrelationship of individuals. The 'social' that is being used in this discussion is the notion of attitudes and practices of many individuals. If we consider this argument a little longer we can begin to see two aspects of it: in the first place, that this denigrates human intervention by equating human interaction with spontaneous social forces, and in the second place, the anti-essentialism of this view ends up being fetishistic about the individual in society.

To illustrate this first point, I return to Polly Toynbee's article on black muggers. In her view, the violent response of young black people is simply a reaction to the attitudes of other people, the white criminals. As each group is meant to react and react again to the other on a cultural level so the presentation of the development of difference is mystified in a chicken-and-egg relationship. The culture, however much a reaction to previous situations, is presented as outside our understanding and beyond our control. Polly Toynbee cites Dr Robert Reiner of the LSE articulating this idea:

> 'Once a particular racial underclass is developed, it is difficult to undo the damage. "If you suddenly created jobs in these black areas, you wouldn't stop the crime overnight. People develop a certain set of alienated attitudes and many of them may be lost for ever."'[9]

The responses of young blacks to the surrounding racialised culture are perceived as something that cannot be reversed and rather as something that becomes fixed attitudinally. *Their* reactions appear to be shaped by *their* consciousness of *their* surroundings, and in the process it seems as if *their* consciousness has become warped and twisted. What presented itself as a society-wide explanation reduces to a characterisation particular to young black men. According to the commentators the reactions of young blacks are rational. And furthermore, this 'rationality' has created the violent culture of mugging.

Like the so-called 'alienated Asians' of the 1995 Bradford riots, their identity, separate from the rest of society is seen as not only cultural, consensual, but also, as a consequence, irredeemable. Since the young Asians have reacted consciously, so it seems, to their conditions, so, in the process, they have shaped their cultural consciousness to be violent and antagonistic. But this viewpoint misses the key question: why do racial divisions arise out of this society? Instead, in the tospy-turvy world of Reiner and Toynbee, what they imagine to be the rational decisions of young blacks lead inexorably to violent crime. In fact, the workings of capitalist society are not even, but uneven, institutionalising discrimination and difference at many levels. It is these real social divisions which lay the basis for racial conflict. Without the consideration of this material context, reason is equated with spontaneity and uncontrolled reaction serves as the indictment of consciousness.

But why do the new social theorists equate conscious action with spontaneous forces? This question brings me to my second point on how anti-essentialism ends up becoming fetishistic not about society, which needs to be understood, but about the individual in society.

The starting point of the modern social theorist is the individual standpoint before the impact of social forces. It is true that many of the modern 'communitarian' thinkers polemicise against the selfish individualism of the 1980s. And some theorists, in this way, reject the idea of a pre-set individual with natural rights and see the individual rather as formed and educated through society.[10] But since the communitarians' concept of society does not significantly advance on the sociological concept of society as merely an aggregation of individuals, the means by which the individual is shaped in society remains at the level of communication. As in Jurgen Habermas' society of communicative activity, the social forces are reduced to the sum of conscious interactions. Lacking a conception of society in its totality, both its objective material character and its idealised and mystifying expression, the social constructionist is forced to account for an uneven and increasingly decrepit society in the realm of ideas and attitudes. Put bluntly, without a theory to explain the failures of capitalist society, the theory ends up blaming human beings for those failures.

As a consequence, the structure of society becomes normalised. Individuals are thus considered as abstract, discoursing individuals, before they are seen as having a position in society. Marx identified this confusion and explained that:

> 'These relations are not those between one individual and another, but between worker and capitalist, tenant and landlord, etc. Eliminate these relations and you abolish the whole of society; your Prometheus will then be nothing more than a spectre without arms and legs.'[11]

Since social relations are the one thing in society that go unquestioned today, so the individual has been taken out of the context of his position in society. The recent criticisms of society, therefore, focus on aspects of society without their connection to the underlying social relations. As the social has been reduced to intersubjectivity so the problems in society have been redefined to mean the problems of consciousness.

Many modern theories emphasise the importance of 'context' and 'specificity' but, in the absence of a deeper social theory, these words imply only local and individual. The anti-essentialist dismisses any attempt to uncover underlying causes, and thus reifies and fetishises the individual. For example, they see 'lifestyles' and 'consumer society' instead of social divisions and capitalism. This outlook fetishises the personal—because it can only see the individual in some preordained form—outside of the social forces oper-ating in society. This perspective starts with the individual in the supermarket faced with choices and options. It forgets the arrival at the supermarket—the means by which people get there; by foot, by car, with 10 pence or £10 in their pocket created by a job or no job.

This outlook is then the context where anti-humanism can reign supreme. Having taken the individual out of his relationship with society all we can see is the chaotic world impacting upon the individual. Furthermore, the absence of any critique of the market, particularly when capitalist dynamic is at such a low ebb, means that human intervention is perceived as peculiarly destabilising. Even the effect of attempting to understand society seems potentially disintegrative. Each outlook tends to confirm the lack of coher-ence in the way that society operates and exacerbates tensions and conflicts. The 'risk society', so often mentioned, emphasises more than anything the dangers of any attempt to take control—because the oft-criticised social envi-ronment we have today is presented as the legacy of previous actions.

In conclusion, new social theory reproduces what is happening around us, providing a (distorted) reflection of society but failing to explain it. In brief, modern social theories express the way that man makes society and, at the same time, is not in control of society. The real social processes of capitalism do reproduce the social system but not systematically. The process of capital-ism *is* sporadic, localised and uneven. The human reaction to the deficiencies of the market is political activity. The social theorists see this political activity, not as a response to market failure, but as the actions that have created society and, as these policies really have failed, so the theorists have attributed that failure to the disastrous consequences of human intervention.

In this way, the modern theorists thus see the world as it really is. They see policy failure as failure. They see today's divisions and conflicts as the disastrous effects of the collective projects of the past. Their theories are the expression of alienation because they see the society created by human beings as having taken on a life of its own and then fetishise it. Society really is a product of man's activity, but the new concept of the 'social', with its attendant idea that society is the aggregation of individuals, is the alienated understanding of this society. By reappropriating Marx's theory of alienation, and developing a new critique, there is a way for us to set forth humanism in this anti-humanist climate and challenge this modern mysticism.

NOTES

1   Zygmunt Bauman, *Modernity and the Holocaust,* Polity Press, 1989, p11

2   Andrew Calcutt, 'Uncertain judgement: a critique of the culture of crime' given
     as a paper in this seminar series and reproduced in this volume.

3   Cited in Fergus C Wright (Ed), *Population and Peace: A Survey of International
     Opinion on Claims for Relief from Population Pressure,* International Institute of
     Intellectual Cooperation, International Studies Conference for Peaceful
     Change, League of Nations, Paris, 1939, p264

4   James Heartfield, 'Marxism and social construction' given as a paper in this
     seminar series and reproduced in this volume.

5   *Newsweek,* 13 February 1995

6   *Newsweek,* 13 February 1995

7   *Newsweek,* 13 February 1995

8   Polly Toynbee, *Independent,* 8 July 1995

9   Polly Toynbee quoting Dr Robert Reiner of the LSE in *Independent,* 8 July 1995

10   See Charles Taylor, *Sources of the Self,* Verso, 1991

11   Karl Marx, *Poverty of Philosophy,* p112 cited in Georg Lukacs, *History and Class
     Consciousness,* Merlin Press, 1971, p50

Index